Economics with Heterogeneous Interacting Agents

New Economic Windows

More information about this series at http://www.springer.com/series/6901

Alessandro Caiani · Alberto Russo
Antonio Palestrini · Mauro Gallegati
Editors

Economics with Heterogeneous Interacting Agents

A Practical Guide to Agent-Based Modeling

Springer

Editors
Alessandro Caiani
Università Politecnica delle Marche
Ancona
Italy

Antonio Palestrini
Università Politecnica delle Marche
Ancona
Italy

Alberto Russo
Università Politecnica delle Marche
Ancona
Italy

Mauro Gallegati
Università Politecnica delle Marche
Ancona
Italy

Additional material to this book can be downloaded from http://extras.springer.com.

ISSN 2039-411X ISSN 2039-4128 (electronic)
New Economic Windows
ISBN 978-3-319-44056-9 ISBN 978-3-319-44058-3 (eBook)
DOI 10.1007/978-3-319-44058-3

Library of Congress Control Number: 2016947920

Printed on acid-free paper

This Springer imprint is published by Springer Nature
The registered company is Springer International Publishing AG Switzerland

To Maurizio Mariotti

Foreword

This book emerges from a workshop activity of a research group on Agent Based Models at the Dipartimento di Scienze Economiche e Sociali at the Universitá Politecnica delle Marche, Ancona, which includes—in addition to the four editors—Leonardo Bargigli (Florence), Ermanno Catullo, Eugenio Caverzasi, Fabio Clementi (Macerata), Annarita Colasante, Corrado Di Guilmi (Sydney), Lisa Gianmoena, Federico Giri, Ruggero Grilli, Simone Landini (Tourin), Luca Riccetti (Rome), and Gabriele Tedeschi (Castillon). For many years, we have divided the very few honours and numerous research squabbles, exploring unknown research territories with many friends from different disciplines.

Financial and scientific contributions of the various European projects—in particular, SYMPHONY and FINMAP, DiSES and INET have allowed the survival of the youngest in years of financial famine that has deeply affected the Italian universities.

The book is intended for graduate and Ph.D. students, but also undergraduates with a minimal knowledge in computers and economics, and in general people curious in computational science and Agent Computational Economics, can enjoy it. Despite the fact that the reader will be guided step by step in the simulation, it is not an ACE guide for dummies and almost elementary computer skills are preferred—or at least to know how to switch on a PC. Hopefully the Groucho Marx dictum will be exaggerated: A 4-year-old child could understand this book. Run out and find me a 4-year-old child. I can't make head nor tail out of it.

We have had a lot of "laboratory mice", the students of advanced macro at UNIVPM and the participants in the Summer Schools on ABM, on September 2014 and September 2015.

Our gratitude goes also to Domenico Delli Gatti, Alan Kirman, Giulia Iori, Thomas Lux, Maria Cristina Recchioni and J. Barkley Rosser.

While this book was in its very final stage of compilation, our beloved friend and colleague Maurizio Mariotti passed away. We dedicate the book to him knowing that nothing will replace his kind generosity and are happy to have shared many days illuminated by his “buondì” and beaming smile

Ancona
May 2016

Alessandro Caiani
Alberto Russo
Antonio Palestrini
Mauro Gallegati

Contents

Contributors

Leonardo Bargigli Dipartimento di Scienze per l'Economia e l'Impresa, Università di Firenze, Florence, Italy

Alessandro Caiani Dipartimento di Management, Università Politecnica delle Marche, Ancona, Italy

Ermanno Catullo Dipartimento di Scienze Economiche e Sociali, Università Politecnica delle Marche, Ancona, Italy

Fabio Clementi Dipartimento di Scienze politiche, della comunicazione e delle relazioni internazionali, Università di Macerata, Macerata, Italy

Ruggero Grilli Dipartimento di Scienze Economiche e Sociali, Università Politecnica delle Marche, Ancona, Italy

Antonio Palestrini Dipartimento di Scienze Economiche e Sociali, Università Politecnica delle Marche, Ancona, Italy

Luca Riccetti Facoltà di Economia, Dipartimento di Management, Sapienza Università di Roma, Roma, Italy

Alberto Russo Dipartimento di Management, Università Politecnica delle Marche, Ancona, Italy

Gabriele Tedeschi Departament d'Economia, Universitat Jaume I de Castellon, Castellón, Spain

Introduction

One of the main problems that economics has faced—one could say right from the very beginning—is how billions of agents, with different tastes and abilities, coordinate with each other without any central control. The dominant economic theory has covered several paths, which model agents who interact indirectly. On the one hand, the approach in Walras's Elements Walras (1874)—and in the version of Arrow (1951), Debreu (1951), Arrow and Debreu (1954)—where a market auctioneer is provided with all the information—the single agents only know their own payoff and utility functions—and coordinates the market through the vector of prices. On the other, the equilibrium context without any coordinating figure, where information is distributed among the agents as in Dynamic Stochastic General Equilibrium (DSGE) approach. Both can be thought of as models for interacting agents, but only the second can aspire to become a paradigm for methodological individualism because, in the first it is crucial to model at the micro level in order to have an exact aggregation at the macro one (see the discussion in Chap. 1).

A model of such "interactions" among economic agents is nothing else but a "map" of the world. In microeconomic models, the agents meet in various markets and follow rules of behaviour, based on axioms or on empirical evidence (from which the modeller can obtain simple rules of the thumb). Agents and markets are the fundamental constituents also of every micro-founded macro model. If this is true, it seems to us that micro models are all agent-based and that their differentiation occurs at a following level, when considering information about the world for which the map is built. In traditional models it is assumed that one has a complete characterization of individual preferences. Or plainly speaking, one knows exactly what economic agents want. Payoff and utility function existence theorems were extracted from this hypothesis Debreu (1954), Debreu (1960), Diamond (1965), making it possible to represent the preference scheme of economic agents with scalar objective functions for which the maximum value exists.[1]

[1]Unfortunately, those same assumptions give rise to the Sonnenschein–Mantel–Debreu theorem Sonnenschein (1972), Debreu (1974), Mantel (1974) that demonstrates how many properties at the

From here follows the whole traditional approach to macroeconomics and micro-founded finance. An argument in Muth (1961) further elaborated by Lucas (1972), Lucas (1976) affirms, in fact, that if the economist assumes to be able to represent the preferences of individuals then, in the model, it must be assumed that the same individuals know their preferences and behave so as to get the best they can (optimization) given the information they have at their disposal about the world. In other words, in traditional models the fact that agents optimize is a mere consequence of the initial hypothesis, made by the scholar, of knowing the preference scheme of the agents who are the object of the analysis.

Agent-based literature, on the other hand, aims to study economic phenomena in their complexity; taking into account joint distributions of individual characteristics, the direct and not only indirect interactions and therefore the way in which economic networks are made and changed. Hence, it cannot assume to be able to perfectly represent the preferences and therefore to have an exact knowledge of the objective functions. The starting point of each agent-based analysis is a description of the rules of behaviour, that is, the map between the actions and the information set available to them in which a partial knowledge of the objective functions is included. These rules can be derived from empirical work, from economic experiments, from studies carried out in disciplines other than economics (psychology, sociology, etc.) or from a purely normative analysis. In other words, what would the aggregated relations be if the agents followed certain kinds of rules, which have had important results in auction models (Tesfatsion and Judd 2006).

From the beginning, the agent-based literature had to face the Lucas critique (Lucas 1976). When one wants to assess the effect of an economic policy one has to take into account that the latter will enter the information set of agents, changing their behaviour. This could result in a neutralization of the economic policy or its much lesser effect than expected ex ante. Agent-based models, to respond to the Lucas critique, have often resorted to the use of learning algorithms and switching mechanisms between different rules to take account of the effects of economic changes in the environment on the behaviour of agents. On the other hand the solution proposed by Lucas, based on the use of rational expectations, runs into a potentially worse problem than what had motivated it, since in order to work it has to assume that agents have perfect knowledge, perfect rationality, and almost infinite computing capabilities. "Satisfactory" adaptivity, bounded rationality and behaviour (instead of optimizing) are thus a typical feature of agent-based models: the agents can change their mind during the simulation and often change the rule. Given the only partial knowledge, ex ante, of the objective function there can only be an update, ex-post, on the basis of the results. A rule resists so long as it "works", that is produces good results. Otherwise it will be changed. Let's give a simple example. Suppose we want to divert a stream of ants marching straight towards our

(Footnote 1 continued)
micro level disappears at the macro one, when aggregating. An important consequence is that many properties of an aggregate variable may be generated both by optimizing agents and non-optimizing agents.

house. The Lucas critique would tell us that we cannot simply put an obstacle in their path, or at least it might not be sufficient. The ants could go round it and continue undeterred towards our house. In an agent-based perspective we should study the ways ants bypass obstacles—and thus change the "local" rule of movement when they encounter an obstacle—depending on the size and shape of the latter: a macrofoundation of microeconomics.

This book guides the reader in the world of such agent-based models (ABM) and of the technicalities that need to be solved to evaluate the effect of different rules and their switching. One thing must immediately be made clear. The current agent-based literature is vast and is not just about economics. Our review of the techniques will inevitably be biased towards the work and the problems that our research group has had to face and resolve in more than 20 years of analysis, producing numerous scientific publications. When we refer to agent-based models, the reader must always keep in mind this explanatory bias.

That said an ABM, then, is a computational model, populated by many heterogeneous agents interacting with each other from the bottom—bottom up—that is, without a central coordinator. These interactions produce emergent results in which the aggregate result is different from what it would be if each agent were isolated from the others, that is, without feedback or externalities (see the review on aggregation made in Chap. 1). In ABM economic results can be aggregated, and in particular added together to calculate the GDP, consumption and investment, and in general also the distributions (see the analysis of distributions made in Chap. 4) and economic networks can be studied. These economic statistics are difficult to obtain using traditional approaches and analysis of economic networks is virtually absent.

For a macroeconomist that the GDP is the sum of individual activities is something perfectly familiar: as shown in Chap. 1, even though the approaches are different, a DSGE model could give similar results to an ABM in terms of aggregate dynamics. After all, even a DSGE model is populated by many agents who interact and the results of these interactions produce economic results, and if we add up these results we obtain the GDP and so on. Our argument is that by giving up the assumption of perfect knowledge of the objective function (except for exogenous disturbances), one can describe a much richer set of phenomena than with the DSGE models. Obviously there are important differences between ABM and DSGE, even in the pre-analytical vision. It is however possible, in principle, to pass from an ABM to a DSGE through successive simplifications that identify, unless there are stochastic disturbances, the objective functions. One only has to impose the demand–supply equilibrium, that there are one or more representative agents (or that the distribution of individuals in the period t + 1 can be computed), that the agents maximize an objective function bound to some balance sheet, that from an agent-based model it is possible to theoretically obtain a DSGE. In other words, an important difference between the two approaches is the information and computational capabilities of the agents.

If the information is incomplete the future becomes uncertain while asymmetry leads to interaction. This, however, is not harmless, since economic agents are strategic agents and with their actions change the structure (and the laws: not by chance does one speak of empirical regularities). Moreover, with heterogeneity one interacts locally and the "system" becomes endogenous.

In an ABM, the interactions are governed by rules of behaviour that the modeller codifies directly in the individuals who populate the environment. In an ABM, the behaviour is the point in which a modeller begins to make hypothesis. The DSGE modellers make assumptions about what an optimizing agent wants, compatibly with budget and resource constraints, and represent these wishes with concave real-valued functions defined over convex sets. Based on the combination of objectives and constraints, the behaviour is derived by solving the first-order conditions and when necessary also the second-order conditions. The reason why economists set their theories in this way—making assumptions about the goals and then drawing conclusions about the behaviour—is that they assume that the allocations, decisions and choices are guided by individual interests. Decisions and actions are carried out with the aim of reaching a max-min goal. For consumers, this usually regards utility maximization; a purely subjective assessment of well-being. For businesses, the goal is typically to maximize profits. This is exactly where rationality, for DSGE, is manifested in economics. In a nutshell, in DSGE models the modeller sets the objective function and the consequent maximization generates the rules. In the ABM the modeller sets directly the behavioral rules given empirical evidence and experiments that should control the degrees of freedom. The introduction of information problems in the Walrasian model is only apparently harmless for the externalities and non-convexity deriving from it. The issue of asymmetric information assumes that the agents are different from each other (Greenwald and Stiglitz 1993). According to Leijonhufvud (1981) this distinction is a condition sufficient to generate failures in coordination. In particular, whether information is complete or not, if it is evenly distributed, banks and businesses would become a single aggregate where every debt–credit ratio is cancelled and money has no role to play. The game theory has also shown that rational behaviour can generate multiple equilibria. Along the same lines, it can be argued that if there is asymmetric information the problems of adverse selection prevent a decentralized system from reaching Pareto-optimal positions (Akerlof (1970), Stiglitz and Weiss (1981)), thus giving rise to market failures.

The Arrow–Debreu works established conditions to have a Pareto optimum: the information need not be perfect; it can be incomplete provided it is exogenous, that is, the beliefs must not change as a result of the agents' actions. In short, there must be no direct interaction. The case in question is represented by a central actor (the auctioneer) and the connections going from him to all agents. Instead, when information is imperfect the single agents will come into direct contact, that is, there will be links between agent and agent.

It must be recognized that if there is information asymmetry, the agents interact directly with each other outside the market, stimulated by profits. In that case, however, the Walrasian star type of network presents serious difficulties. And of course the idea of a representative agent has to be abandoned. Which is not only a problem of fallacy of composition, or of aggregation: it is that with interaction aggregate behaviour is no longer a linear summation, but a nonlinear process that emerges from the individual one and as such is endowed with properties that are different from that of the single constituent parts. The ABM approach aims precisely to describe, in a reduced scale, the behaviour of single individuals and bring out the aggregate properties.

Chapter 1 will analyze in detail the ABM approach compared to the traditional one mentioned above. The idea of this chapter is to give a set of tools necessary to understand the construction of two economic models developed in Chaps. 2 and 3. The chapter opens with a discussion on the problems of aggregation of macroeconomic models. To be honest, such a discussion would not be strictly essential in the ABM models which implement a bottom-up approach that takes into account the distribution of the agents in each period. Aggregation is performed at the end of each period by simply adding or calculating the per capita values. It is, however, important to be aware of this problem which must, instead, be solved in the construction of traditional models. The chapter continues with a comparison between the traditional models and the ABM approach showing the advantages of the latter in the analysis of distribution evolution regarding the features and choices of agents and in the analysis of economic networks. The second session of the chapter analyzes in detail the "box of tools" necessary to the ABM economist. In particular, it illustrates the choices of consumption and production, the expectations, the matching between demand and supply of credit and the entry–exit of companies from a market.

Chapter 2, using the tools of Chap. 1, describes step by step the construction of an educational version of the agent-based model published in Riccetti et al. (2013). The model analyzes the interaction between the distribution of the companies that produce a homogeneous good with external sources of funding and the banking system which is also heterogeneous. Although this is a "toy model", its description proposes a twofold goal: (1) on the one hand it allows us to show how the tools described in the first chapter can be used to build an existing model in the literature and (2) shows the basics of computer programming.

A few words must be spent about the use of programming languages. When two of the editors of this book were young, virtually every economic model had to be analyzed analytically. Certainly it could be simulated and this was a possible strategy of analysis: simulation was performed in order to understand the properties which later were analytically demonstrated. Today many models, both standard and agent-based, are impossible to be analyzed analytically. The attack strategy to the economic problem has been completely reversed. Maybe one can analytically analyze a very simplified version in order to understand the basic properties, but the one and true model can only be studied numerically. Therefore, it is necessary to strongly invest in one or more programming languages (MATLAB/Octave, R, Fortran, C, C++, Python, etc.). The choice of the second chapter fell on R because it is open-source, with a good learning curve (the language is similar to MATLAB even though Octave is closer) and rich in statistical functions with which to analyze the results of an economic model; functions like those also described in Chap. 4. The chapter is packed with exercises in R that provide a thorough knowledge on programming techniques and on the construction of an economic model which is, of course, the ultimate goal of this book.

In Chap. 3, instead, we chose to use the most classic and fastest programming language, C. This is because we believe that for the most complex economic models the choice of fast programming languages (as well as Fortran and C++) is hardly avoidable. Investing in one or more of these compiled languages is a choice, perhaps not necessary, but which we strongly recommend to students, graduate students, young researchers who are interested in the subjects of this book. Chapter 3 presents the construction of a simplified agent-based model drawn from the publications of Tedeschi et al. (2009), Tedeschi et al. (2012b). The model represents, in a stylized form, the operation of a financial market in order to reproduce the most important statistical regularities we observe in financial time series. The main mechanism of the model is the endogenous mechanism of imitation, via a preferential attachment rule (Barabási and Albert 1999) in which the agents are more likely to imitate the choices of others who have generated higher profits in the past. The aims of this chapter are (1) to show how using the classic and fast programming language C it is possible to build an agent-based model for financial markets; (2) how agent-based modelling allows to analyze direct interaction phenomena that generate financial networks and make them evolve.

The book ends with Chap. 4, a valuable chapter for those who study agent-based economic models, but not only. This chapter describes density and probability functions which are useful to represent empirical distributions of individuals and businesses depending on their characteristics. Also illustrated, and implemented in R, is their estimation procedure. They are all "heavy-tail" distributions in the sense of having heavier tails than normal and than their derivatives. This is one of the most robust stylized economic facts that agent-based models must and can explain. In reality the probability of extreme events is higher, and often much higher, than that implied by Gaussian distributions.

Alessandro Caiani
Annarita Colasante
Antonio Palestrini
Alberto Russo
Mauro Gallegati

Chapter 1
Getting Started: The Aggregation Conundrums and Basic Toolkits of Agent Based Modeling

Ermanno Catullo, Antonio Palestrini and Gabriele Tedeschi

1.1 Understanding Heterogeneity and Interaction in Economic Models

1.1.1 Aggregate Models with Boundlessly Rational Agents

From the very beginning macroeconomics analysis tried to understand aggregate relationships (GDP, Consumption, Investments, etc.). The most famous one is the Keynesian relation between aggregate consumption at time t, C_t and aggregate income, Y_t

$$C_t = F(Y_t) = \bar{C} + cY_t \tag{1.1}$$

where $\bar{C}$ is the autonomous component of consumption and c is the marginal propensity to consume.[1]

[1]These aggregate relation was later modified by Friedman (1957) and Ando and Modigliani (1963) in $C_t = F(Y_{pt})$ where Y_p is permanent income.

E. Catullo (✉) · A. Palestrini
Dipartimento di Scienze Economiche e Sociali, Università Politecnica delle Marche, Piazzale Martelli 8, 60121 Ancona, Italy
e-mail: ermanno.catullo@gmail.com

A. Palestrini
e-mail: a.palestrini@univpm.it

G. Tedeschi
Departament d'Economia, Universitat Jaume I de Castellon, Avenida de Vicent Sos Baynat, s/n, 12071 Castellón, Spain
e-mail: gabriele.tedeschi@gmail.com

A. Caiani et al. (eds.), *Economics with Heterogeneous Interacting Agents*, New Economic Windows, DOI 10.1007/978-3-319-44058-3_1

These kind of relationships were motivated by behavioral rules such as the Keynes' observation that marginal consumption of a family/individual is a fraction of disposable income.[2]

The problem with this starting approach to macroeconomic analysis is that, because of the lack of micro data, such behavioral rules were not motivated by empirical or experimental analysis[3] but just common sense. Furthermore, was not clear at the very beginning the aggregation problem we face in analyzing aggregate variables (see next section).

During the 70s, the discussion in macroeconomics stressed the necessity of a micro-foundation of macroeconomic theories. In other words, the economic relations have to be specified at the micro-level, then there is the aggregation step and finally the computation of the (determinate) rational expectation solution of the aggregate model. This approach produced a huge amount of literature but with important limitations: first, the theoretical assumptions at the base of modern neoclassical macroeconomic models (such as, DSGE models) have been increasingly challenged. Secondly, the use of representative agents prevent to analyze the joint distributions of individual characteristics/choices and the network topology of agents decisions, which can be crucial both in an explanatory and normative perspective.[4]

This latter aspect also implies that the aggregation procedure employed in the standard literature is logically valid only under particularly restrictive hypothesis, as we discuss in the next section.

The first set of criticisms instead challenges one of the milestones of neoclassical macroeconomic: the idea that agents are perfectly informed, perfectly rational, and take their decisions through an optimization process of some objective function. In this respect, the agent-based approach, in a sense, is a continuation of the mid of the past century analysis recognizing the problems of the concept of *perfect rationality*. In the 1950s there was the first attempt to discredit the assumptions of the Neoclassical Economic theory. Without any doubt, Herbert Simon and Maurice Allais were the first authors who shed light on the inadequacy of the axiomatic approach of the Neoclassical Economics. The main critiques raised by Simon and Allais focused on the idea that in the process of individual decision making two factors should be taken into account: cognition and psychological aspect.

Simon (1957) highlighted the fact that agents have limited capacity of calculus and they have no sufficient computational capability to find the optimal solution. Simon, in fact, introduced the concept of *bounded rationality* which implies that agents are not able to use the optimization process to reach their goal. Assuming that individuals

[2]In Keynes' words (Keynes 1936) a "psychological law of consumption".

[3]The field of Experimental Economics aims at investigate individual behaviors. In this field data are collected through laboratory or field controlled experiment as in physic or biology in which the phenomenon under observation is the choices of human beings. Running an experiment means to create a controlled environment to examine some questions of interest. This method has a great advantage with respect to the use of existing data set, i.e. researchers are able to isolate the impact of the variable under investigation and, most important, they are able to observe real individual's choices or preferences.

[4]Think about the importance, of inter-bank networks or firm-bank credit networks today.

are boundedly rational implies that agents usually simplify the complex problem by decomposing the entire process of choice into sub-problem and, using a step-by-step process, they are able to find the so-called *satisficing solution*. Allais (1953) shed light on the importance of the psychological aspect of choices. He proposed an experiment on individual preferences and the results show that agents systematically violate the independence axiom of the Expected Utility.

For these reasons, the agent-based literature tries to extrapolate simple behavioral rules (such as consumption, production, investment rules) from microeconomic surveys, empirical analysis and experimental economics, rather than deriving agents' choices from the optimization of an a-priori objective function subject to certain types of constraint.

Although econometric estimations techniques, microeconomic stylized facts, direct observations and case-studies still provide a fundamental guide in shaping agents' behavior, as well as in validating models results, over the last decades the Agent Based Modeling literature has increasingly looked at behavioral and experimental economics in order to study the actual mechanisms at the base of agents' decision in a variety of economic context (e.g. financial market operations, investment and production, consumption). The *experimental economics literature* dates back to the seminal work of Vernon Smith[5] (see Smith (1965)) while the 2002 Nobel Prize Daniel Kahneman is considered as the "father" of behavioral economics. Admittedly, as pointed out by Bardsley (2010), the boundary lines between experimental and behavioral economics is thin. However, the field of behavioral economics is broader in that it includes contributions concerning the investigation of human behavior with different technique, i.e. not only through the experimental procedure.

The approach proposed by Smith, which is replicated in many other recent studies like Lei et al. (2001), Stöckl et al. (2010), Haruvy et al. (2007) and Palan (2013), are able to capture the individual behavior in the market. On the other hand, the approach proposed by Kahneman, focuses on the search of the so-called *heuristics* used by agents in making their choices. Heuristics are a *rules of thumb* used as a shortcut for solving the decision problem. These kind of rules emerged from the investigation using lab experiment and, it has been shown, that the adoption of these heuristics brings agents to make predictable errors called *biases*. Some of the well-known heuristics are: (i) availability (Tversky and Kahneman 1973) by which a decision maker relies upon knowledge that is readily available rather than examine other alternatives or procedures; (ii) representativeness (Kahneman and Tversky 1972) which implies a distortion of the probability associated of an event; (iii) framing effect (Tversky and Kahneman 1989) which highlights the importance of the framing within which a situation is presented; (iv) loss aversion (Kahneman and Tversky 1979) that shows that people feel losses more deeply than gains of the same value.

The link between experimental or, more in general, behavioral economics and the agent based model is given by these heuristics. Indeed, the results of experiment are useful to extrapolate behavioral rules which is often used to calibrate or validate agent based model. These models, populated by heterogeneous interactive agents, need a

[5] The Nobel Price in 2002 for his research in experimental economics.

micro-foundation because their results are emergent from the interaction dynamics of many economic units. Unfortunately, one of the important assumption of many agent-based models is that agents are not, and cannot be, perfectly rational and this obviously implies that the micro rules cannot be based on the use of utility functions.

To overcome the problem, it is possible to implement behavioral rules observed in the laboratory. These rules could be useful to calibrate the model and/or to validate the results of the agent based simulation. On the of the first and the most important contribution that show how to use the experimental results to calibrate a model is that by Roth and Erev (1995). In this work authors take into account the results from three well-known experimental game and use these information to construct a dynamic model. One of the significant work on the use of experimental evidence to validate a model is that by Anufriev and Hommes (2012), which focuses on macro experiment on asset and commodity markets and they extrapolate the behavioral rules observed in these fictitious markets to construct an agent based model.

Although an exhaustive survey of the experimental economics literature is beyond the objective of the present book, there is a tighter and tighter relationship between agent based modeling and behavioral experiments. Duffy (2006) is probably the main contribution in this field, providing a significant number of examples of how Agent Based Models can be employed to replicate the properties emerging from experimental data.

The present chapter aims at sketching out a (non-exhaustive) survey of the behavioral rules employed in the ever growing AB literature. These behaviors will be presented and discussed making reference to the different functional block of AB models to which they pertain, such as production, investment, consumption and saving, pricing, expectations, finance behaviors. Then, we will show how to implement some of these behavioral rules into simplified AB didactic models.

Before moving to the core of the book, however, we deserve in the next section some attention to the problem of aggregation in economic analysis with the aim of highlighting the limitations faced by standard approaches in macroeconomics and finance, and how the AB approach presented in the book allow to address them. In the same wake, Sects. 1.1.4–1.1.6 then make a brief comparison of the two methodologies.

1.1.2 The Aggregation Problem

What C_t, and Y_t, of the above sub-section, exactly mean? What is an aggregate variable? Technically, a variable X_t at time t is an aggregate variable if it is a function of the distribution of the micro-variable x_{it} where i is the index of agent-i. That is

$$X_t = h(x_{1t}, x_{2t}, \dots, x_{Nt})$$

The function h, like in the consumption-income example, almost always means sum ($\sum_i x_{it}$) or per capita ($N^{-1} \sum_i x_{it}$). The justification of the aggregate relation is an economic theory at the micro level claiming that individual consumption is a function of income.

Suppose for every individual consumption at time t is $c_{it} = m_{it} y_{it}$; it depends on the income y_{it}, and marginal propensity to consume m_{it}. By assumption there is no autonomous level of consumption. Then, choosing the sum aggregator ($h = \sum$), we have

$$C_t = \sum_{i=1}^{N} c_{it} = \sum_{i=1}^{N} m_{it} y_{it} \tag{1.2}$$

that it is not a functional relation between C_t and Y_t; i.e., C_t depends on the entire distribution of y_{it}. This is known in the literature as the *aggregation problem*. If the distribution is stable and N "big" then we can, using the properties of the sample covariance function $Cov(\bullet, \bullet)$, do the following algebraic computation: start with the definition

$$Cov(m_{it}, y_{it}) = N^{-1} \sum_{i=1}^{N} m_{it} y_{it} - \bar{m}_{it} \bar{y}_{it}$$

where $\bar{m}_{it} = N^{-1} \sum_i m_{it}$ and $\bar{y}_{it} = N^{-1} \sum_i y_{it} = Y_t / N$ are averages. Then multiplying by N

$$NCov(m_{it}, y_{it}) = \sum_{i=1}^{N} m_{it} y_{it} - \bar{m}_{it} Y_t$$

and solving for $\sum_{i=1}^{N} m_{it} y_{it}$, using the consumption definition in Eq. (1.2) we arrive at the aggregate relationship

$$C_t = N\, Cov(m_{it}, y_{it}) + \bar{m}_{it} Y_t.$$

Under the assumption of a stable joint distribution between m and y the relation exists, but

1. is a function of the moments of the distribution. In other words, when the relation exists it depends on properties of agents' distribution. The implication for an economic model, and so for the agent-based framework in particular, is that to have a stable aggregate relationship individuals can change their characteristics over time;
2. is different from the micro-relationships. Provided we have a convergence to an asymptotic distribution the aggregate function may be different from the micro relation. Note that, in the micro consumption-income function there is no constant, whereas we find it in the aggregate relation. Without considering the aggregation problem we may erroneously interpret the aggregate constant as an autonomous consumption that is not present in the micro relation by assumption.[6]

[6]A famous example of the importance of point 2 is the aggregate relation between output and inputs in the basic modern new-keynesian models with sticky prices in a monopolistic competition

The reason to discuss the aggregation problem in this book is to stress an important distinction between standard macroeconomic analysis and the agent-based framework. The former assume the existence of stable aggregate relationships, then specifies preferences (using the utility function representation), payoffs (with an objecting function, usually a profit) and technology and finds the dynamics of the model computing the maximum value in the payoffs/preferences set. In the latter, instead, behavioral rules and technology are specified and then computed the dynamics of the model and the aggregate variables using the appropriate function h (usually the sum). In doing so, in every period is also computed the agents' joint distribution of every characteristics that can be compared with empirical joint distributions.

For the sake of completeness, in the following section we briefly describe the standard approach used in macroeconomics and finance. In other words, following Heathcote et al. (2009) and Guvenen (2011), and the G. Violante's Macroeconomic Theory II course (www.nyu.edu; New York University) we briefly discuss the conditions under which it is possible to obtain the first step of a standard approach; an exact macro-relation between aggregate variables *independent from movements of distributions*.

1.1.3 The Standard Approach and the Aggregation Problem

The simplest macroeconomic model is made of N_f firms and N_c consumers in a *perfect competitive environment*. As said above, the standard approach specifies the objecting function and derive the behavior of the agents computing the maximum value. Let's start with the firm.

1.1.3.1 Firms

Suppose that the production function of the firm is characterized by:*CRS technology* (capital, k_{it}, and labor, l_{it}) and *aggregate uncertainty* Z_t, that is

$$Z_t F(k_{it}, l_{it}).$$

In equilibrium, the production function is also real revenue of the firm. Total cost is

$$w_t l_{it} + r_t k_{it}$$

where w_t is real wage and r_t is the real interest rate. Firms maximize their profits (revenues–costs)

(Footnote 6 continued)
environment. Because of firms setting different prices the aggregate relation between output and input is different from the micro one. Thanks to the Calvo price setting mechanism it is possible to compute the macro function depending also on a price dispersion (see Christiano et al. 2010).

$$Z_t F(k_{it}, l_{it}) - w_t l_{it} - r_t k_{it}$$

computing the first order conditions[7] with respect to capital and labor

$$Z_t F_k(k_{it}, l_{it}) = r_t$$

$$Z_t F_l(k_{it}, l_{it}) = w_t$$

using the CRS property of the production function.

They obtain

$$\frac{F_k(k_{it}/l_{it}, 1)}{F_l(k_{it}/l_{it}, 1)} = \frac{r_t}{w_t}$$

implying that capital-labor ratios are equal across firms, that is

$$k_{it}/l_{it} = K_t/L_t.$$

An important consequence of this result is that the firm's chosen amount of labor and capital are the same fraction, say λ_i, of their respective aggregate counterpart,

$$l_{it} = \lambda_i L_t$$

and

$$k_{it} = \lambda_i K_t.$$

Given this result we can easily compute the aggregate production function

$$\sum_i Z_t F(k_{it}, l_{it}) =$$

$$= \sum_i Z_t F(\lambda_i K_t, \lambda_i L_t) =$$

$$= \sum_i \lambda_i Z_t F(K_t, L_t) =$$

$$= Z_t F(K_t, L_t) \sum_i \lambda_i = Z_t F(K_t, L_t).$$

[7]This approach needs well defined optimization problems; concave objecting functions evaluated on a convex support.

In words, the aggregate production function exists[8] and is equal to the micro function.

In the next sub-section we discuss "the other side of the sky"; i.e., consumer's decisions.

1.1.3.2 Consumers

In order to analyze consumption it becomes crucial defining under what conditions the aggregate consumption do not depends on the wealth distribution avoiding the aggregation problem?

Gorman (1953, 1961) studied conditions under which aggregate consumption $C = \sum_i c_i(p, a_i)$ is distribution independent; that is - given the functional relation between consumption and prices, say p, and wealth, say a_i - for every couple of agents i and j the following equation holds

$$\frac{\partial c_i}{\partial a_i} = \frac{\partial c_j}{\partial a_j}.$$

The equation says that agents have same marginal propensity to consume out of wealth implying a linear function consumption choice

$$c_i = n_i(p) + m(p)a_i.$$

Note that the intercept may differ across agents, but the slope coefficient must be the same.

Gorman proved that this is the case when the consumers indirect utility function,[9] is (affine) linear

$$v_i(p, a_i) = \alpha_i(p) + \beta(p)a_i$$

To have this specification (also called *Gorman polar form*) preferences have to be *quasi-homothetic*.[10]

[8]The above derivation exploits the fact that the production function has CRS (λ_i can be factor out) and the sum of the fractions λ_i sum to 1; that is $\sum_i \lambda_i = 1$.

[9]The indirect utility function, say v_i is the utility function, say u_i, evaluated at the optimal solution, $c_i^*(p, a_i)$; that is $v(p, a_i) = u(c_i^*(p, a_i))$.

[10]By definition quasi-homothetic preferences generate affine Engel curves in wealth or income. The mathematical definition of an homothetic function $f(x)$ where x is a vector is the following: given two vectors x_1 and x_2, if we have that they obtain the same value $f(x_1) = f(x_2)$ then they produce the same value when multiplied by the same positive number k, i.e. $f(kx_1) = f(kx_2)$. The economical intuition is that consumption of any good is always a given fraction of wealth or income independent of its level.

In standard macro models, in order to find the optimal consumption rule, they solve the following problem[11]:

$$\sum_{t=0}^{\infty} \beta^t u(c_{it})$$

s.t.

$$\sum_{t=0}^{\infty} p_t c_{it} \leq p_0 a_{i0}.$$

As before, p_t = actualized prize of commodity bundle, a_{i0} = real initial wealth.

Utility functions, the preferences representation, often used in macro model are homothetic, like $u(c_{it}) = \log c_{it}$ that is a particular case of $u(c_{it}) = c_{it}^{1-\sigma}/(1-\sigma)$. They become quasi-homothetic if there is a subsistence level $\bar{c}$; i.e., $u(c_{it}) = (c_{it} - \bar{c})^{1-\sigma}/(1-\sigma)$.

Nevertheless, even though the homotheticity guarantees the Gorman's conditions there is still a problem. Note that, analogously to the firms' common technology assumption, parameters $\bar{c}$, β, and σ are the same across firms. Standard macroeconomics, in a sense, assumes also that agents' behavior remain the same exchanging rich and poor.[12] This is a strong restriction as it is the assumption of homothetic preferences that are really powerful in the aggregation of consumer choices. To make an example, computing the first order conditions (derivative with respect to c_{it}) with a log utility function we get

$$\beta^t u'(c_{it}) = \lambda_{i0} p_t \quad \Rightarrow \quad \beta^t c_{it}^{-1} = \lambda_{i0} p_t.$$

Solving for c_{it}

$$c_{it} = \frac{1}{\lambda_{i0}} \frac{\beta^t}{p_t}.$$

and substituting the budget constrain we can solve for $\frac{1}{\lambda_{i0}}$

$$\frac{1}{\lambda_{i0}} = (1-\beta) p_0 a_{i0}$$

implying that also c_{it} is linear w.r.t. initial wealth, that is

$$c_{it} = \frac{(1-\beta) p_0 \beta^t}{p_t} a_{i0}.$$

Finally, summing across agents we have

[11] See below the comparison between agents' behavioral rules in standard macroeconomics and in the agent based literature.

[12] Like in the famous 1983 movie "Trading Places" with Eddie Murphy!

$$\sum_{i=1}^{N_c} c_{it} = C_t = \frac{(1-\beta)p_0\beta^t}{p_t} A_0.$$

a linear relation between aggregate consumption and aggregate initial wealth exactly equal to the micro relation.

To sum up, with *quasi-homothetic preferences*, *CRS technology*, *complete markets* and *aggregate uncertainty* we can bypass the endowments heterogeneity problem building an aggregate relation that is exactly equal to the micro-relation. As a gift of these assumptions, we can find the solution of the complete model by solving the aggregate counterpart (called the *analogy principle* by Theil (1954); i.e., the centralized solution to the decentralized economy[13]:

Consumer:

$$\max E_0 \sum_{t=0}^{\infty} \beta^t u(C_t)$$

s.t.

$$\sum_{t=0}^{\infty} p_t C_t \leq p_0 A_0$$

Firm: Maximize profits using the aggregate technology

$$Z_t F(K_t, L_t).$$

Some final remarks can be done at the end of this simple introduction to the aggregation problem in the standard macro approach: (1) When the economic model fulfills conditions for a perfect aggregation, still there is a distribution. Simply, it doesn't matter for the variables modeled and their relationships. But what about if we are interested in fiscal policies? We have to compute the distribution. (2) In steady state the distribution is indeterminate. (3) An important assumption difficult to relax is complete markets (no frictions). (4) When we change some of the hypothesis, the exact aggregation does not hold anymore. In analyzing the distribution, standard macro models allow the introduction of heterogeneity but in 1 dimension (typically income) and at a very high computational cost (Krueger et al. 2015). These methods are not able to analyze networks of agents. For example firm-bank relationships.[14] In Chap. 3 there is an example of modeling bank-firms relationships.

[13] A deep analysis of the aggregation problem can be found in Browning et al. (1999), Heathcote et al. (2009), and Guvenen (2011).

[14] An example of an agent-based model analyzing firm-bank network using a Japanese dataset is Catullo et al. (2015).

1.1.4 A Didactic Example Comparing ABM with the Standard Approach

Suppose we want to analyze aggregate consumption. One possibility is to relay on the empirical literature saying, for example, that this relation is approximately linear with a coefficient in a certain range. Let's say $\{c_{it} = 0.5y_{it}, c_{it} = 0.6y_{it}, c_{it} = 0.7y_{it}, c_{it} = 0.8y_{it}, c_{it} = 0.9y_{it}\}$. Then heterogeneous agents, in an agent-based model, may try different specifications of the linear relation in the range coming from micro-survey. Choices of the agents can switch over time according to a feedback mechanism such as the *reinforcement learning* suggested in Tesfatsion (2006) using a utility function at time t. Essentially, is a *fitness function* reinforcing strategies with a good record. Consumers may use a utility function, say U_i, to update how good a consumption strategy is compared to the others. The consumers' information sets Ω_{it} contain x_{it} = {past consumption, incomes they earns}, n_{it} = {information on consumption of neighbors}.

Similarly, to implement a fitness function, a firm may use profits, given technology $y_{it} = f_i(k_{it}, l_{it}, z_{it})$ (output as a function of capital, labor and productivity) to decide in every period the best strategy in a given set.

The productivity variable z_{it}, possibly different among firms, follows a *Markov process*. In this problem, the information set is $\Omega_t = \{x_t, e_t, n_{it}\}$ where $x_t = (k_{it}, z_{it-1}, technology)$, e_t is the information that markets are perfectly competitive, and n_{it} collect information of past decisions of other firms.

Focusing the analysis on the consumption part of the model, during the simulation we record the distribution $\{f_1, f_2, f_3, f_4, f_5\}$, where the f_j $(j = 1, 2, 3, 4, 5)$ is the fraction of agents choosing, respectively, 0.5, 0.6, 0.7, 0.8, 0.9. This enable us to compute the final (last period) average choice or average marginal propensity to consume

$$\bar{c} = 0.5f_1 + 0.6f_2 + 0.7f_3 + 0.8f_4 + 0.9f_5$$

but also the median and others quantiles statistics. Same analysis can be done regarding firms choices.

How this methodology relates to the standard macroeconomic approach? As we said, we need to assure aggregation simplifying the problem. For example, in standard macroeconomics is usual the assumption of a representative consumer and a representative firm to compute the equilibrium rational expectation solution.

This lead to the well-known *optimal growth model* derived solving the aggregate maximization problem for the consumer i

$$\max E_0 \sum_{t=0}^{\infty} \beta^t U(C_t) \tag{1.3}$$

$$K_{t+1} = Y_t + (1 - \delta)K_t - C_t \tag{1.4}$$

with the firm's production function defined by the following equation[15]

$$Y_t = F(K_t, z_t) \tag{1.5}$$

where, again, z_t follows a *Markov process*. In this problem the information set is $\Omega_t = \{x_t, e_t\}$ where $x_t = (K_t, z_{t-1})$ and e_t is the information that market are perfectly competitive.

FOC with respect to C_t and K_{t+1} give the Euler equation

$$U'(C_t) = \beta E_t U'(C_{t+1})(F_k(K_{t+1}, z_{t+1}) + 1 - \delta).$$

To solve the model assume a Cobb-Douglas production function

$$Y_t = F(K_t, z_t) = z_t K_t^{\alpha} \tag{1.6}$$

$\delta = 1$ and condition for perfect aggregation of consumer decisions (homothetic preferences), such as

$$U(C_t) = \ln(C_t).$$

The solution of the problem is the consumption rule

$$C_t = (1 - \alpha\beta)Y_t. \tag{1.7}$$

We can calibrate this rule with numbers given from empirical studies. For example α is around 1/3 and β is in the range (0.9,1), say $\beta = 0.95$. This gives the linear optimal rule

$$C_t = 0.68Y_t. \tag{1.8}$$

that can be expressed in per-capita terms (with N agents), $y_t = Y_t/N$ and $c_t = C_t/N$

$$c_t = 0.68y_t. \tag{1.9}$$

The problem with this result is that it is optimal only under the simple environment specified and the assumptions made. Nevertheless, in principle the two approaches may give the same result. In other words, even though the two methodologies are different, it is possible that in the agent-based model

$$\bar{c} = 0.68.$$

In this very particular case we can conclude that agents and firms' heterogeneity, direct interaction in consumption and production choices (e.g., herding behaviors) are not important in explaining aggregate dynamics.

[15] Note that, to simplify the analysis, we assume a constant level of labor.

1.1.5 Behavioral Rules and Aggregation in ABM

In this part, having seen the stringent conditions to use the standard approach, let's return to the main topic of the book: The agent-based methodology.

The definition of an agent-based model is not simple, given that there many types in the economic literature and, more important, they are not confined to economic sciences. A broader enough definition is the one used in Tesfatsion et al. (2014) (p. xx): *An agent-based model (ABM) is a discrete-time space modeling of a system populated by agents whose successive interactions drive all system events over time.*

Here the direction in constructing the model is, in a sense, reversed. Dynamics comes first and then aggregation is derived. The interaction is though behavioral rules and market interaction or direct interaction between agents.

The agent-based approach is similar and different to the standard macro approach. It is similar because models start with a detail description at the micro level. It is different because (1) agents' behavioral rules are not derived from optimization, but from empirical analysis, surveys and experiments in economics; (2) markets descriptions richer representations (even though still simplified) of real markets; (3) to build the dynamics of the model is not necessary the preliminary aggregation step. The aggregation is computed ex-post enabling the analysis to deal with possibly non stable aggregate relationships. Finally, (4) it is taken seriously the possibility of direct interactions between agents and the consequent network analysis.

Point 4, together with the fact that the methodology derive agents' joint distribution, is the main key strength of the agent-based analysis.

Returning to behavioral rules, at a very broad level what is important for the choice of an economic agent is his/her information set or state at time t,

$$\Omega_{it} = \{x_{it}, e_{it}, n_{it}\}$$

made of 3 components. The vector x_{it} collects individual characteristics (preferences, technology, etc.), in e_{it} there are external signals (knowledge of the market in which they operate, news by media or public authorities, etc.), and n_{it} is the neighborhood of agent-i that he/she observes. All the variables are predetermined or exogenous; i.e., observable variables at the time t of the agent's choice.

A rule is an

(action/choice) given the (state/information set) at time t.

Agents behave rationally in the sense that learn from their mistakes or rules have a feedback structures. This may produce a switching between different rules as described in Hommes (2013) given a feedback rule that usually reinforces strategies giving higher payoffs in the past. In AB models the environment is complex[16] and

[16]The complexity of an Economic System and the necessity to build the model as an evolving comprehension of it by the agents is expressed with the notion of the *Economy as an Evolving Complex System* in Arthur et al. (1997), Blume and Durlauf (2005), Arthur (2006) and with the *Bottom-up Adaptive Macroeconomics* in Delli Gatti et al. (2011).

it is difficult to find the optimal rule.[17] This is the reason for the use of micro and experimental evidence with some reinforcement learning mechanism. This notion of rationality is better specified using the definition of *constructive rationality* in Tesfatsion et al. (2014). There is constructive rationality when the agent' action/rule can be expressed as a function of the state at time t. This means that when in the state there are consideration of future events those have to enter as anticipations; i.e., function of the state at time t. The strong notion of rational expectations in the Muth (1961) sense is a fixed point of the feedback actions-anticipations.

In the following sub-section there is an example of this approach. In this section are described also algorithms used in the agent-based literature to match demand and supply of goods, services and financial assets. In other words, when a firm produces something it needs to find someone to sell it. When a firm needs labor services it has to find skilled people working for me. To find a job this firm needs to search for a vacancy, etc. Finally, there is a description of firms' entry-exit stochastic processes implemented in the agent-based literature.

In the following section, to give some insights into the agent-based approach and compare it with more traditional approaches, we show a didactic model analyzing consumption choices.

1.1.6 Aggregation in ABM with Network Effects

In this final part we want to give an intuition of what are the implications of direct interaction or network effects in agents' decisions (the part n_{it} missing in standard macroeconomic models).

Let N be the number of agents and Θ a $N \times N$ time invariant matrix of links between agents. In the theory of graph its transpose Θ^T is the weighted adjacency matrix whose ij-entries θ_{ij} represent the strength of the link between agent-i and agent-j (in case such link exists). Obviously, we consider only links between different agents, so that the elements in the principal diagonal θ_{ii} are all zero.[18]

In other terms, in the following we assume that agents'decision regarding a choice variable, say c_{it} are linked together so that what happens to an agent-i affects in future periods agent-j.

Suppose that the information set at time t, Ω_{it}, contains individual characteristics, x_{it}, and the choice made by the others agents in previous period. In other words, the part n_{it} contains the vector $c_t = [c_{1t}, \dots, c_{Nt}]^T$.

---

[17]Nevertheless, there are agent-based models in which agents derive the behavioral rules optimizing. Examples are the works of Delli Gatti et al. (2003, 2005a) analyzing the macroeconomic consequences of the heterogeneity implied by the framework in Greenwald and Stiglitz (1993). In this line of research, firms maximize profits considering the expected cost of the bankruptcy event.

[18]This is a standard assumption for adjacency matrices in graph theory, meaning that agents have no self-loops. A more detailed analysis, with self loops, is in Palestrini (2013).

To simplify the analysis assume additivity. Suppose that agent-i rule may be represented by the following linear equation

$$c_{it} = \sum_{j=1}^{N} \theta_{ji} c_{jt-1} + \gamma x_{it} \tag{1.10}$$

where x_{it} $(i = 1, \ldots, N)$, the individual characteristic, enter in the rule with parameter γ and $\sum_{j=1}^{N} \theta_{ji} c_{jt-1}$ is the herding component in agents' decision. The parameters θ_{ij}, as said above, are weights measuring how strong are links between agent-i and agent-j.

Putting all the x_{it} in the vector $x_t = [x_{1t}, \ldots, x_{Nt}]^T$, we may write the system of equations

$$c_t = \Theta c_{t-1} + \gamma x_t. \tag{1.11}$$

According to the above equation agent-i's choice may be explained by the links with other agents at time $t-1$ according to the time homogeneous $N \times N$ matrix of weighted links Θ and by an individual characteristic.

In macroeconomic models we are interested in the dynamic of aggregate variables, that we may measure as the mean of the agents (the aggregator function h) at time t, that is

$$\bar{c}_t = \frac{1}{N} \sum_{i=1}^{N} c_{it}$$

By taking the average of vector components in Eq. (1.11), the aggregate dynamics becomes:

$$\bar{c}_t = \frac{1}{N} \sum_{i} d_i^{+} c_{it-1} + \gamma \bar{x}_t \tag{1.12}$$

where d_i^{+} is the sum of the column-i of the matrix Θ known as the *outer degree* of agent-i in graph theory.

This simple analysis shows two important points: (1) Direct interaction may generate persistence in aggregate agents' choice. (2) In order to understand the aggregate dynamics, we need to study the *degree distribution of agents* together with, as stressed in Chap. 4, the joint distribution of individual characteristics.

The most important tools used in macroeconomic to build an agent-based model are described below. In particular, we briefly illustrate how to model individual demand and supply in real and financial parts of the economy and their matching; the introduction of political economy "actors" (Government and Central Banks); the analysis of innovation processes and, finally, it discusses how to model firms' entry-exit processes. Moreover, we show basic tools used in financial agent-based model: micro-foundations and behavioural rules to reproduce traders' strategies, microstructure to model market transaction mechanisms.

1.2 Basic Macroeconomic Agent Based Tools

1.2.1 Macroeconomic Building Blocks

This chapter illustrates some basic building blocks of macroeconomic agent based models extracted from few seminal works. These building blocks are made by a set of behavioral and interaction rules that are associated to particular events that are repeated during the simulations of the model.

Figure 1.1 illustrates a typical sequence of events of an agent based simulation model. Agents make decisions in two steps, first they formulate expectations and after they make production and exchange choices. Indeed, a simulation may start with agents making expectations on which production choices are based, determining their production scale and the demand for loans. Then, in the credit market, loan demand matches bank loans supply. Moreover, firms may use internal resources and credit to increase their profit through technological improvement augmenting their productivity or the quality of the good produced. Finally, consumers choose the share of their income they want to consume and buy firms' final goods.

Therefore, the economic system evolves according to agent behaviors and interactions but it is also influenced by the decisions of public actors as the government

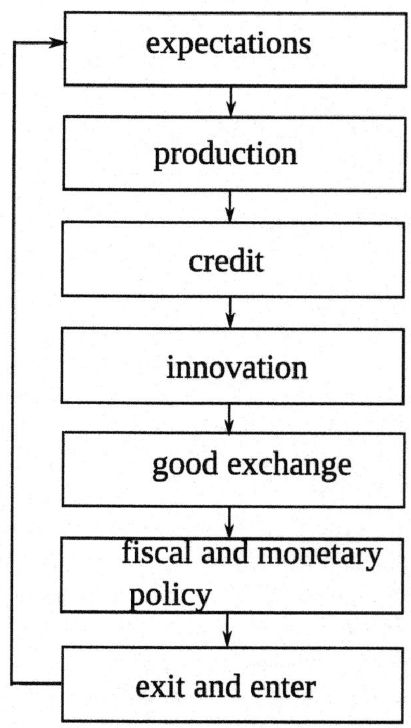

Fig. 1.1 Simulation schema

and the central bank. Government collects taxes and sustains the economy through public expenditure. While, the central bank manages the monetary policy.

Besides, the model has to regulate entry and exit of agents. Indeed agents may go bankrupt and, thus, they exit from the market, while new agents may enter.

Then, the building blocks we focus on are: expectation formation the formulation of production and credit, innovation process, the consumption process, the role of government and central bank, enter and exit conditions conclude.

1.2.2 *Expectations*

Agent behaviors are determined by expectations on the future dynamics of the economy. For instance, firms may fix selling price according to their individual expected demand or consumers decide their reserve price according to expectations on average prices.

Agent based models usually describe the economic environment resulting from the interaction of heterogeneous agents as complex adaptive system in which agents have bounded rationality and follow heterogeneous behaviors and expectations. According to Gigerenzer et al. (2000), it is possible to conceive agent behaviors as the result of the application of particular behavioral rules or heuristics based on a reduced informational set. Agents may test different rules and choose the one that gives better results.

Following the expectation structure developed in Brock and Hommes (1997), Anufriev and Hommes (2012) are able to replicate experimental data on asset prices through simulation allowing agents to formulate their expectation (p^e_{t+1}) on prices according to different heuristics which consider both the expectation (p^e_t) and the effective realization of the asset price (p_{t-1}):

1. Adaptive heuristic:
$$p^e_{t+1} = p^e_t + w(p_{t-1} - p^e_t) \tag{1.13}$$
in case $w = 1$, we have the so called "naive" expectations $p^e_{t+1} = p_{t-1}$, agents expectations are equal to the previous realization
2. Trend-Following Heuristic:
$$p^e_{t+1} = p_{t-1} + \gamma(p_{t-1} - p_{t-2}) \tag{1.14}$$
with $\gamma > 1$, the higher γ the stronger the impact on trends on expectations
3. Anchoring and Adjustment Heuristic:
$$p^e_{t+1} = 0.5(p_f + p_{t-1}) + (p_{t-1} - p_{t-2}). \tag{1.15}$$
where p^f is a fundamental level of the price that may be used as an anchor, for instance p^f may be the average of the past realizations, $p^f = (1/t)\sum_{j=0}^{t-1} p_j$.

Each agent measures the performance ($U_{h,t-1}$) of all the h heuristics in predicting the price realization p_{t-1}:

$$U_{h,t-1} = -(p_{t-1} - p^e_{h,t-1})^2 + \eta U_{h,t-2}. \tag{1.16}$$

where η is a measure of the value given on past performance of the heuristics, thus the probability of choosing an heuristic $n_{h,t}$:

$$n_{h,t} = \delta n_{h,t-1} + (1-\delta)\frac{exp(\beta U_{h,t-1})}{Z_{t-1}} \tag{1.17}$$

where Z_{t-1} is a normalizing factor ($Z_{t-1} = \sum_{h=0}^{H} exp(\beta U_{h,t-1})$) and $0 \leq \delta \leq 1$ determines the inertia of the impact of each rule in the agent choice among the different heuristics.

In Dosi et al. (2015) the approach proposed by Brock and Hommes (1997), Anufriev and Hommes (2012) is followed to determine firm investments according to their demand expectations, which derive from an heuristic chosen among different rules. Dosi et al. (2015) do not find that heuristic heterogeneity have a strong impact on systemic results even if they influence in a significant way output volatility.

1.2.3 Production and Credit

Production choices depends on firms' expectations. Different approaches are used to determine the quantity of goods firms produce, one of these is fixing a desired production scale through profit maximization or through adaptive rules. For instance, in Delli Gatti et al. (2005b, 2010b) firms production level (Y_{it}) depends on expected profit minus bankruptcy costs. Expected profit ($E(\pi_{it})$) increases with production scale (Y_{it}) and firm net worth (A_{it}) but, at the same time, bankruptcy costs ($C(Y_{it})$) and bankruptcy probability augment with the production level ($\Omega(Y_{it}, A_{it})$):

$$\max_{Y_{it}} \quad V(Y_{it}, A_{it}) = E(\pi(Y_{it}, A_{it}) - C(Y_{it})\Omega(Y_{it}, A_{it}) \tag{1.18}$$

firms fund production through their net-worth and in case their net-worth is not sufficient they ask banks for loans. Indeed, according to the "pecking order theory", information asymmetries result in higher costs for external financing, thus investments are financed though internally generated funds (in this case firm net-worth) and only if internal funds are not enough they resort to debt.

However, if we assume that firm loan demand depends on the trade-off between costs and benefits of debt, the relation between credit and production level can be reversed. According to the "dynamic trade theory approach" firms try to reach a long run level of leverage that resolves the trade off between debt costs and gains Riccetti et al. (2014).

Because of bounded rationality and search costs firms ask for loans to a limited set of banks and credit network matching may derive from loan costs. The interest rate charged on credit depends on financial robustness of both the borrowing firm and the lending bank, in Delli Gatti et al. (2010b) the higher the leverage (measured as the total amount of loans divided by equities) the higher the interest of loans and the lower the quantity of loans received. Thus, the interest rate is computed as:

$$r_{zt} = \alpha A_{zt}^{-\alpha} + \alpha l_{it} \quad (1.19)$$

where A_{zt} is the net-worth of bank z and l_{it} the leverage of firm i at time t, given the α parameter greater than zero. Thus, αl_{it} is the firm specific component: firms that have higher leverage are riskier, thus they pay an higher interest rate. While $\alpha A_{zt}^{-\alpha}$ is the bank specific component: banks with higher net-worth suffer less from single firm failures, thus they may charge lower interest on loans.

More realistic and elaborated approaches are used to determine loan supply according to agents financial robustness. For instance in Caiani et al. (2015) a multidimensional algorithm defines the credit supply based on three pillars of the credit offer: the active management of banks' balance sheet, case-by-case credit worthiness evaluation and the credit worthiness based on operating cash flows. In Assenza et al. (2015) banks estimate a logistic regression of firm bankruptcy probability in relation to firm leverage levels. Thus, thanks to the estimated logistic regression, banks are able to associate to each firm a default probability, which contributes to determine the interest rate charged on loans and the maximum quantity of credit each firm may receive.

Besides, credit network matching may derive from loan costs: firms try to borrow from the cheaper offerer. Following Delli Gatti et al. (2010b), in every period each borrower observes the interest rate of a fraction of the population of lenders. They switch from the previous lender to a new one with a probability p_s:

$$p_s = \begin{cases} 1 - e^{\lambda(r_{new} - r_{old})/r_{new}}, & \text{if } r_{new} < r_{old} \\ 0, & \text{if } r_{new} \geq r_{old} \end{cases} \quad (1.20)$$

where r_{old} is the previous interest rate and r_{new} is the interest rate offered by an other bank, where λ is the intensity of choice. The lower λ the higher the preference for preserving the previous credit relation, thus with low λ credit network configuration tend to be more stable.

1.2.4 Innovation

Agent based models describe the economic world as a complex adaptive system characterized by out of equilibria dynamics and uncertainty. Therefore, agent based models may be an appropriate methodology for analyzing innovation processes.

which are essentially dynamic and tend to break equilibria. Moreover, technological change is characterized by uncertainty and agent heterogeneity in the dual process of generation and appropriability of knowledge (Dawid 2005).

In Dosi et al. (2010), technological change takes the form of productivity improvements of capital goods. In the capital good sector, technological change derives from firms' efforts in both imitation and innovation. The probability of innovating is related to the strength of the expenditure in *R&D* (RD_{it}), which depends on firm previous sales $S_{i,t-1}$:

$$RD_{it} = \nu S_{i,t-1} \tag{1.21}$$

with $0 < \nu < 1$. Expenditure in innovation is divided between innovation (IN_{it}) and imitation (IM_{it}):

$$IN_{it} = \xi RD_{it} \tag{1.22}$$

$$IMit = (1 - \xi) RD_{it} \tag{1.23}$$

innovation occurs in two steps, the first step expresses the probability of innovating, thus access or not to innovation:

$$\theta_{in}^{it} = 1 - e^{-\zeta_1 IN_{it}} \tag{1.24}$$

with $0 < \zeta_1 \leq 1$, if the firm succeed may improve its productivity (B_{it}) or the efficiency of the instrumental good it produces (A_{it}):

$$A_{it}^{IN} = A_{it}(1 + x_{it}^{A}) \tag{1.25}$$

$$B_{it}^{IN} = B_{it}(1 + x_{it}^{B}) \tag{1.26}$$

where x_{it}^{A} and x_{it}^{B} are extracted from a beta distribution $Beta(\alpha_1, \beta_1)$ over a support between -1 and 1.

Similarly imitating probability depends on IM_{it}

$$\theta_{im}^{it} = 1 - e^{-\zeta_2 IM_{it}} \tag{1.27}$$

with $0 < \zeta_1 \leq 1$, this gives the probability of imitating one of the firm in the market.

A similar approach is followed in the Eurace model (Cincotti et al. 2010), where firms that produce final goods may introduce also good quality improvements. Firms estimate the potential gains of increasing quality, considering sales of goods with different quality levels and then they choose the amount of money they want to invest in research and development devoted to quality improvement. Therefore, the higher the number of worker employed in innovation the higher the probability of incremental good quality growth.

An other interesting approach to the innovation process is the one proposed by Gilbert et al. (2002), where innovation is conceived as the variation of basic components of a technology the "kenes": "kenes" may be combined in different way and their effectiveness may be improved through time, leading to a new technology which is valued according a fitness function. Firms that are able to employ better "kene" combinations are the one that make higher profits and thus may survive or increase their dimensions. Moreover, in order to increase their effectiveness, firms may create collaboration and network to share their "kenes".

1.2.5 Consumption

In macroeconomic agent based models, a basic distinction may be made between models that treat consumption as "supply driven" and models that define specific consumption behaviors.

In "supply driven" models the demand for goods is on average in line with the supply, while at individual level firms are subject to idiosyncratic price shocks: higher (lower) prices represent a relatively high (low) demand. In Delli Gatti et al. (2005b) the individual selling price is given by a random extraction from a uniform distribution around an average level ($P_{it} = u_{it} P_t$) with $E(u_{it}) = 1$. Therefore, price random variations are a manifestation of firm demand uncertainty.

While, consumption is endogenous, for instance, in Riccetti et al. (2014), where each agent chooses the desired consumption (c^d_{ht}) according to a simple behavioral rule:

$$c^d_{ht} = c_1 w_{ht} + c_2 A_{ht} \tag{1.28}$$

thus, consumption depends on the wage received (w_{ht}) and on wealth (A_{ht}). Given the desired consumption, each consumer buys the cheaper goods it finds considering a limited set of observable firms. Consequently firms compete through their selling price (p_{it}), which is adapted following the dynamics of the inventories ($\tilde{y}_{it}$):

$$p_{it} = \begin{cases} p_{i,t-1}(1 + \alpha U(0,1)), & \text{if } \tilde{y}_{it} = 0 \text{ and } y_{i,t-1} > 0 \\ p_{i,t-1}(1 - \alpha U(0,1)), & \text{otherwise} \end{cases} \tag{1.29}$$

Indeed, when a firm has inventory ($y_{i,t-1} > 0$) it was not able to sell all its production, thus this firm will reduce the selling price. In any case, the minimum price is equal to production cost. Similarly, in Caiani et al. (2015), firms change adaptively the selling price modifying their mark-up on marginal costs. If inventories overcome a certain threshold firms reduce the mark-up and thus the selling price, while on the contrary if inventories are too low they increase the mark-up.

Some agent based model proposes a more detailed description of the final good markets. For instance, the Eurace model (Cincotti et al. 2010) describes consumption decisions as a three steps process. First of all households choose the amount of their income they want to consume and, thus, saving according to their liquidity level an to income volatility, indeed higher income volatility implies a more prudential consumption pattern. The second step is the mall choices. Firms bring their product to malls and consumer choose the mall where they want to go for shopping selecting the once with lower prices and higher good quality. Finally, in a randomly selected order consumers buy the goods that offer a good quality price combination.

1.2.6 Government and Central Bank

Government and central bank in macroeconomic agent based model play a critical role in stabilizing the economy adopting countercyclical measures and providing liquidity to the system.

Government collects taxes from firms, banks and consumers in the form of wealth and income taxes. At the same time, government may assume public employs, buy goods or provide public transfers. For instance, in Caiani et al. (2015), government assumes a given number of worker as public employees and provide unemployment benefits, thus government expenditure assume a countercyclical pattern: during recession the amount of taxes collected decreases because incomes go down and, conversely, government pays unemployment benefit and sustains household income through unemployment benefits. Public deficits are funded through the emission of bonds, which are bought by commercial banks or by the central bank. At the same time, central bank provides liquidity to the economy and fixes the discount interest rate.

Moreover, government and central bank may be conduct bail- in procedure in case of bank failures or may provide funds for the enter of new agents in the system if there are not enough private recourses.

Although government and central banks are crucial in the functioning of the artificial economies, their importance is essential in the formulation of monetary and fiscal policies. Indeed, changing the discount interest rate value or the supply of money impact on the micro and macro dynamics, giving us insights into the importance of monetary measures and the channels through which they are transmitted into the economic system.

Conversely, it is possible to test the effects of different fiscal policy regimes on the economic system. For instance varying the tax burden, the expenditure amount or varying the specification of particular expenditure measures as unemployment benefits, minimum wages or minimum income.

1.2.7 Exit and Enter

The dynamic of the population of agents is strictly connected with aggregate dynamics and with meso patterns. For instance, the enter and exit of firms and banks impact on aggregate output dynamics but also on the evolution of the credit network and on the distribution of agent size.

The exit rule is related with the failure procedure, usually when the net-worth of an agent is negative this agent fails and, thus, exits from the market. Moreover, firms may fail if they have not enough liquidity to pay for their input and to repay the service of their debt (Caiani et al. 2015).

Costs of failure may fall on banks, indeed legal expenditure may reduce the share of credit that banks are able to recuperate from a firm failure. In Riccetti et al. (2014), the recovery rate is the percentage of loans provided by a bank that is given back by the failing firm, this is computed as the ratio between assets and loans of the bankrupted firm decreased by a fixed amount for the legal expenditure. The recovery rate have a significant impact on the dynamic of the credit network influencing the amount of bad debt a bank may suffer, considering as bad debt the share of the loan that is not recovered by the lending bank after the failure of the borrowing firm. Thus, firm failure, through bad debt, may trigger bank failures, which in turn, may lead to a credit contraction having sharp effect on output.

Failed agents are replaced by new entries. Thus, it is necessary to establish the number of new enters and their size. In Delli Gatti et al. (2005b) the number of entering firm depends on the interest rate charged (r_{t-1}), which influence profitability, the higher the interest rate, the lower the profit rate and thus the lower the incentive to enter the market. Thus, the probability to enter $P(entry)$:

$$P(entry) = \frac{\bar{N}}{1 + exp[d(\bar{r}_{t-1} - e)]} \tag{1.30}$$

where d and e are parameters and $\bar{N}$ is greater than one.

The size of the entering firms is given by a drawn from a uniform distribution centered on the mode of incumbent firms. In effect, in many agent based models the number of agents is given, thus every agent that fails is substituted by another agent, while the size of the agents and their target leverage vary according to some average measures. For instance the size, expressed by the net-worth, may be related to the average, median or the mode of the other firms or, even, may be equal to an initial value adjusted by the level of prices (Riccetti et al. 2014; Caiani et al. 2015).

1.3 Basic Financial Agent Based Tools

1.3.1 Financial Building Blocks

Following the previous section, we present some basic building blocks of financial agent based models extracted from few seminal works. In this regard, some clarifications are important. Firstly, many behavioral rules shown in the previous chapter are also appropriated to describe financial markets or, in some cases, have been

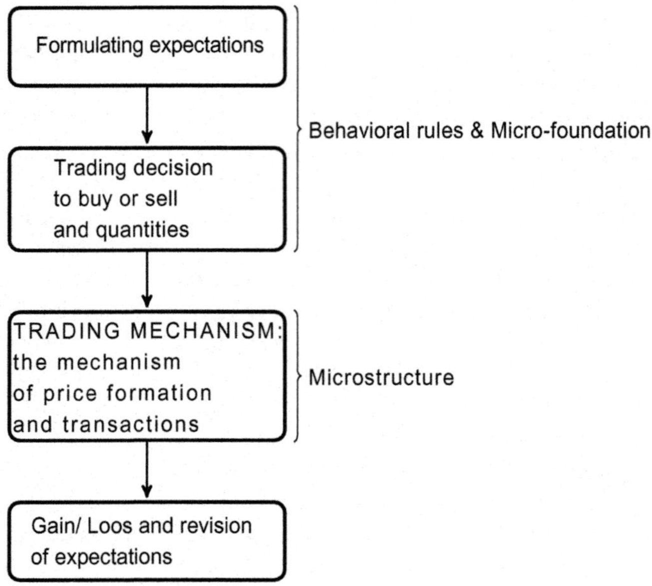

Fig. 1.2 Simulation Schema in financial models

borrowed from financial models.[19] Indeed, the high availability of financial data and their high frequency have facilitated the identification of important behavioral rules (Vaglica et al. 2008). Then, many markets illustrated in the previous chapter are themselves financial systems. For instance, consumption, saving, investment and credit demand/supply are financial decisions. Whether, in the previous section we have analyzed some financial strategies in order to see their impact on the real economy, here we deal with the stock market as a "closed market", purely speculative.[20]

As Fig. 1.2 shows, the typical sequence of events of a financial agent based model may be divided into two main blocks. First, traders formulate their expectations on future stocks price. These beliefs, which may be derived from a classical micro-foundation or through some other behavioral rule, identify some investor features. Specifically, according to the expectation, the agent decides whether to buy or sell, his price and quantity. Once formulated expectations, agents enter the market trying to buy or sell the desired amount of stocks. The mechanism of price formation, that is the detail of how exchanges occur in financial markets, defines the market

[19]Specifically, expectations and adaptive behaviors described in the Chapter 2.5 are driven from financial models (Brock and Hommes 1998).

[20]When a modeler wants to create a multi-markets model, where agents act in different environments, such as, for instance, the consumption or the stock market, it is useful to remember that we are dealing with the same individual which, although in a market is a consumer and in the other one an investor, should have consistent and coherent strategies and behavioral rules in the two different systems. In other words, if an agent is "rational" in a market, he must apply the same behavior in all the other environments where he operates.

microstructures. In this regards, stock markets can be organized in different ways. There are, for example, supply demand in-balance markets which require the presence of a market maker, double action and order-driven markets. Among the several financial agent-based models, some works have paid more attention in reproducing the behavioral rules of traders (Brock and Hommes 1998; Lux and Marchesi 2000; Kirman 1993), others, instead, have focused the analysis on the market microstructures (Iori 2002; LiCalzi and Pellizzari 2003; Raberto et al. 2001; Tedeschi et al. 2009). Very few models, however, have jointly combined agents' microfoundation with markets' microstructures (Chiarella et al. 2009; Tedeschi et al. 2012c).

1.3.2 *Microfoundations and Behavioural Rules*

Several behavioural rules have been introduced in order to reproduce traders' strategy in stock market. The modeler could use a plausible and realistic rule of thumb or a more sophisticated microfoundation derived from the maximization of some utility function. Since the stylized financial model present in Chap. 3 reproduces a system where traders use rules of thumb in order to form their expectation, here the analysis focuses on the maximization of an utility function.

It is commonly accepted, in the financial markets, that traders must be described as risk adverse players. To this end, different utility functions can be used ranking from the CARA utility function (Chiarella et al. 2009; Tedeschi et al. 2012c) to the mean-variance one (Kirman 1993; Brock and Hommes 1998). In this section we present the well-known microeconomic analysis on the traders' behaviour introduced by Kirman (1991, 1993) and, later used in several papers of Brock and Hommes (1998).

The advantage of introducing this behavioral rule depends not only on its many theoretical applications, but also on the several estimation procedures which have tested it (Alfarano et al. 2005; Boswijk et al. 2007; Recchioni et al. 2015).

The model introduced by Kirman describes the trend of a foreign exchange rate by considering the opportunity that traders can switch between two different behavior. Kirman borrows the idea of switching from the observation of the ants' behaviour. When, indeed, ants face two different but identical food sources, very often a great number of them, about 80 % concentrate on one of the food sources, whilst only the remaining 20 % on the other. Moreover, after some time these proportions suddenly switch. Kirman proposes a dynamic stochastic model able to explain this asymmetric aggregate behaviour and, then, applies it to an exchange market where investors can switch between two strategies, namely the chartist and fundamentalist one.

In this market agents may invest in a risky foreign currency which offers a stochastic dividend y_{t+1} IID with mean $\hat{y}$ or in a risk-free domestic currency with a fixed interest rate $R = (1 + r) > 1$. The Utility function which the agents maximize is mean-variance: $U^i(W^i_{t+1}) = E_i(W^i_{t+1}) - \sigma^i V_i(W^i_{t+1})$, with E_i and V_i the conditional expectation and variance of wealth in t+1 respectively. Wealth dynamics is given by $W^i_{t+1} = RW^i_t + (s^e_{i,t+1} + y_{t+1} - Rs^e_{i,t})d^i_t$. The agent i's foreign currency demand is so:

$$d_t^i = \frac{s_{i,t+1}^e + \hat{y} - (1+r)s_t}{2\alpha\sigma_i}, \tag{1.31}$$

where 2σ represents risk aversion, $s_{i,t+1}^e$ agent i's expectation about the exchange rate s_{t+1}, $\hat{y}$ is the mean of the IID dividend process and $\alpha = V(s_{t+1} + y_{t+1})$.

The equilibrium for the exchange rate with rational expectations is given by:

$$s* = \frac{y - 2\alpha\sigma X_t}{r}, \tag{1.32}$$

with X_t supply of foreign exchange. In the case with n_t fundamentalists and 1-n_t chartists, the market equilibrium is, indeed,

$$n_t d^f + (1 - n_t)d^c = X_t. \tag{1.33}$$

Let us define $s_{f,t+1}^e$ and $s_{c,t+1}^e$ the expectations of fundamentalists and chartists on the next period's exchange rate s_{t+1}, such as:

$$s_{f,t+1}^e = s_{t-1} + v(s * - s_{t-1}), \tag{1.34}$$

and

$$s_{c,t+1}^e = s_{t-1} + g(s_{t-1} - s_{t-2}), \tag{1.35}$$

with $0 \le v \le 1$ and $g \ge 0$. Fundamentalists believe that the exchange rate will move back to its fundamental value s*. The speed of this process depends on v: if v is equal to 1, then, fundamentalists expect the exchange rate to jump to its fundamental value s* immediately otherwise, if v = 0, fundamentalists expect the exchange rate to follow a random walk. In the case of chartists, indeed, Kirman focuses on g = 1.

Substituting Eqs. (1.34) and (1.35) in the market Eq. (1.33) and defining $x_t = s_t - s*$ like the deviation of s_t from the fundamental benchmark, Kirman finds the equilibrium exchange rate:

$$(1 + r)x_t = [1 - vn_t + g(1 - n_t))]x_{t-1} - g(1 - n_t)s_{t-2}. \tag{1.36}$$

Furthermore a Markov chain explains the evolution of $n_t = k_t/N$. When all agents are fundamentalists, $n_t = 1$, the Eq. (1.36) yields

$$x_t = \frac{1 - v}{1 + r}x_{t-1}, \tag{1.37}$$

which is a stable linear system with eigenvalue $\lambda = (1 - v)/(1 + r)$; otherwise, if all individuals are chartists, $n_t = 0$, the Eq. (1.36) is

$$x_t = \frac{1 - g}{1 + r}x_{t-1} - \frac{g}{1 + r}x_{t-2}. \tag{1.38}$$

For $g = 1$ the Eq. (1.38) has complex eigenvalues which become unstable when g increases beyond $1 + r$, that is, when chartists expect the change in exchange rate to be larger than the risk free gross return.

To sum up, when the market is dominated by fundamentalists, the exchange rate is stable and pushed towards its fundamental value, s*. Otherwise, when the market is governed by chartists, the exchange rate is stable only if $g \leq 1 + r$.

1.3.3 Market Microstructure

Once defined the investor decision-making process, we have to model how transactions happen in the market. The role of market design has been widely explored in economic literature and, as Stiglitz (2004) has underlined "one of the recent revolutions in economics is an understanding that markets do not automatically work well and that design matters". Several papers have pointed out the influence of exchange rules on the allocative efficiency Bottazzi et al. (2005), Gode and Sunder (1997), Sallans et al. (2003), for example by analyzing the most favorable market architecture in maximizing agents' outcome Milgrom (2004), Pogrebna (2006), Kirman et al. (2008).

Following the pioneering Santa Fe Artificial Stock Market, SF-ASM (LeBaron et al. 1999), several artificial markets have been developed to explain the impact that market design has on traders' behaviors and performances Chiarella and Iori (2002), LeBaron and Yamamoto (2008), Lux (1998). These models show how agents can change their strategies when they are coordinated via market mediated interactions. The role that market structure plays in determining the agents' strategies and their performance is, therefore, essential. To this regards, financial AB models use two main categories for describing the mechanisms of price formation. On the one hand, some models implement realistic exchange mechanisms, such as double actions Raberto et al. (2001), order-driven or negotiated markets Chiarella and Iori (2002), Tedeschi et al. (2009), Tedeschi et al. (2012a). In these markets traders, once decided if they are buyers or sellers and their respective purchase and sale prices (called bids and asks respectively), meet and directly bargain prices and quantities in a very decentralized way.

Let's analyze, for example, the stylized negotiated market proposed by Tedeschi et al. (2012a). Buyers enter the market sequentially in a random order. Once the buyer is in a market, he meets a finite number of sellers at random. He buys first from the seller offering the lowest price (provided, of course, that his reservation price is lower than the asked price). If the supply available at the cheapest asking price is not sufficiently large to fulfill his order, the agent buys all the quantity available at the asking price and then moves on to check the second lowest asking price, iterating the process until he has no more good to buy, or there are no more good for sale among sellers the buyer links with. If the order can only be partially filled, the buyer is rationed. Sellers deal with buyers on a "first come, first served" basis. This market is characterized by a continuous decentralized search, generating out-of-equilibrium dynamics. Due to the absence of any exogenously imposed market-clearing mechanism, the economy is allowed to self-organize towards a spontaneous order with persistent involuntary unsold good and excess individual demands. The market price, used in this model, corresponds to a classic Paasche index. For each day t: $\bar{p}_t = \sum_{i=1}^{N}(p_t^i(\frac{q_t^i}{\sum_{i=1}^{N} q_t^i})$, where p_t^i is given by the price at which a transaction occurs, q_t^i the quantity sold in that transaction, and N the number of transactions made in t. If no new transection occurs, a proxy for p_t^i is given by the previous traded price.

In Chap. 3, the reader can find a more sophisticated market microstructure, where we present an order-driven book.

On the other hand, other models implement a stylized exchange mechanism based on a supply demand in-balance Brock and Hommes (1998), Kirman (1991), Lux and Marchesi (2000). These models allow traders to effect all wished transactions. Specifically, the exchanges are regulated by the equilibrium prices vector, which guarantees the realization of all transactions without implementing any direct exchange via market mediated interaction.

Chapter 2
A Simple Model of Business Fluctuations with Heterogeneous Interacting Agents and Credit Networks

Leonardo Bargigli, Alessandro Caiani, Luca Riccetti and Alberto Russo

2.1 Getting Started: Implementing a Toy Model

In what follows we firstly describe and then implement and simulate a very simple model, that is a simplified version of Riccetti et al. (2013), by using **R**.[1] In the original paper, a multitude of heterogeneous firms and banks interact in the credit market. Firms want to produce and sell a homogeneous commodity in the goods market and, in order to finance production, they need credit from banks. Firms look at a random

[1] Readers who already have good programming skills may quickly read this section and then go to the next one in which many steps of the implementation procedures are similar though proposed in a more complicated environment.

L. Bargigli
Dipartimento di Scienze per l'Economia e l'Impresa, Università di Firenze,
Via delle Pandette, 9, 50127 Florence, Italy
e-mail: leonardo.bargigli@unifi.it

A. Caiani (✉)
Dipartimento di Management, Università Politecnica delle Marche,
Piazzale Martelli 8, 60121 Ancona, Italy
e-mail: alessandro.caiani@univpm.it

L. Riccetti
Facoltà di Economia, Dipartimento di Management, Sapienza Università di Roma,
Via del Castro Laurenziano 9, 00161 Roma, Italy
e-mail: luca.riccetti@uniroma1.it

A. Russo
Dipartimento di Management, Università Politecnica delle Marche, Piazzale Martelli 8,
60121 Ancona, Italy
e-mail: alberto.russo@univpm.it

A. Caiani et al. (eds.), *Economics with Heterogeneous Interacting Agents*,
New Economic Windows, DOI 10.1007/978-3-319-44058-3_2

subset of potential partners (due to imperfect information) and then choose the most convenient bank (i.e. the bank charging the lowest interest rate); as a consequence, an endogenous network of credit interlinkages evolves over time. The model shows the emergence of business fluctuations and highlights both the role of financial fragility and network structure in shaping economic dynamics.

The model we are going to develop and analyze is, however, a very simplified version of Delli Gatti et al. (2010a), so that we can thought of it as a "toy model". Such a minimal model, however, can be very useful to understand the basic features of modeling and programming, even though we cannot use it as a guide for economic analysis and policy. For instance, we only take into account agents' *heterogeneity*: firms differentiate along time due to idiosyncratic shocks and individual decisions (for instance, the investment choice). Instead, we do not consider *interaction* which is one of the central feature of a complex economic system to be analyzed by building and simulating agent-based models. However, this characteristic will be introduced in an improved version of the model in Sect. 2.2.

2.1.1 Model Theoretical Setup

We model a simplified economy in which, time after time, *heterogeneous firms* decide how much to invest on the basis of previous profits. In this way firms accumulate capital which is used to produce a homogeneous (perishable) commodity sold at a *stochastic price*. The economic system is composed of N firms ($n = 1, 2, \dots, N$). We analyze this economy for a time span of T periods ($t = 1, 2, \dots, T$). At the beginning, firms have an *initial endowment* of net worth A_0 (the same for all firms).[2]

2.1.1.1 Investment, Capital and Financial Structure

In every period t, each firm invests an amount of resources which is proportional to past realized profits, $Z_{n,t-1}$:

$$I_{n,t} = \gamma Z_{n,t-1} \tag{2.1}$$

where $\gamma > 0$, say the *investment accelerator*, is a time-invariant parameter, uniform across firms.

Based on investment decisions, firms accumulate capital[3]:

[2]Consider that even though we will talk about business fluctuations and the like, we are developing a partial dis(equilibrium) model, which is not a stock-flow consistent macroeconomic model. Initial conditions are not stock-flow consistent as well.

[3]For the moment, we assume that there is no depreciation of capital. In Sect. 2.1.4.1 we introduce a depreciation rate.

$$K_{n,t} = K_{n,t-1} + I_{n,t} \tag{2.2}$$

From the financial point of view, capital is covered by both internal resources – the net worth $A_{n,t}$ – and external finance – a bank loan $B_{n,t}$:

$$B_{n,t} = \begin{cases} K_{n,t} - A_{n,t} & \text{if } K_{n,t} > A_{n,t} \\ B_{n,t} = 0 & \text{otherwise} \end{cases} \tag{2.3}$$

We assume that there is a (passive) banking system which provides credit to firms (then, the supply of credit is equal to the demand of credit by construction).

2.1.1.2 Production and Pricing

Firms produce a homogeneous commodity by using a single input, that is capital. In particular, production is proportional to capital:

$$Y_{n,t} = \phi K_{n,t} \tag{2.4}$$

where $\phi > 0$, say the *capital productivity*, is a time-invariant parameter, uniform across firms.

The price $p_{n,t}$ at which firms sell the homogeneous goods Y is a stochastic variable. For the sake of simplicity, we assume that the price is given by a constant, that is the parameter $\bar{p}$, plus a stochastic variable with unitary mean and a *uniform distribution* in the interval $(0, 2)$. Let's also assume that firms sell all the produced output at the stochastic price:

$$p_{n,t} = \bar{p} + U(0, 2) \tag{2.5}$$

2.1.1.3 Profits

As a first approximation, we assume that the cost of capital $r > 0$, say the *interest rate*, is a time-invariant parameter, uniform across firms.

Then, the *n-th* firm's profit is:

$$Z_{n,t} = p_{n,t} Y_{n,t} - r K_{n,t} = (p_{n,t}\phi - r) K_{n,t} \tag{2.6}$$

which implies that dividends are proportional to the interest paid on the bank loan (that is, the cost of self-finance is equal to the cost of external finance).

Based on the realized profit, firms update their net worth:

$$A_{n,t+1} = A_{n,t} + Z_{n,t} \tag{2.7}$$

2.1.1.4 Entry–Exit Process

Firms may default if they become insolvent: if $A_{n,t+1} < 0$, then the firm goes bankrupt and leaves the economy.[4] For the sake of simplicity, we assume a *one-to-one replacement* mechanism according to which bankrupted firms are replaced by new entrants with an initial net worth equal to A_0.

Finally, *aggregate variables* are obtained by summing up individual variables.

2.1.2 Implementing the Model Using R

In the previous section, we described the setup of the model. Now, we want to implement such a model in the computer by using an appropriate software, that is **R**. Before that, however, it can be useful to think about the *algorithmic structure* of the model we developed.

There are two main blocks to be considered: (i) the list of *parameters* and the *initial conditions* of variables; (ii) the *sequence of events*, that is in which order the equations of the model should be considered to have an effective algorithm to be implemented.

As for the first block, we should consider the following elements:

- Parameters: γ, ϕ, r, and $\bar{p}$. N firms (indexed by n); T periods of time (indexed by t);
- Firms' variables: A (net worth), Z (profit), I (investment), K (capital), B (debt), Y (production), P (price);
- Initial conditions ($t = 1$): set $A = 1$ and $K = 1$ for all firms and pick up N random number from a U(0,1) to initialize Z; set all other variables to zero.[5]

Now, we can describe the sequence of events running in the model, for each firm ($n = 1, 2.., N$) and in every period of time ($t = 1, 2, \ldots, T$):

1. Investment choice: $I = \gamma Z_{-1}$
2. Capital accumulation: $K = K_{-1} + I$
3. Production: $Y = \phi K$
4. Debt: $B = K - A_{-1}$; $B(B < 0) = 0$
5. Stochastic price: $P = 2U(0, 1) + \bar{p}$
6. Profit: $Z = PY - rK$
7. Net worth: $A = A_{-1} + Z$
8. Entry–exit process: $Z(A < 0) = 0$; $K(A < 0) = 1$ $A(A < 0) = 1$;

As you can see, the algorithm is such that each event in which a variable is updated (for instance, the investment choice at the first step of the sequence) occurs before the

[4]In this case, the banking sector would suffer from a non-performing loan; however, we are not modeling such a process related to the banking system's balance sheet in this simplified model.

[5]For now, we are not considering aggregate variables.

same variable is involved in the updating of another variable in a subsequent step (for instance, capital accumulation at the second step).[6] The events are then organized according to a sequential order that excludes the presence of simultaneous events.[7]

2.1.2.1 The R Code

In general, the algorithmic structure of the model we presented can be implemented in any computational language. Our choice is to provide a way of implementing it in **R**. We provide the simulation code of the "toy model" in the 6 following steps:

1. Open a new file in **R**-Studio.[8] Therefore, the starting point is a blank page.
2. The first line of the code could be

```
#Toymodel
```

   where the symbol # is used to comment the line of code (that is, if preceded by that symbol, the line of the code is not compiled by the software).
3. Then, we can set the time span and the number of agents,

```
#SET TIME SPAN AND NUMBER OF FIRMS
#Number of simulation periods
Time <- 1000
#Number of firms
Ni <- 100
```

   where the symbol <- is equivalent to the symbol = (for instance, we could also write `Time = 1000` instead of `Time <- 1000`)
4. and the parameter setting:

```
#PARAMETER SETTING
#Investment accelerator
gamma <- 1.1
#Capital productivity
phi <- 0.1
#Interest rate
r <- 0.1
#Random price constant
Pbar <- 0.01
```

---

[5]It is worth noticing that the first step, that is the investment choice, is based on a lagged value of another variable, that is past profit, which is available at the beginning of the time period t from the computations of the previous period $t-1$.

[7]This does not mean that, in general, it is not possible to simulate simultaneous events in an agent-based model.

[8]To simplify some tasks it could be useful to install **R**-Studio (on the top of **R**) so to use this platform as the programming environment. However, this is not a necessary step: one can just install and employ **R** to write the code in a text file and then run it with the *Source* button.

where the values assigned to parameters are "reasonable" numbers that should lead to "acceptable" simulation results (that is, broadly resembling the actual behavior of some economic variables). Given that we are working with a "toy model", parameters are not empirically calibrated nor simulation output is validated against actual micro and macro data. We will discuss this issue later in the chapter.

5. The next step is the allocation of variables and the setting of the initial conditions:

```
#ALLOCATING VARIABLES AND INITIAL CONDITIONS
#Firms' net worth
A <- matrix(data=1,ncol=1,nrow=Ni)
#Firms' capital
K <- matrix(data=1,ncol=1,nrow=Ni)
#Firms' debt
B <- matrix(data=0,ncol=1,nrow=Ni)
#Firms' investment
I <- matrix(data=0,ncol=1,nrow=Ni)
#Stochastic price
P <- matrix(data=0,ncol=1,nrow=Ni)
#Firms' production
Y <- matrix(data=0,ncol=1,nrow=Ni)
#Firms' profit
Z <- matrix(2*runif(Ni)+Pbar,ncol=1,nrow=Ni)
#Aggregate production
YY <- matrix(data=0,ncol=1,nrow=Time)
```

where each variable is allocated as a matrix with $ncol$ columns and $nrow$ rows and the initial conditions are given by the number inserted in $data$. For instance, the matrix A is a $nrow * ncol$ matrix where all elements are equal to 1, while the matrix B is a $nrow * ncol$ matrix where all elements are equal to 0; instead, the initial conditions for Z are such that each element of this matrix is picked at random from a uniform distribution with support $(Pbar, Pbar + 2)$.
All the matrices allocated, but YY, refer to firms' variables: each of these matrices has 1 column ($ncol = 1$) and Ni rows ($now = Ni$, that is the number of firms we inserted above). This implies that we do not record the past values of firms' variables, as time elapses. We will see in a while how to implement a model in which some variables depend on their own one-period lagged value or the one-period lagged value of other variables.
The matrix YY is allocated with 1 column and a number of rows equal to $Time$ (that is, the number of simulation periods inserted above): this is a matrix that we will use to report the level of aggregate production.

6. Now, we can implement the sequence of events according to the algorithm described above:

```
#SEQUENCE OF EVENTS
for (t in 2:Time) {
   I <- gamma * Z #Investment choice
   K <- K + I #Capital accumulation
   Y <- phi * K #Production
   B <- K - A #Debt
```

```
    B[B<0] <- 0 #Self-financed firms
    P <- 2*runif(Ni)+ Pbar #Stochastic price
    Z <- P * Y - r * K #Profit
    A <- A + Z #Net worth
    Z[A<0] <- 0 #Entry condition
    K[A<0] <- 1 #Entry condition
    A[A<0] <- 1 #Entry condition
    YY[t] <- sum(Y) #Aggregate production
}
```

where `for (t in 2:Time) {` opens a cycle according to which in every period of time t (going from 2 to $Time$, while $t = 1$ has been already used to initialize variables) the lines of code included in curly brackets are executed. Within this cycle, a sequence of event occurs from the investment choice to the entry–exit conditions and the computation of aggregate production. For instance, the first line of code within the cycle regards the level of investment: in the model, the level of investment at time t depends on the past level of the profit, given the parameter γ. This holds for each firm. Instead of opening another cycle, this time across firms,[9] we update a whole matrix, for instance I, by using the other matrices and parameters, for instance $I = \gamma Z$. By multiplying each element of the matrix Z by the parameter γ we update all the elements of the matrix I in a single operation (thus avoiding a `for` cycle). Following the example, it is worth to note that when the matrix Z is used to update the matrix I, the elements of the first matrix are those calculated at time $t - 1$ (at the beginning, that is for $t = 2$, data in Z are initial conditions). Once the matrix I is updated, its new values are used to update another matrix, for instance K. Therefore, when we write that $K = K + I$, this means that the values we find in the matrix K (coming from the previous period of time) and the new level of investment I, give rise to new elements in the matrix K (then, we write the new elements of K on the top of old values of the same matrix). In the same way, we update all the firms' variables. Accordingly, we do not record individual variables as time elapses (though this possibility remains open), which allows us to speed up the computation (that becomes a relevant topic when working with large models). Once the new values of matrix K are obtained, we can also compute firms' production multiplying this matrix by the productivity parameter ϕ.
Given that the level of debt for each firm depends on capital accumulation and net worth, that is $B = K - A$, for some firms we could obtain a "negative debt", which is a value we do not want to consider. In the line of code, `B[B<0] <- 0`, it is written that negative values are substituted with 0, meaning that some firms are self-financed. Once that stochastic prices are computed, we can calculate firms'

[9] A possible implementation of such a cycle could be: `for (n in 1:Ni) { I(n,t) = gamma * Z(n,t-1) }`.

profits that, in turn, are added to past net worth to obtain the updated level of firms' net worth.

The line of code `Z[A<0] <- 0` means that the profit of the firms for which we observe a negative net worth is set to zero, which is a very simple way to implement a *one-to-one replacement* of defaulted agents with new entrants. Therefore, the elements of the matrix Z which corresponds to elements of the matrix A with negative values, i.e. bankrupted firms, are re-initialized to a number that in this case is zero (obviously, more complicated entry–exit conditions may be considered). In the same way, we reset the values of matrices K: in this case, the entry condition is equal to 1. Once the previous steps has been done, we can set all the negative elements of A equal to 1.[10]

Finally, we compute an aggregate variable as total production, i.e. the sum of firms' production.[11]

2.1.3 Simulating the Model

Clicking on the *Source* button makes the computer to run the code. In order to visualize some result, we can add a plot of a variable. For example, we can display the time series of aggregate production.

- The following line of code should be added after the closing of the `for` cycle, that is at the bottom of the code:

```
#PLOTTING AGGREGATE PRODUCTION
plot(2:Time, YY[2:Time,1],type="l",ylab="YY",xlab="t")
```

  where `2:Time` are the x coordinates in the plot, `YY[2:Time,1]` are the y coordinates, `type="l"` means that we use a line plot, `ylab="YY"` is the label of the y-axis, and `xlab="t"` is the label of the x-axis.

If you run the code again, now you get the plot (or at least a similar one) with aggregate production (see Fig. 2.1).

We can add some other plots to enrich the graphical analysis of the model.

[10] It is worth to note that the last variable to be updated, according to entry–exit conditions, has to be A, because this matrix is used to check other matrices for negative values of firms' net worth (that is, when some of the values of the matrix A can be negative yet).

[11] Other aggregate variables can be computed in a similar way.

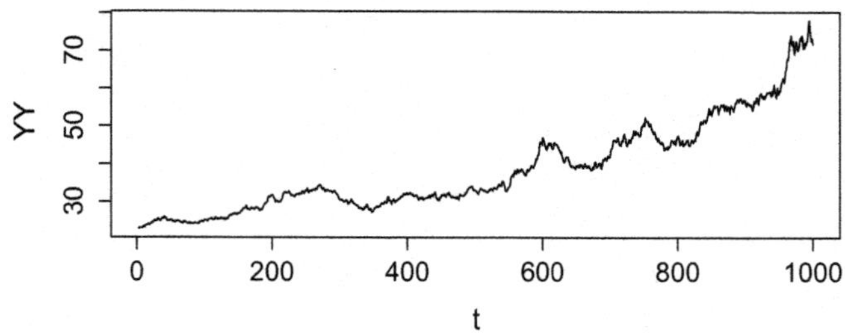

Fig. 2.1 Aggregate production

- For instance, we can add the following lines of code just after the computation of aggregate production:

```
AA[t] <- sum(A) #Net worth
BB[t] <- sum(B) #Debt
```

and, then, we can insert the command to plot these variables at the bottom of the code, say after the plotting of aggregate production:

```
#PLOTTING AGGREGATE NET WORTH
plot(2:Time, AA[2:Time,1],type="l",ylab="AA",xlab="t")

#PLOTTING AGGREGATE DEBT
plot(2:Time, BB[2:Time,1],type="l",ylab="BB",xlab="t")
```

Figure 2.2 displays the output of the last line of code.

2.1.3.1 Random Numbers

If you want to reproduce exactly the same plot displayed in Fig. 2.1 (as well as the same plots for the other variables), you should set the *seed* of the pseudo-random number generation process equal to 15.[12]

- Therefore, we can insert the following line of code, just after the parameter setting:

```
set.seed(15)
```

This allows the programmer to have control on the stochastic variables which are introduced in the model. Indeed, when you set a given seed to initialize the sequence of pseudo-random numbers, you get always the same sequence of *random* values in

[12]This is an arbitrary choice we make for providing an example. Obviously, you can set the seed you prefer, though only 15 allow you to reproduce exactly the simulation presented in this section. More on random numbers can be found below, when this topic will be analyzed within an extended modeling framework.

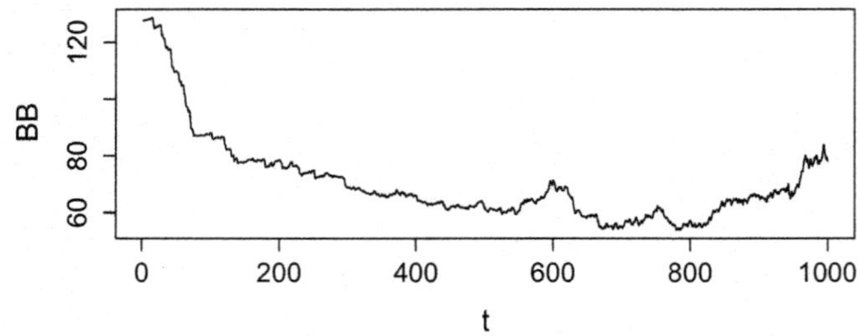

Fig. 2.2 Aggregate debt

the model. This means that given the parameter setting and the initial conditions, you may reproduce exactly the same simulation results every time you insert a certain seed. Accordingly, changing the seed gives rise to a different sequence of pseudo-random numbers and (slightly) different simulation results.[13] For these reasons, we talk of pseudo-random numbers and not of truly random numbers. This is a very important feature that we will further analyze below.

Before proceeding with the next section, set the value of the parameter γ equal to 2 in the **R** code (as requested in the first exercise presented in the appendix of the chapter).

2.1.4 Some Variations

In this section we consider two simple modifications to the code developed until now.[14] The first change introduces a depreciation rate, while the second modification (to be built upon the previous one) considers an endogenous rate of interest which depends on the riskiness of firms (as proxied by their leverage). Practically, you can start from the code as developed until now and follow the instructions below.

[13]However, changing the seed should not lead to significant differences in the qualitative behavior of the model; indeed, if qualitative results greatly differ from one simulation to another this would mean that model dynamics are too much sensitive to stochastic variables and thus that the model does not represent a good tool for analyzing any phenomenon. As we will see later, instead, qualitative results may change when varying parameter values or introducing some modifications of the model.

[14]You may check the correspondence between the code you developed following the instructions and the code in the file `toymodel.R` we provide in the appendix to the book. If all steps were followed accurately, including the exercises, the two codes should match. Now, you can save your own file and then use the same code to create a new file in which implement the modifications suggested in this section. Alternatively, you may open the file `toymodel.R` and start from it to practice this section.

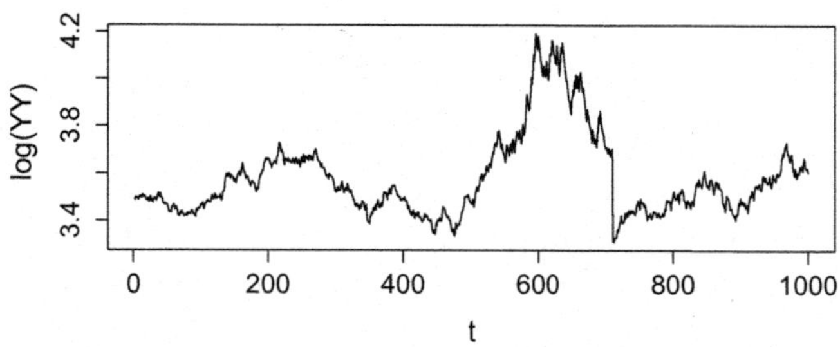

Fig. 2.3 Logarithm of aggregate production

2.1.4.1 Depreciation of Capital

Now we take into account the role of *capital depreciation* and introduce another couple of changes.

- We introduce the parameter δ, that is the depreciation rate. Let's set $\delta = 0.05$. Accordingly, we have to add it to the parameter setting:

```
#Depreciation rate
delta = 0.05
```

- Let's assume that there is *no investment* in case of negative profits. To implement this rule, we can insert the line of code:

```
I[I<0] = 0
```

  after the determination of investment and before the equation for capital accumulation.
- Finally, we can plot the *logarithm* of aggregate production (see Fig. 2.3). To obtain the plot we can write:

```
plot(2:Time, log(YY[2:Time,1]),type="l",
ylim=range(log(YY[2:Time])),col=1,ylab="log(YY)",xlab="t")
```

  We can modify in the same way the plots for aggregate net worth and debt.[15]

2.1.4.2 An Endogenous Rate of Interest

Building upon the model as it has been implemented and modified until now, let's now assume that the *interest rate* is no longer a parameter. In this modified version,

---

[15] After the modifications introduced in this subsection the **R** code should correspond to that in the file `toymodelmod.R`.

we want to introduce an interest rate which is firm-specific, that is the interest rate of the firm n at time t is given by the following equation:

$$r_{n,t} = \bar{r} + \bar{r}(B_{n,t}/A_{n,t-1})^{\bar{r}} \tag{2.8}$$

where $\bar{r}$ is a positive parameter (constant and uniform across firms). Accordingly, the interest rate for the single firm is now given by two components:

- a fixed component $\bar{r}$ that could represent the *policy rate* set by the central bank;
- a variable component, e.g. a *risk premium*, according to which the higher the leverage the larger the interest charged on the firm.

To implement these changes, after having removed the old parameter r from the code,

- we should add the parameter $\bar{r}$ and set a value for it, for instance, 0.075; hence, we can write

```
rbar=0.075 #Interest rate
```

  as the last line of the parameter setting.
- Then we can introduce the new equation representing the interest rate (just before the computation of profits)[16]:

```
r <- rbar + rbar*(B/A)^rbar #Interest rate
```

- In order to construct a multiple plot with four panels (see Fig. 2.4) – the logarithm of aggregate production, the average leverage, the logarithm of aggregate net worth, and the logarithm of aggregate debt – we can substitute the old lines of code regarding plotting with these new ones:

```
layout(matrix(c(1, 3, 2, 4), 2, 2))
layout.show(4)
#PLOTTING AGGREGATE PRODUCTION
plot(201:Time, log(YY[201:Time,1]),type="l",
ylim=range(log(YY[201:Time])),col=1,ylab="log(YY)",xlab="t")
#PLOTTING AGGREGATE DEBT
plot(201:Time, LEV[201:Time,1],type="l",
ylim=range(LEV[201:Time]),col=1,ylab="leverage",xlab="t")
#PLOTTING AVERAGE LEVERAGE
plot(201:Time, log(AA[201:Time,1]),type="l",
ylim=range(log(AA[201:Time])),col=1,ylab="log(AA)",xlab="t")
#PLOTTING AVERAGE INTEREST RATE
plot(201:Time, log(BB[201:Time,1]),type="l",
ylim=range(log(BB[201:Time])),col=1,ylab="log(BB)",xlab="t")
```

[16]For the sake of simplicity, we are keeping the (not so realistic) assumption that firms pay a remuneration on their own capital which corresponds to the interest rate on external debt.

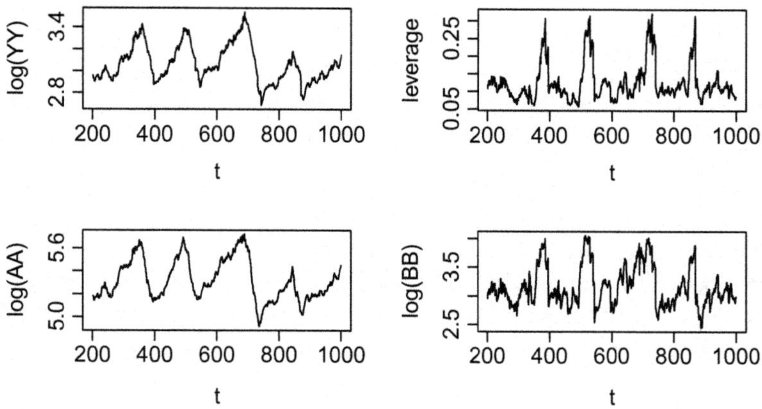

Fig. 2.4 A multiple plot with the logarithm of aggregate production, the average leverage, the logarithm of aggregate net worth, and the logarithm of aggregate debt

The main result shown by the modified version of the toy model is *cyclicality*, which is related to the presence of a simplified *financial accelerator* mechanism. Indeed, all the variables plotted in Fig. 2.4 exhibit a "business cycle" pattern. The accumulation of net worth leads the firms to produce more along an expansionary phase; to further increase production, firms expand their debt; this makes the leverage to rise until a peak; here the level of debt with respect to net worth becomes "excessive" (the cost of capital rises a lot, thus resulting in negative profits) and the cycle reverted.[17]

2.1.5 *Multiple Simulations*

In this section we explain how to implement a set of multiple simulations of the model we developed until here. Very often the motivation for simulating a model is that we want to understand its typical behavior, independently of the sequence of pseudo-number we introduce to account for stochastic factors. The idea is then to simulate the model a certain number of times – say MC which stays for Monte Carlo simulations – by starting each time from a different initial seed of the pseudo-random number generation process. In order to make it as simple as possible, we start with only three simulations of the model.

- First of all, we have to set the number of simulations. Then we can modify the beginning of our code as follows.

```
#SET TIME SPAN, NUMBER OF FIRMS AND NUMBER OF SIMULATIONS
#Number of simulation periods
```

[17]The reference file after these modifications is `toymodelmod2.R`.

```
Time <- 1000
#Number of firms
Ni <- 100
#Number of multiple simulations
MC <- 3
```

- In order to record the relevant output of each simulation, we have to add a new dimension to aggregate variables. Consider, for example, aggregate production. This matrix has already a time dimension, with a number of rows ($nrow$) equal to the number of simulation periods ($Time$), while the number of columns was set to one. Now, we set the number of columns ($ncol$) equal to the number of multiple simulations (MC):

```
#Aggregate production
YY <- matrix(data=0,ncol=MC,nrow=Time)
```

  The same procedure can be followed for other aggregate variables like the average leverage, aggregate net worth and debt (we do not modify the allocation of individual variables).
- Then, we can insert a new `for` cycle after the allocation of aggregate variables and before individual variables:

```
for (mc in 1:MC) {
```

  This cycle has to be closed after the other one (over simulation periods).
- Another change to make consists in adding the new dimension (that is, the number of multiple simulations MC) to all aggregate variables within the *main program*; for example,

```
YY[t,mc] <- sum(Y) #Aggregate production
```

- Finally, we can plot the output of the three simulations, for instance the aggregate production, in a single plot as follows:

```
plot(2:Time, YY[2:Time,1],type="l",ylim=range(0,max(YY)),
ylab="YY",xlab="t")
lines(2:Time, YY[2:Time,2],type="l",
ylim=range(0,max(YY)),lty=2, lwd=2)
lines(2:Time, YY[2:Time,3],type="l",
ylim=range(0,max(YY)),lty=3, lwd=2)
}
```

  In this plot we display the output of the first simulation as the default (continuous) line, the output of the second simulation as a dashed line (by setting `lty=2`) and the third simulation as a dotted line (by setting `lty=2`; moreover, the second and third line are thicker than the default line, which is due to `lwd=2`). As you can see (Fig. 2.5), the three simulations exhibits a similar behavior of aggregate

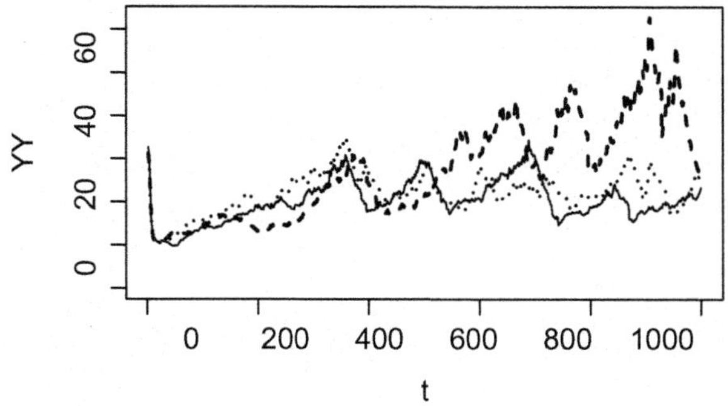

Fig. 2.5 Three simulations of the model (with different seeds of random numbers)

production, while the differences are due to the role of stochastic factors.[18] In order to deepen the analysis of the model through multiple simulations, in the next section we implement a larger computational experiment.

2.1.6 A "Large" Computational Experiment

In this section we perform a computational experiment with 100 multiple simulations. In this case we cannot assess the similarity or the differences among simulations by simply plotting them together in a single graph. Instead, we need to collect statistics from multiple simulations so to summarize model dynamics.

- First of all, set $MC = 100$ in the **R** code.
- We can delete the lines of code related to the plots built in the previous section.
- After the closing of the `for` cycle over multiple simulations, we can compute the mean and the standard deviation of some variables across multiple simulations so to analyze the average evolution of the system and whether this represents its typical behavior, independently of stochastic factors whose influence is measured by the volatility around mean values.

```
#COMPUTE MC MEAN, STANDARD DEVIATION AND CONFIDENCE INTERVALS
meanYY = matrix(data=0,nrow=Time,ncol=1)
stdYY = matrix(data=0,nrow=Time,ncol=1)
YYup = matrix(data=0,nrow=Time,ncol=1)
YYdown = matrix(data=0,nrow=Time,ncol=1)
for (t in 1:Time) {
   meanYY[t] = mean(YY[t,])
   stdYY[t] = sd(YY[t,])
}
YYup = meanYY + 2*stdYY
YYdown = meanYY - 2*stdYY
```

[18] The reference file for this section is `toymodelMC.R`.

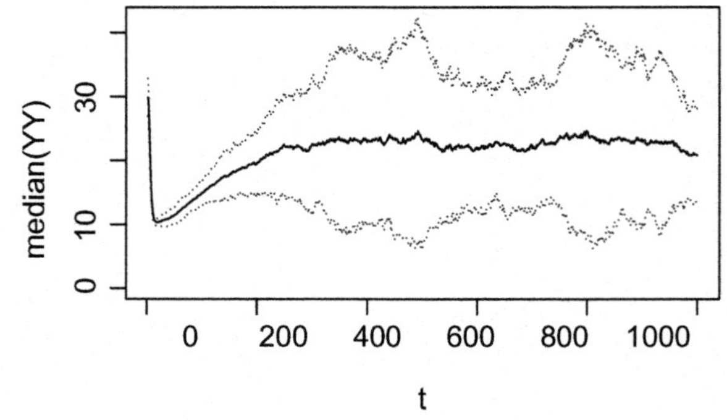

Fig. 2.6 Median aggregate production (*continuous line*) and confidence bars (*dotted line*) built on median absolute deviation (MAD)

With these lines of code we firstly allocate the new variables, then we compute the average aggregate production (`meanYY`) and its volatility (`stdYY`) across multiple simulations; finally, we add two confidence bars (`YYup` and `YYdown`).

The average and the standard deviation of simulated variables could be substituted by more accurate measures (which are less sensitive, for instance, to outliers). In order to get some robust statistics of multiple simulations we can compute the *median* and the *median absolute deviation* (MAD).

Figure 2.6 displays the median and two confidence bars built on MAD.[19]

2.1.7 Sensitivity Analysis

Simulation results depend on the value of parameters. In order to assess the sensitivity of model dynamics to parameters, we can perform another type of computational exercise, that is a sensitivity analysis. The aim is to understand how simulation results vary when changing the value of a parameter (keeping the values of others unchanged). In what follows we describe how to implement a sensitivity analysis on the parameter $\bar{p}$.[20] For the sake of simplicity, we only run three simulations of the model with three different values of the parameter.

- In the parameter setting, set the initial value of the parameter to be analyzed equal to zero:

```
\Pbar <- 0
```

This is just to initialize the parameter under investigation.

[19]The implementation of the large computational experiment with robust statistics is provided in the file `toymodelMC100mad.R`. We suggest to look at this file only after the Exercise 4 presented in the Appendix of the chapter has been done.

[20]You can follow a similar approach in order to assess the sensitivity of the model to other parameters.

- Then, add the following line of code just after the `for` cycle over multiple simulations:

```
#SENSITIVITY ANALYSIS
Pbar <- Pbar + 0.005
```

  Accordingly, for each simulation the value of the parameter is incremented by the amount 0.005, starting from 0 before multiple simulations start. This means that we are exploring model dynamics for three values of the parameter: 0.005, 0.01, 0.015.
  After the above line of code, you can also add the instruction

```
print(Pbar)
```

  so to display on the screen the value of the parameter in each simulation.
- In order to isolate the effect of the parameter we should move the setting of the random number seed (`set.seed(15)`) from outside to inside the `for` cycle over multiple simulations (for example, just before of just after the code of the previous point). As a result, the sequence of pseudo-random numbers will be the same in the three simulations of the sensitivity analysis. This is very important to avoid that results are the effect of both changing random numbers and parameter values.[21]

2.1.8 A Policy Experiment

Although the model we developed is too simple to be used for the explanation of the complex economic reality and for providing effective policy suggestions, in this section we describe how to implement a policy experiment within our computational framework. Let's analyze the effect of monetary policy due to an increase of the policy rate $\bar{r}$: for instance we want to simulate a permanent increase from 0.075 (the initial values of $\bar{r}$) to 0.1 for $t > 500$.

- The first step is removing $\bar{r}$ from the parameter space (we can also remove plotting commands implemented before).
- In order to analyze the effects of different levels of the interest rate on the economic system, we can set $MC = 2$ so that we have a baseline scenario (with a fixed policy rate, that is $\bar{r} = 0.075$) and a treatment involving a policy change ($\bar{r} = 0.075$ until $t = 500$, $\bar{r} = 0.1$ for $t > 500$). To implement such a computational experiment we can add the following lines of code just after the opening of the `for` cycles over simulation periods:

[21] The file corresponding to this section is `toymodelSens.R`.

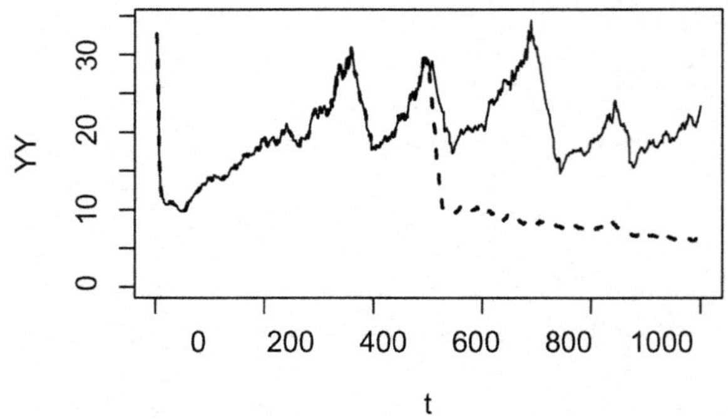

Fig. 2.7 Baseline model (*continuous line*): $\bar{r} = 0.075$. Treatment (*dashed line*): for $t \leq 500$, $\bar{r} = 0.075$; for $t > 500$, $\bar{r} = 0.1$

```
#SIMULATING THE POLICY CHANGE
if (mc>1 & t>500) {
    rbar = 0.1   #Interest rate
    } else {
    rbar = 0.075 #Interest rate
  }
```

- Finally, we can plot the results of the policy experiment:

```
#PLOTTING AGGR. PRODUCTION WITH AND WITHOUT THE POLICY CHANGE
plot(2:Time, YY[2:Time,1],type="l",
ylim=range(0,max(YY)),ylab="YY",xlab="t")
   lines(2:Time, YY[2:Time,j],type="l",
   ylim=range(0,max(YY)),lty=2,lwd=2)
```

Figure 2.7 shows the output of the two simulations: the baseline scenario with a fixed policy rate is plotted in black; the treatment with the policy change is in dashed line. As you can see (and as expected after a restrictive monetary policy), the increase of the policy rate, implying a rise of the interest rate paid by firms on loans and then reducing profits and the accumulation of firms' net worth, result in a decrease of aggregate production.[22]

In order to assess the robustness of our finding, in other words if the difference between the two simulations after the policy change is statistically significant, we should perform multiple simulations. For example, we can implement a computational experiment with 100 simulations of the baseline scenario and 100 simulations of the policy treatment. The result of such an experiment is summarized in Fig. 2.8 which shows that the median of aggregate production after the policy rate hike decreases significantly; moreover, the median production and the corresponding confidence bars in the policy treatment are below those of the baseline scenario.

[22]The reference file for the first part of this section is `toymodelPolicy.R`.

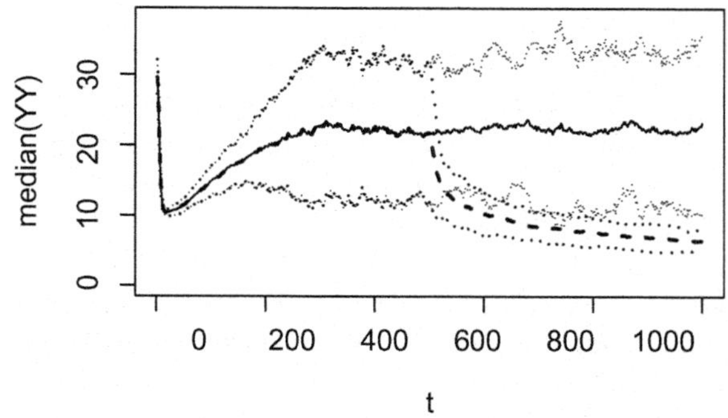

Fig. 2.8 Baseline model (*continuous line* with *dotted bars*): 100 simulations with $\bar{r} = 0.075$. Treatment (*dashed line* with *dotted/thicker bars*): 100 simulations with $\bar{r} = 0.075$ for $t \leq 500$ and $\bar{r} = 0.1$ for $t > 500$

Many other changes can be introduced and various computational experiments could be implemented even in this simplified framework.[23] In the remaining part of the chapter a more complex version of the toy model we described, implemented and simulated until here will be proposed. Some steps in the implementation of the code will be similar to the ones proposed above, though there will be more details on agents' behavior, market structures and computational aspects. In particular, the next model includes more types of agents (e.g. heterogeneous firms and banks) and allows for direct interaction among them (e.g. credit interlinkages between firms and banks). Moreover, a practical guide to empirical calibration will be provided.

2.2 Going Further: Heterogeneous Agents and Credit Networks

In this section we simulate a simplified version of the model published in Riccetti et al. (2013). That model tries to reproduce how business cycle fluctuations can be enlarged by different self-reinforcing mechanisms.

First of all, a negative shock on firms' output makes firms less willing to invest. The investments decrease reduces the overall output in a vicious circle.

This positive feedback mechanism can be further expanded by financial factors that are called "financial accelerator" in the economic literature. In particular, Bernanke and Gertler (1989, 1990, 1995), Kiyotaki (1997), and Bernanke et al. (1999) show the presence of a positive feedback mechanism that Riccetti et al. (2013) call "leverage accelerator": the mentioned negative shock on firms' output makes banks less willing to loan funds, with a consequent credit constraint and/or an increase of the interest rate, forcing firms to lower leverage and thus investments and output. For this reason, even a crisis that starts in the financial sector can turn into a recession.

---

[23]The complete implementation of the policy experiment described in the second part of this section is provided in the file `toymodelMC100madPolicy.R`. We suggest to look at this file only after the Exercise 6 in the appendix has been done.

Riccetti et al. (2013), following Delli Gatti et al. (2010a), consider another self-reinforcing mechanism, called "network-based" accelerator. The network-based financial accelerator highlights that the presence of a credit network may produce an avalanche of bankruptcies. Indeed, the bankruptcy of a firm may bring "bad debt" that affects the net worth of banks, which can go bankrupt, with a consequent credit crunch. Even if they manage to survive, as usually happens, they could react to the deterioration of the net worth reducing the available credit and/or increasing the interest rate to all their borrowers (Stiglitz and Greenwald, 2003, p.145), making firms incur additional difficulties in servicing debt and thus increasing the weakness of the whole non-financial sector. Therefore, in every case, the non-financial sector weakness turns into financial fragility and this turns again into non-financial sector fragility, in another vicious circle.

Given these premises, the model presented here is based on two features: a firm capital structure able to represent a leverage cycle, and the interaction between firms and banks through the credit network.

As for the firm capital structure, the economic literature presents many theories, but the empirical literature finds contrasting evidence to support them. To model in a reliable way the leverage cycle, we decide to apply the "dynamic trade-off theory". In this theory, firms actively pursue target debt ratios even though market frictions temper the speed of adjustment. In other words, firms have long-run leverage targets, but they do not immediately reach them, instead they adjust toward them during some periods. Dynamic trade-off seems to be able to overcome some puzzles related to the other theories, explaining the stylized facts emerged from the empirical analysis (Flannery and Rangan, 2006; Frank and Goyal, 2008, 2014; Marinsek et al., 2015). Moreover, Graham and Harvey (2001) conduct a survey where they evidence that 81 % of firms affirm to consider a target debt ratio or range when making their debt decisions. Following this theory we assume that firms have a "target leverage", implying that a growing firm will balance the increasing capital with increasing debt exposure, thus creating in good periods the basis for the subsequent crisis.

As for the bank-firm credit network, in the current model we simplify the structure of Delli Gatti et al. (2010a) avoiding the trade-credit relationship among firms, and we simplify the structure compared to Riccetti et al. (2013) avoiding a multiperiodal debt structure and the possibility for firms to obtain credit from more than a single bank. Therefore, every firm has a single link.

The current model presents many other simplifications compared to Riccetti et al. (2013), such as for the interest rate setting, for the computation of bank deposits (without reserves), for the computation of bank costs, for the recovery rate on non-performing loans, and for the firm decision to increase or to reduce the target leverage. We will explain the simplified model framework in detail in the following section.

2.2.1 Model Setup

Our economy is composed by two markets: credit and goods. We focus on the former and we sketch the latter.

The credit market is populated by firms and banks. Firms, that produce consumption goods and ask credit to banks, are indexed by i $= 1, 2, \ldots,$ I. Banks extend credit to firms and are indexed by z $= 1, 2, \ldots,$ Z.

On the market for consumption goods there are consumers and firms. However we make simplifying assumptions. In practice, we suppose that consumers buy all the output that firms sell at a firm-specific stochastic price fluctuating around a common average. Prices are exogenously determined by a random process, following Greenwald and Stiglitz (1993). This simplifying assumption makes us unable to analyze inflation dynamics. Therefore our monetary policy experiments cannot investigate the usual trade-off between inflation and output growth. Moreover, our analysis is confined to business cycle issues because there are not growth-enhancing factors as population growth, labor productivity evolution, technological progress, and so on.

The rationale of the model is simple: the net worth of firms is the "engine" of fluctuations for the economic output, indeed we assume that the scale of production of firms is a function of their net worth. Firms' net worth is influenced by exogenous prices on goods market: prices determine firms' profits, which affect the accumulation of firms' net worth and their financial fragility. Indeed, next to this exogenous dynamics, there is the focus of the model, that is the dynamics of the credit market network, in which firms and banks interact. As already explained, a negative shock to a firm affects the credit relationship between the firm and the bank: if the shock is large enough, the firm may be unable to fulfill debt commitments and may go bankrupt. In a networked economy, the bankruptcy of a firm may bring "bad debt" - i.e. non-performing loans - that affects the net worth of its lending bank, which can also go bankrupt or, if it manages to survive, will react to the deterioration of its net worth increasing the interest rate to all its borrowers. Hence, borrowers may incur additional difficulties in servicing debt. We want to highlight that the structure of the network of credit relationships evolves endogenously due to a decentralized mechanism of interaction: in every period each firm looks for the bank with the lowest interest rate. Thus, interest rates (that are the prices in the credit market) have two important roles: (i) influence profits, which affect the accumulation of net worth and financial fragility, (ii) shape the evolving topology of the credit network.

Now we can introduce the equations used to model our economy.

2.2.1.1 Firms Production and Capital Structure

We assume that the level of production of the ith firm at time t, $Y_{i,t}$, is an increasing concave function of its net worth $A_{i,t}$:

$$Y_{i,t} = \phi K_{i,t}^{\beta} \tag{2.9}$$

where $\phi > 1$ and $0 < \beta < 1$ are parameters uniform across firms and $K_{i,t}$ is the total capital of the firm, composed by the sum of net worth and debt ($B_{i,t}$): $K_{i,t} = A_{i,t} + B_{i,t}$. This is a "financially constrained output function", because β is less than 1. The concavity of the financially constrained output function captures the idea that there are "decreasing returns" to financial robustness. Following Greenwald and Stiglitz (1993), this function can be thought as the solution of an optimization problem of firms' expected profits net of expected bankruptcy costs.

The level of debt $B_{i,t}$ is a function of the net worth and of the leverage (defined as debt/net worth):

$$B_{i,t} = A_{i,t} leverage_{i,t} \tag{2.10}$$

Within the theoretical framework of the dynamic trade-off theory, we assume that all firms have a target leverage. The target leverage is set by firms following an adaptive behavioral rule according to which the current leverage level is equal to the previous level modified by a random percentage increase (decrease) when the expected revenue is larger (smaller) than the interest paid on bank loans $R_{z,i,t}$. Therefore, for instance, a firm is prone to invest more (increasing the leverage) if it expects to borrow money from the bank at a low cost (a low interest rate paid) and to invest this money with a high revenue.

We assume that the firm expectation about the future revenue is the simplest, adaptive with no memory: the firm forecasts the same revenue of the last year: $p^e_{i,t+1} = p_{i,t}$.

Therefore the target leverage is set in the following way:

$$\begin{cases} leverage_{i,t+1} = leverage_{i,t}(1 + adj \cdot u) \text{ if } p_{i,t} > R_{z,i,t} \\ leverage_{i,t+1} = leverage_{i,t}(1 - adj \cdot u) \text{ if } p_{i,t} \leq R_{z,i,t} \end{cases} \tag{2.11}$$

where adj is a parameter that sets the maximum leverage change between the two periods and is multiplied by a random number drawn by a uniform distribution between 0 and 1: $u \sim U(0, 1)$.

The target leverage changes among firms and over time given the evolution of $p_{i,t}$ and $R_{z,i,t}$: firms are heterogeneous for their size, given by their net worth, but also for their target leverage.

With this capital structure, a firm that has some reinvested profits, increasing $A_{i,t}$ and $leverage_{i,t}$, asks banks an increasing debt amount to keep the leverage at the desired level: the debt is built during the growth periods. We can also hypothesize that this mechanism is driven by the bank side: banks are willing to lend money to profitable firms and firms use the available money; the reverse is true when firms have losses: banks constraint the amount of credit and firms are forced to reduce their debt exposure (credit crunch).

2.2.1.2 Firm-Bank Interaction

In every period, every firm asks for an amount of debt which is determined as explained in the previous section.

Each bank sets a different interest rate on loans and these differences imply that firms sometimes change bank to obtain a lower interest rate, as we will explain.

We assume that the zth bank adopts the following rule in setting the interest rate on loans to the ith borrower:

$$R_{z,i,t} = rCB_t + \underbrace{\gamma A_{z,t-1}^{-\gamma}}_{\text{Bank-specific}} + \underbrace{\gamma \frac{(leverage_{i,t})}{1 + \frac{A_{i,t-1}}{Max\{A_{j,t-1}, j=1,\ldots,N_{firms}\}}}}_{\text{Firm-specific (risk premium component)}} \tag{2.12}$$

Thus, the interest rate is composed by three parts:

1. the policy rate set by the central bank: rCB_t;
2. a bank-specific term that decreases with the financial soundness of the bank (proxied by the zth bank's networth $A_{z,t}$). If the bank is strong from the financial point of view, it will be eager to extend credit at more favorable terms to increase its market share. This is in line with the assumption made by Delli Gatti et al. (2010a) and the references therein included;
3. a firm-specific term that incorporates a risk premium increasing with borrower's leverage, and discounted for larger firms (the denominator ranges between around 1 for very small firms and 2 for the largest one). Indeed, on one hand, the required risk premium has to reward the bank for the default risk borne (positive relation between interest rate and leverage, that is positively related to the default risk) and, on the other hand, a larger firm could have more bargaining power in order to reduce the interest paid.

The presence of this endogenous risk premium in the interest rate is a channel of our financial accelerator.

Initially, the credit network, i.e. the links among firms and banks, is random. Afterwards, we follow a "strategic link formation" approach (Jackson, 2008): in every period each borrower observes the interest rates of a number χ of randomly selected banks. We assume that the firm changes bank with a probability ps of switching to the new lender that is increasing (in a non-linear way) with the difference between R^{new} (the interest rate set by the observed potential new bank) and R^{old} (the previous bank's interest rate), only if it finds another bank that charges an interest rate lower than the actual. In symbols:

$$\begin{cases} ps_{i,t} = 1 - e^{\lambda(R_{z,t}^{new} - R_{z,t}^{old})/(R_{z,t}^{new})} \text{ if } R_{z,t}^{new} < R_{z,t}^{old} \\ ps_{i,t} = 0 \text{ otherwise} \end{cases} \tag{2.13}$$

where $\lambda > 0$ (for the calibration of this parameter, see Sect. 2.3). As a result, the chosen bank is not changed every period. In this way, we model the sticky connection between a borrower and its bank, due to the so called switching costs, largely described in the financial literature. A low λ is able to reproduce a credit network with high switching costs and a consequent strong stickiness, and vice versa for a high value of λ.

With this mechanism, the topology of the network evolves continuously and endogenously due to the changing interest rate charged by the banks. Indeed, large banks can charge lower prices and therefore attract more new partners. As a consequence, their profits go up and their net worths increase, making room for even lower interest rates in the future and attracting more new partners. This positive feedback mechanism gives rise to a right-skewed distribution for banks' degree: some banks are characterized by a relatively high number of links ("hubs") and many others have a small number of connections.

The partner's selection mechanism could have interesting effects on the whole system. Indeed, when a negative shock hits a node - for instance a firm goes bankrupt - the lender of the bankrupt firm faces a bad debt that reduces its net worth, therefore it reacts by raising the interest rate charged to all the other borrowers. This interest rate hike may induce the borrowers to switch to banks who offer more favorable conditions, with two effects: on one hand avoiding the spreading of the shock to these firms that change partner, mitigates financial instability; on the other hand, further weakening the bank that suffers the initial default, and amplifying the market concentration, with an increasing risk of a following stronger spread of the financial instability.

2.2.1.3 Net Worth Evolution and Bankruptcies

In every period, each firm draws its stochastic gain on a unit of output $p_{i,t}$, that contains the revenues net of the expenses for producing the output itself (but for financial costs). We assume $p_{i,t}$ is a variable distributed as a Normal with α mean and variance var_p: $p_{i,t} \sim N(\alpha, var_p)$. A high realization of $p_{i,t}$ can be thought of as a regime of high demand which drives up the relative price of the commodity in question, while a low or negative realization of $p_{i,t}$ represents a regime of low demand, that may even push the firm to default.

This value is very important because it is used to set the target leverage as already seen in Eq. (2.11), and because it determines the firm's profit. Indeed, after drawing $p_{i,t}$, firm i is able to compute its profit with the following equation:

$$Pr_{i,t} = p_{i,t} Y_{i,t} - R_{z,i,t} B_{i,t} \tag{2.14}$$

The profit determines the evolution of the firm net worth $A_{i,t}$:

$$A_{i,t+1} = A_{i,t} + Pr_{i,t} \tag{2.15}$$

If $A_{i,t+1} < 0$, the firm goes bankrupt. Given Eq. (2.15), the firm defaults if it incurs a loss (negative profit) and the loss is big enough to deplete net worth: $-Pr_{i,t} > A_{i,t}$.

However, in order to keep the number of firms in the model fixed, when a firm goes bankrupt, we assume that a new firm enters in the market. The incoming firm has:

- a very small random net worth $A_{i,t} \sim U(0, 2)$, in order to reduce the stock-flow inconsistency and to avoid an exogenously driven economic recovery;
- a target leverage $leverage_{i,t} = 1$;
- a price $p_{i,t}$ sampled from $N(\alpha, var_p)$;
- a randomly selected partner bank on the credit market.

In case of default, the lending bank suffers a loss, but it does not lose all the loan amount, because we consider the recovery rate (RR) and, consequently, we compute the loss given default rate LGD, that is 1-RR. In particular,

$$LGD_{i,t} = \frac{-(A_{i,t} + Pr_{i,t})}{B_{i,t}} \tag{2.16}$$

It is important to consider the LGD[24], that it is one of the components of the credit risk models, with the probability of default (PD) and the exposure at default (EAD), because it has very relevant implications for the stability of the banking system, that we are going to analyze.

In every period, we also compute the profits of all the banks:

$$Pr_{z,t} = \sum_{i \in \Phi_z} R_{z,i,t} B_{i,t} - rCB_t D_{z,t} - c \cdot A_{z,t} - bad_{z,t} \tag{2.17}$$

where:

- deposits $D_{z,t}$ are the outstanding credit less the net worth: $B_{z,t} - A_{z,t}$;
- parameter c represents bank's fixed cost;
- bad debt $bad_{z,t}$ represents non-performing loans computed as the sum of all the credit lent to firms gone bankrupt in period t, multiplied by the loss given default rate (LGD) evaluated with Eq. (2.16) for each defaulted firm.

The rationale of Eq. (2.17) is simple: the first addend is the bank's revenue, that is the sum of the interests paid on their debts by firms that don't default. The second addend is the interests paid to depositors; for simplicity, we assume that all banks pay the same interest rate, that is equal to the policy rate set by the central bank. The third addend represents some fixed bank's costs proportional to bank's size. The last addend, as already said, is the loss due to non-performing loans.

As for firms, banks' profits are needed in order to compute banks' net worth $A_{z,t}$ evolution:

[24]For instance, a firm with net worth A equal to 10 and debt B equal to 20, has an initial capital K equal to 30. If the profits are −15, the firm defaults because its net worth goes below zero (it is −5). However, it has a capital equal to 30 − 15 = 15; this amount can be recovered by the lender that loses only 20 − 15 = 5. The LGD is equal to $\frac{-(10-15)}{20} = \frac{5}{20} = 25\,\%$.

$$A_{z,t+1} = A_{z,t} + Pr_{z,t} \tag{2.18}$$

Again, if $A_{z,t+1} < 0$, that is if $-Pr_{z,t} > A_{z,t}$, the bank defaults. Also in this case, for simplicity, we keep the number of banks fixed, therefore we assume that a new bank enters in the market. The incoming bank has a very small random net worth $A_{z,t} \sim U(0, 2)$ and takes the links of the defaulted bank (even if it is immediately in the new contest for maintaining and acquiring customers).

2.2.2 *Implementing the Model with* R

2.2.2.1 Preliminary Steps

Computer simulation, or computational modeling, involves representing a model as a computer program. Different programming languages differ under a number of possible dimensions such as the symbolic language adopted (i.e. the syntax), the programming paradigm employed (e.g. object oriented programming, functional-procedural programming, or a mix of the two), the way of organizing and structuring the scripts, the performance, etc. However, regardless the programming language adopted, when it comes to execution, a computer program is an ordered sequence of instructions. Therefore, at its bottom line, an AB model can be conceived as a flow of sequential instructions executed by the computer. Through debugging, a modeler might potentially browse through this entire flow, by executing one by one the entire chain of commands which constitutes the simulation. The inherent sequential nature of AB models rises an important issue for the model-building process: that of timing.

Before starting to write the code of the model, we thus have to carefully think about the sequence of events taking place within each round of the simulation. That is, we have to figure out the exact order in which agents will be asked to employ their heuristics in order to take specific decisions, such as production planning, credit demand/supply determination, prices or interest rates setting, expectations computation, and to perform specific actions, such as consuming, buying goods, choose suppliers. Similarly, we also need to specify when variables employed in the model are updated (for example, firms' and households' wealth, firms' profits, etc.). Indeed, heuristics are generally expressed as functions of specific sets of variables, some of which are computed as the outcome of other heuristics. For example, the matching protocol on the credit market requires firms to know the interest rate on loans offered by banks, that should therefore be computed before the matching occurs.

Thinking about the intra-period order of events is also a convenient way to spot possible inconsistencies in the logical structure of the model, which may ask for some revision of the model itself. This preliminary step hence represents a convenient expedient to deepen the modeler's awareness about the logical structure of the model and avoid time wasting mistakes in the ensuing implementation stage. Nevertheless, the more complex a model is, the more complicated the task of identifying ex-ante the most suitable sequence of events to take place might be. Leakages in the theoretical and time structure of the model may emerge both during the implementation, debugging, and simulation phases, asking for a revision of the model. The model-building procedure is thus a backward and forward process from the model theoretical specification to the model practical implementation.

Another important preliminary aspect that modelers should take into account before starting to write the code of a model relates to the report variables that will be employed to analyze the model dynamics. At a first approximation these are mostly represented by either aggregate variables (such as GDP, aggregate consumption, inflation rates), pertaining to the economic system as a whole, or micro variables (individual firms' credit, households' income, firms' size), referring to individual agents' characteristics. However, in AB models there is often a further class of variables which are somehow in the middle serving as a bridge between the micro and macro layers, thereby pertaining to a meso-economic analysis. Within this group we find variables and statistics expressing features of specific groups of agents or economic sectors. These are for example data related to firms' rates of growth and size distributions, income and wealth distributions within the households sector or between different subset of it (e.g. workers vs capitalists), or measures of markets concentration. Another very important group of meso-variables are those related to economic networks linking agents both within the same sector and across different sectors: credit networks between borrowers (households and firms) and lenders (banks), commercial networks linking suppliers (firms) to customers (households in the case of consumption goods, or other firms in the case of intermediate goods, such as machineries), financial stocks network linking investors in financial assets (banks, firms, or households) to liability holders (e.g. banks and firms issuing bonds or shares) are typical examples of economic networks one might be interested to analyze through an AB model. Degree (weighted or unweighted) distributions, nodes centrality measures, clustering indexes, average paths length and diameters, and many other topological measures are then computed to analyze the features of economic networks emerging from the simulations and to assess their impact on the system dynamics and stability.

In order to compute all these different types of statistics one needs to employ very different types of data generated by the model that in turn have to be stored in the computer memory using different types of objects such as vectors, matrices, lists, or arrays.[25] For example, the dynamics of GDP in a single simulation can be tracked by a vector of values whose elements corresponds to GDP levels in each period of the simulation. On the contrary, storing the information to track the evolution of an economic network over the simulation time-span may ask for more complex data structure, as in each period of the simulation the network will be represented by an adjacency matrix whose entries are numbers expressing the presence of a link between two agents, or the strength of that link (for example, a bank's exposition towards each specific borrower). In addition, AB models are usually executed as Monte Carlo simulations in order to check the robustness of results and assess across-

[25] These are the most common objects employed for collecting data in the vast majority of programming languages.

runs variability. Sensitivity analysis on model parameters and scenario analysis are often performed to analyze the behavior of the model under different set-ups, or to assess the effects of exogenous shocks or policy interventions. This asks to find suitable ways to store across-runs information.

Thinking about the structure of the reports used to store these information is thus an important preliminary steps in implementing a model for at least two reasons: first, modifying the structure of the objects employed to store our artificially generated data once the model has already been implemented may be tricky, in particular when these objects are employed by some agents' heuristics in the model, as it is often the case. In these cases, we need to revise every piece of code containing a reference to the modified report object (for example the indexing in a vector, a matrix, or an array). Besides being time-demanding, this revision is also likely to be a source of bugs. Second, notwithstanding the ever growing performance of computers of last generation, we are still facing a trade-off between the amount of data that are stored in the computer memory during simulations and the speed of executions of the code representing the model. One should then be in principle as parsimonious as possible in choosing which simulation data are useful for analyzing the model dynamics, and should then be kept in the memory of the computer, and which data should instead be neglected, or deleted, as soon as they have been employed in the execution of the model.

2.2.2.2 Order of Events in the Simplified Credit Model

The simplified model presented in the previous section is open to several possible orderings of the events taking place within each round of the simulation. A simple expedient that can help in identifying a suitable ordering is to abstract from the specific functional form of each heuristics and just focus on the variables employed to calculate the value of the dependent variable controlled by the heuristic. For example, the bank-specific component of the interest rate is a function of the stock of wealth of the bank at the end of the previous period: $R_{b,t} = \gamma A^{\gamma}_{b,t-1}$. Therefore we can simplify by saying that $R_{b,t} = f(A_{b,t-1})$. Similarly, we know from the definition of the matching protocol that firms will select within their randomly drawn set of potential lenders, the bank offering the lowest interest rate on loans. The behavioral rule followed to set the firm-specific component of the interest rate is the same for all banks and it is a function of the $leverage_{i,t}$, of $A_{i,t-1}$, and of $Max\left\{A_{i,t-1}\right\}_{i=1}^{N_f}$. Therefore, firms' selection of the supplier on the credit market will be based just on the bank-specific component of the interest rate offered by potential partners. If we define $link_{f,b}$, where f stands for "firms" and b for "banks", a vector of dimension $(1 \times N_f)$ where the ith element is the index corresponding to the bank selected by firm i through the matching protocol, we have that: $link_{f,b}[i] = f(R_{b,t})$ with b varying in the set of potential partners of firm i. From this simple reasoning we can conclude that the rule to set the banks-specific component of interest rates on loans should be called before the matching process on the credit market, whereas the determination of the overall interest rate paid by firms on loans should come after both the determination of the banks' specific component and the selection of lenders by firms. By applying the same reasoning to all the functions of the model we can derive an intra-period ordering of events:

1. Banks compute their bank-specific interest $R_{b,t} = f(A_{b,t-1})$
2. Matching mechanism on the credit market: $link_{f,b} = f(R_b)$
3. Firms update their target leverage $leverage_{i,t} = f(p_{i,t-1}, Rb_{i,t-1})$
4. Firms compute their demand for loans $B_{i,t} = f(leverage_{i,t}, A_{b,t-1})$
5. Firms compute total financial capital $K_{i,t} = f(B_{i,t}, A_{i,t-1})$
6. Firms compute desired output $Y_{i,t} = f(K_{i,t})$
7. Firms update the price $p_{i,t}$ (stochastic)
8. Firms compute their specific interest rate: $R_{i,t} = f(R^*_{b,t}, leverage_{i,t}, A_{i,t-1}, Max\left\{A_{i,t-1}\right\}_{i=1}^{N_f})$
9. Firms compute profits $Pr_{i,t} = f(p_{i,t}, Y_{i,t}, R_{i,t}, B_{i,t})$
10. Firms update their net wealth $A_{i,t}$ and check whether they default or not $fall_{i,t} = f(A_{i,t})$
11. We compute the loss-given default ratio for each firm $LGD_{i,t} = f(A_{i,t}, B_{i,t})$
12. Banks' compute deposits $D_{b,t} = f(A_{b,t}, B_{b,t})$
13. Banks compute bad debt $bad_{b,t} = f(B_{b,t}, fall_{i,t}, link_{i,b})$
14. Banks compute profits $Pr_{b,t} = f(R_{i,t}, D_{b,t,B_{b,t}}, A_{b,t}, bad_{b,t})$
15. Banks update their net wealth and check whether they default or not $fall_{b,t} = f(A_{b,t})$

Notice that this is only one of the possible orderings for the simplified model depicted in this chapter. For example, any other position for the matching mechanism would be good as well provided that it is located after the bank-specific interest component setting, and before the firms' overall loan interest rate determination. Similarly, while the inner ordering of the block of operations going from the determination of firms' leverage to the determination of firms' output cannot be modified, as each one of these heuristics uses the output of the previous one to compute its own output, the model would not change if we moved the entire block to the top of the sequence.

Finally, let us notice that there is still an event to add to our ordering of events which is not related to any behavioral rule of agents, but rather to the replacement of defaulted agents. This can be added indifferently at the end of the simulation round or at the beginning of the next one. In our implementation we follow the convention of replacing agents at the beginning of the next period.

0. Defaulted firms/banks replacement

In the implementation of the model that follows, we will refer to the ordering presented in the previous scheme. The code corresponding to the model presented is written in **R**.

2.2.3 *Implementing the Model in R*

2.2.3.1 The General Structure of the Program

Figure 2.9 shows a relatively simple but quite general way to structure the code of a model in order to execute it as a Monte Carlo experiment. In a nutshell, the flow of execution of the program can be subdivided in three major blocks:

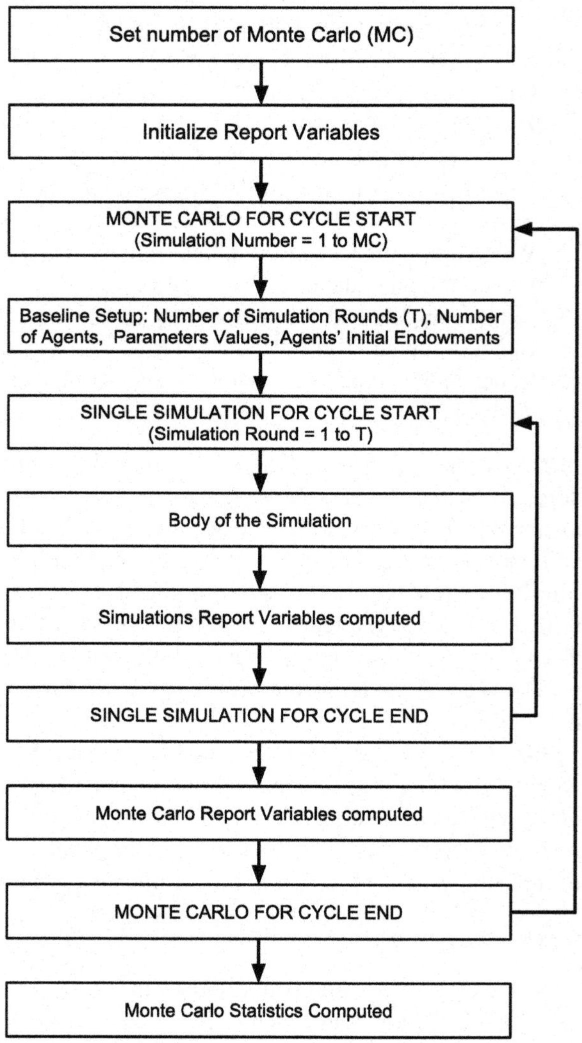

Fig. 2.9 Code structure

- *The Monte Carlo Setup*. The first block of code contains the commands to set the number of the Monte Carlo simulations, declare the variables that will be employed to track the results of the Monte Carlo experiment, and possibly set other simulation features that will be kept invariant across the single runs of the Monte Carlo experiment.
- *The Monte Carlo "For" cycle*. It creates a loop in which the attributes of the single simulation runs are set and then the simulations are executed. The loop terminates when the desired number of Monte Carlo simulations has been executed.
- *The Simulations "For" cycle*. Within each iteration of the Monte Carlo loop a single simulation run is executed. The latter is expressed as well as a "For" cycle, where each iteration represents a single period of the simulation. The block of commands contained in this cycle thus defines the sequence of events and actions of agents occuring within each simulation period.

Figure 2.9 also shows that, according to their type, report variables values may be updated either at the end of each simulation period (e.g. the GDP is computed at the end of each simulation period in order to obtain a time series for GDP for each simulation), or at the end of single simulations runs (e.g. the average GDP rate of growth of the simulation), or at the end of the Monte Carlo loop (e.g. the across-runs standard deviations of GDP average rates of growth).

Having in mind this diagram, we now turn to the implementation in **R** of the model. Instead of showing the entire code of the simulations all at once, and then analyze it, we proceed as if we had to start implementing the model from a blank sheet, introducing one at a time (as far as possible) the blocks identified in Fig. 2.9, so as to highlight the logic followed in programming.

2.2.3.2 Set up of the Monte Carlo Experiment

In this section of the code we set the number of the Monte Carlo simulations to be executed and the values of the behavioral parameters employed in the simulations. The latter are time-invariant and their value is kept constant across all the Monte Carlo simulations, so that we can initialize them once and for all at the top of the script.

As a general rule, in the **R** implementation of the model we will keep the same notation employed in the previous sections though substituting the Greek letters symbols, which are not allowed in **R**, with their names. Using the # we can put brief explanatory comments in the code, to facilitate the reading.

First, we set the number of rounds for each simulation to 1000. We assume that our economy is populated by 500 firms and 50 banks. Then we fix the values for the behavioral parameters of the model.

```
##############BEGIN OF THE SCRIPT###############

#IMPORT LIBRARIES
#No libraries to be imported for the moment
```

```
MC=1 #Number of Monte Carlo Simulations to be executed

#MONTE CARLO INVARIANT PARAMETERS SETTING
#Number of simulation rounds
Time=1000
#Number of firms
Nf = 500
#Number of banks
Nb = 50
#Interest rate parameter
gamma = 0.02
#Number of potential partners on credit market
chi = 5
#Partner choice parameter: intensity of choice
lambda = 4
#Leverage adjustment speed parameter
adj = 0.1
#Production function parameter
phi = 3
#Production function parameter
beta = 0.7
#Firms' price parameter: mean of Normal Distribution
alpha = 0.1
#Firms' price parameter:variance of Normal Distribution
varpf = 0.4
#Central bank's interest rate
rCB = 0.02
#Banks' costs
cB = 0.01
```

After having specified the properties of the Monte Carlo experiment we turn to the initialization of the report variables that will be employed to analyze the model dynamics. Admittedly, at this stage of the implementation process, the modeler typically has just a rough idea of the report variables needed. Therefore, this section of the code is likely to be repeatedly integrated at later stages of development. Yet, we can define a preliminary set of reports that are very likely to be employed in the model analysis. The following block of instructions initializes these reports. Comments clarify the meaning of the variables specified in the next lines of the code. Notice that all these report variables are declared as a matrix of dimension $MC \times Time$ because we want to have a time series for each simulation of the Monte Carlo, tracking the dynamics of the variables over the simulation time span.

```
#(AGGREGATE) REPORTS INITIALIZATION
#Switching rate Report
changeFB = matrix (data = 0, ncol=MC, nrow=Time)
#Aggregate output Report
YF = matrix(data = 0, ncol = MC, nrow = Time)
#Aggregate Banks' NW Report
AB = matrix(data = 0, ncol = MC, nrow = Time)
#Aggregate Firms' NW Report
AF = matrix(data = 0, ncol = MC, nrow = Time)
#Aggregate Debt Report
BF = matrix(data = 0, ncol = MC, nrow = Time)
```

```
#(Simple) Average interest rate Report
RBF = matrix(data = 0, ncol = MC, nrow = Time)
#Aggregate bad debt Report
BAD = matrix(data = 0, ncol = MC, nrow = Time)
#Total firms' defaults Report
FALLF = matrix(data = 0, ncol = MC, nrow = Time)
#Total banks' defaults Report
FALLB = matrix(data = 0, ncol = MC, nrow = Time)
#Aggregate Leverage (BF/AF) Report
LEV = matrix(data = 0, ncol = MC, nrow = Time)
#Aggregate firms' profits Report
PRF = matrix(data = 0, ncol = MC, nrow = Time)
#Aggregate banks' profit Report
PRB = matrix(data = 0, ncol = MC, nrow = Time)
#Aggregate growth rate Report
GR = matrix(data = 0, ncol = MC, nrow = Time)
#(Simple) average price
PF = matrix(data = 0, ncol = MC, nrow = Time)
#Firms' probability of default report
PBF= matrix(data = 0, ncol = MC, nrow = 1)
#Banks' probability of default report
PBB= matrix(data = 0, ncol = MC, nrow = 1)
```

The next step of the implementation process is the declaration of the two nested `for` cycles required to run our experiment, the outer one to launch the series of Monte Carlo simulations, the inner one to execute a single simulation.

```
for (mc in 1:MC) {

#HERE SIMULATION SETUP

for (t in 1:Time) {

#HERE BODY OF THE SIMULATION
}
}
```

Then, we fill these loops with the instructions corresponding to the blocks of commands highlighted in Fig. 2.9.

On the top of the Monte Carlo cycle we define the initial setup of the simulation runs. The first line simply asks **R** to print in the console window the number identifying the Monte Carlo simulation currently running. Then, we set the value of the seed used in the pseudo-random numbers generator algorithm of **R**.[26] Since the purpose of the Monte Carlo method is checking the across-runs robustness of the model properties, we want each Monte Carlo simulation to employ a different sequence of random numbers during the simulation.

[26]A pseudo random numbers generator (PRNG) is a deterministic algorithm which produces a sequence of numbers which has almost the same statistical features of a sequence generated by a random process. The PRNG-generated sequence of numbers is not truly random, because it is completely determined by a relatively small set of initial values (possibly just one) called "seeds". PRNGs are employed in a wide range of applications involving programming and are crucial in simulations applications, in particular when running Monte Carlo experiments.

In principle, this can be achieved simply by setting the value of the random seed at the very top of the code (i.e. before the declaration of the two nested `for` cycles described above). In this case, the PRNG generates a unique sequence of random numbers for the Monte Carlo experiment as a whole, but each simulation draws its pseudo-random numbers from a different slice of this sequence, as shown hereunder where rs_0 is the random seed used by the PRNG and $prn^i_{rs_0}$ is the ith generated pseudo random number in the sequence:

$$\begin{aligned} &PRNG\,(rs_0)\,generated\ sequence{:}\{\underbrace{prn^1_{rs_0}, prn^2_{rs_0}, \ldots, prn^i_{rs_0},}_{Simulation\ 1} \\ &\underbrace{prn^{i+1}_{rs_0}, prn^{i+2}_{rs_0}, \ldots, prn^j_{rs_0},}_{Simulation\ 2} \underbrace{prn^{j+1}_{rs_0}, prn^{j+2}_{rs_0}, \ldots, prn^z_{rs_0},}_{Simulation\ 3} \ldots\} \end{aligned} \tag{2.19}$$

However, there are good reasons to assign to every simulation in the Monte Carlo experiment a different seed. In this case each simulation draws its pseudo-random numbers from a different sequence, each one being generated by the PRNG algorithm initialized with the simulation-specific seed:

$$\begin{aligned} &PRNG\,(rs_0)\,generated\ sequence{:}\{\underbrace{prn^1_{rs_0}, prn^2_{rs_0}, \ldots\}}_{Simulation\ 1}, \\ &PRNG\,(rs_1)\,generated\ sequence{:}\{\underbrace{prn^1_{rs_1}, prn^2_{rs_1}, \ldots\}}_{Simulation\ 2}, \\ &\ldots, \\ &PRNG\,(rs_{MC})\,generated\ sequence{:}\{\underbrace{prn^1_{rs_{MC}}, prn^2_{rs_{MC}}, \ldots\}}_{Simulation\ MC}, \end{aligned} \tag{2.20}$$

Let us stress that given rs_i the sequence of pseudo random number generated by the PRNG is computed in a deterministic way. In other words, given rs_i, the PRGN will always produce the same sequence of pseudo-random numbers. The case for assigning to each Monte Carlo simulation a specific seed is related to the fact that Monte Carlo simulations are only one component of the validation process. Sensitivity analysis should be performed as well in order to check how the behavior of the system changes under different parameters configurations, compared to the baseline scenario. Whereas in doing Monte Carlo we compare different simulations runs to assess *the impact of stochastic components* on the robustness of the model properties, through sensitivity analysis the modeler aims to assess how these properties are impacted by different parameters specifications, *net of stochastic factors*. Therefore, while in doing Monte Carlo on the baseline scenario we compare simulations obtained from different pseudo random number sequences, in doing sensitivity analysis we compare simulations drawing from the same sequence but characterized by a different parametrization. The same reasoning applies when we use the model for normative purposes, performing for this sake either a scenario (e.g. how the model reacts if an external shock hits it) or policy analysis (i.e. what is the effect of a change in a given policy rule).

Keeping this in mind, in our implementation we assign to each Monte Carlo simulation a random seed equal to mc, where this latter indicates the index of the simulation currently running. In this way we ensure that every simulation starts with a different seed - thereby drawing from a different sequence of pseudo random numbers - the first simulation having a random seed equal to 1, the second equal to 2, and so on till the last one which has a seed equal to MC.

```
for (mc in 1:MC) {
print(paste("Monte Carlo N", mc))
set.seed (mc)
```

Then we begin to declare the variables that will be employed in each simulation, setting their initial values equal to 0 for simplicity reasons.[27]

Notice that we declare them as an object of type *matrix* even though we set the number of rows equal to 1, so that each matrix comes down to a *vector*.[28]

In practice, the most convenient way to proceed when declaring the variables of the model is to start by specifying only those variables which are related to agents' initial endowments (for example, agents' initial net worth), and then gradually integrate this

[27]We might as well declare these variables without specifying the initial values, using the following syntax: `variable = matrix (, ncol=numberOfAgents, nrow=1)`. In this case **R** would create a matrix of NA values. The two implementations are absolutely equivalent.

[28]Hence, we might had specified them as vectors as well, using the syntax `variable = vector(mode = "any", length = numberOfAgents)`. Each agent within a specific group (households, firm, and banks) is identified by an index which gives its position within each one of these vectors. So, for example, the ith element of the `Rb` vector declared in the code below always represents the bank-specific component of the ith bank. Notice that this vector representation is somehow related to the fact that in the current specification of the model we do not have any heuristics employing information referring to periods other than current and past ones. However, in a later stage of development we might decide to change some heuristics in a way that they come to depend on the values of some variables over a time span of n past periods. For example, we might change the simple adaptive expectations formation scheme in favor of a rule which defines expectations as a weighted average of the values assumed by the correspondent variable over the last n periods. To allow this rule to work, we should declare the variables on which we want to compute expectations in a format which allows to store the necessary information (i.e. the values of the variable in the last n periods for each agent). In our example this would require to declare the variable as a matrix of dimension $n \times numberOfAgents$. Therefore, in order to keep the declaration of the variables compatible with this and other possible revisions, we preferred to use a *matrix* object rather than a *vector*.

One might in principle decide to keep track of every agent's attributes along the whole simulation, thereby declaring by default the correspondent variables as a matrix of dimension $Time \times numberOfAgents$, regardless the type of heuristics employed. However, let us recall again the programming tenet according to which one should be as parsimonious as possible to avoid useless wastefulnesses of computer memory and slowdowns in execution times.

block of code with the declaration of the remaining variables, as they appear along the implementation of the model.

However for graphical and explanatory reasons, we would like to avoid segmenting the code presentation in too many pieces, as well as having to go backward and forward to integrate or modify blocks of the code already presented in the text. Therefore, hereunder we present the entire block referring to the variables declaration once and for all. Each variable is preceded by a comment providing a brief description of it, as usual.

```
#INITIAL CONDITIONS OF THE SIMULATION RUN
  #Banks specific component of the interest rate
  Rb = matrix(data = 0, ncol = Nb, nrow = 1)
  #Banks' Net Wealth
  Ab = matrix(data = 0, ncol = Nb, nrow = 1)
  #Firms-Banks credit matching
  link_fb = matrix(data =0, ncol = Nf, nrow = 1)
  #Firms' interest rate on loans
  Rbf = matrix(data = 0, ncol = Nf, nrow = 1)
  #Firms' leverage
  lev = matrix(data = 0, ncol = Nf, nrow = 1)
  #Firms' price
  pf = matrix(data = 0, ncol = Nf, nrow = 1)
  #Firms' debt
  Bf = matrix(data = 0, ncol = Nf, nrow = 1)
  #Firms' Net Wealth
  Af = matrix(data = 0, ncol = Nf, nrow = 1)
  #Firms' defaults (1=defaulted,, 0=surviving)
  fallf = matrix(data = 0, ncol = Nf, nrow = 1)
  #Banks' defaults (1=defaulted,, 0=surviving)
  fallb = matrix(data = 0, ncol = Nb, nrow = 1)
  #Loss-given-default ratio
  LGDf = matrix(data = 0, ncol = Nf, nrow = 1)
  #Deposits
  D=matrix(data = 0, ncol = Nb, nrow = 1)
  #Banks' non performing loans
  Badb=matrix(data = 0, ncol = Nb, nrow = 1)
  #Banks' profits
  Prb=matrix(data = 0, ncol = Nb, nrow = 1)
  #Banks' credit link degree
  creditDegree=matrix(data = 0, ncol = Nb, nrow = Time)
```

In order to allow the simulation to start, we have to assign an initial value to some of the variables introduced before. Our initialization block is then concluded by the following set of code lines, where we assume that banks' and firms' start with an initial net worth equal to 10, that the price charged by each firm is a random draw from $N(\alpha, \sigma)$, and that the initial leverage target by firms is equal to 1. In addition, we also assign to each firm a random partner on the credit market. The command `ceiling(runif(Nf)*Nb)` sample `Nf` random numbers from a Uniform Distribution between {0, 1}, then multiply each of them for the dimension of the banks' population (`Nb`) to obtain a sequence of random numbers between {0, `Nb`}, and finally round down each of them to obtain a sequence of `Nf` random integers on the same interval, representing the indexes of the randomly assigned banks.

After the simulation set-up block, the single simulation `for` cycle opens.

```
#INITIALIZE THE VALUES OF VARIABLES REQUIRED TO START THE SIMULATION
  Af[1:Nf] = 10
  Ab[1:Nb] = 10
  pf[1:Nf] = rnorm(Nf)*varpf+alpha
  lev[1:Nf] = 1
  link_fb[1:Nf] = ceiling(runif(Nf)*Nb)

  for (t in 1:Time) {
```

2.2.3.3 The Body of a Simulation

In Sect. 2.2.2.2 we identified one of the possible orderings for the events taking place in each round of the simulation. That sequence will be now employed as a lineup in order to implement the equations of the model presented in Sect. 2.2.1.

Admittedly, we will make only an exception to this implementation schedule: according to our lineup, the first event taking place in each period of the simulation is the replacement of (possibly) defaulted firms and banks. However, since firms' replacement depends on defaults conditions, there are relatively good reasons to postpone the writing of this part of code after that referring to the defaults checking procedures. Since this latter block is located at the end of our lineup, we simply put a comment to remind us to write this part of the program later on, and start instead from event 1 that is the determination of the bank-specific component of interest rates. The line of code presented hereunder thus updates the value of each element of the vector `Rb` by raising it at the power of `(-gamma)` and then multiplying for `(gamma)`, as prescribed by Eq. (2.12).

```
for (t in 1:Time) {
# 0)HERE REPLACEMENT OF DEFAULTED FIRMS & BANKS
    #TO DO
# 1)UPDATE BANK SPECIFIC INTEREST COMPONENT
  Rb = gamma * Ab ^ (-gamma)
```

Having determined the bank-specific component of banks' interest rates on loans, we pass to the implementation of the matching protocol between firms and banks on the credit market. This matching mechanism is implemented using a `for` loop which iterates on the firms' population to ask each firm to select her partner in a random subset of the banks' population. The code representing the matching protocol is the following one:

```
  # 2)MATCHING ON CREDIT MARKET
  for (i in 1:Nf) {
    #SELECT POTENTIAL PARTNERS
    newfb=ceiling(runif(chi)*Nb)
    #SELECT BEST INTEREST AMONG POTENTIAL PARTNERS
    inew = min(Rb[newfb])
    #PICK UP THE INTEREST OF THE OLD PARTNER
    iold = Rb[link_fb[i]]
    #COMPARE OLD AND NEW INTERESTS
    if (runif(1) < (1-exp(lambda*(inew-iold)/(inew)))) {
```

```
        #THEN SWITCH TO A NEW PARTNER
        changeFB[t] = changeFB[t] + 1
        research = which(Rb[newfb]==min(Rb[newfb]))
        #CHECK IF MULTIPLE BEST INTERESTS
        if (length(research)>1){
          research=research[ceiling(runif(1)*length(research))]
        }
        #UPDATE THE LINK
        link_fb[i] = newfb[research[1]]
      }
      else {
      #STICK TO THE OLD PARTNER
        link_fb[i]=link_fb[i]
      }
    }
    #COMPUTE SWITCHING RATE
    changeFB[t]=changeFB[t]/Nf
```

First, the command `ceiling(runif(chi)*Nb)` selects randomly `chi` banks in the banks' population. These represent the potential partners of firm i in the current period. Its outcome is a row a vector of length chi, whose elements are the indexes of the randomly selected banks.

The next line of code first subsets the vector of banks' bank-specific interest rate components by picking up only the elements corresponding to selected banks (`Rb[newfb]`), and then identifies the lowest interest offered using the `min()` function of **R**.

In the following line of code `link_fb[i]` gives the ith element of vector `link_fb`, that is the index of the old partner of firm i on the credit market.[29] `Rb[link_fb[i]]` thus picks up the interest rate of the old partner.

The remaining part of the above block of commands then compares the two local variables `iold` and `inew` to asses whether firm i sticks to the old partner or switches to the new one. `1-exp(lambda*(inew-iold)/(inew))` calculates the probability of switching to the new potential partner, based on the interest rates of the old and new banks. The condition in the `if` statement thus mimics the Bernoulli experiment based on this probability. If the outcome of this experiment is positive, the borrower switches to the new partner. In this case, the counter of firms which have decided to switch to another partner `changeFB[t]`[30] in the current period t, which had been initialized to 0, is increased by one. Then we identify the index of the selected bank: first, we employ the **R** function `which` in the command `research = which(Rb[newfb]==min(Rb[newfb]))` which returns the position in the sub-vector `Rb[newfb]` of the element having the minimum interest rate. Notice however that it might be the case - though very unlikely - that there are more than a bank offering the minimum interest rate in the set of potential partners. In this case, the length of vector `research` will be greater than 1. Before updating the `link_fb[i]` vector is thus convenient to add a procedure to check for this possibility which reduces the `research` vector to a vector with just one element, randomly

[29] In the first period of the simulation this is the index of the bank which was randomly assigned to i in the initialization of the simulation.

[30] This counter will be employed to calculate the aggregate switching rate.

drawn from the original one. Finally, we assign to `link_fb[i]` the index identifying the selected bank. When the firm sticks to the original partner, `link_fb[i]` is kept constant. For clarity reasons, we made it explicit in the code, though the `else` statement could indifferently be omitted from the code without affecting the implementation of the model.

Finally, we calculate the switching rate on the credit market for the current period.

After having selected the bank to ask for credit, firms update their target leverage. The code is quite intuitive: first we define a vector `u` composed of `Nf` numbers randomly drawn from a $U(0, 1)$, which represent the stochastic components of the heuristics updating the leverage targets. Then, following Eq. (2.11) we increase or decrease the leverage according to whether the firm's past period price was higher or lower than the interest paid in the past period. The related block of commands also highlights a very practical feature of **R** which allows to subset a vector of a given dimension based on a comparison of the elements of two other vectors of the same dimension, as in the following example, where `a` and `b` are the vectors whose elements are to be compared and `c` is the vector to be subset:

```
> a=c(2,10,25,3,7)
> b=c(1,11,24,4,8)
> c=c(10,20,30,40,50)
> c[a>b]
[1] 10 30
```

In the above example only the first and third elements of `c` are selected as the condition `a>b` is verified only when we compare the first and third elements of `a` and `b`. Accordingly, in the case of `lev[pf>Rbf]`, we subset the vector `lev` by picking only those elements which have the same position of the elements in vectors `pf` which are greater of the correspondent elements in `Rbf`. This sub-setting technique is thus especially helpful when implementing rules which ask to do something conditional upon something.

```
# 3) FIRMS UPDATE LEVERAGE TARGET
  #RANDOM SAMPLE FROM U(0,1) FOR EACH FIRM
  u = runif(Nf)
  #IF PRICE>INTEREST INCREASE LEVERAGE
  lev[pf>Rbf] = lev[pf>Rbf] * (1 + adj*u[pf>Rbf])
  #OTHERWISE...
  lev[pf<=Rbf] = lev[pf<=Rbf] * (1 - adj*u[pf<=Rbf])
```

The next three intra-period steps are the computation of firms' demand for loans, the evaluation of total financial capital available to fund production, and the determination of firms' output. The lines of code referring to this events are relatively straightforward, as their implementation does not present any programming peculiarity, so that we just present them without discussing.

```
# 4)DETERMINE DEMAND FOR LOANS
  Bf = lev * Af
# 5)COMPUTE TOTAL FINANCIAL CAPITAL
```

```
  Kf = Af + Bf
# 6)COMPUTE (FINANCIALLY CONSTRAINED) OUTPUT
  Yf = phi * Kf ^ beta
```

Firms then update their price by sampling from a Normal distribution: the function `rnorm(N)` gives as outcome a vector of `N` random numbers drawn from a Gaussian Normal distribution which are then multiplied by `varpf` and summed to `alpha` to obtain a draw from a Normal α, var_p, as prescribed by the model.

```
# 7)UPDATE THE PRICE
  pf = rnorm(Nf) * varpf + alpha
```

Firms compute the interest rate they have to pay on loans following Eq. (2.12).

```
# 8)COMPUTE THE INTEREST RATE CHARGED TO FIRMS
  Rbf = rCB + Rb[link_fb] + gamma*(lev) / ((1+Af/max(Af)))
```

The code presented below shows another useful technical trick which allows us to update the `Rbf` vector at once without having to write a `for` cycle iterating on his elements. The trick is based on the possibility provided by **R** of creating a vector by selecting the elements of another one based on a third vector of indexes as in the following example, where `a` is our original vector and `b` the vector of indexes:

```
> a=c(2,10,25,3,7)
> b=c(3,1,4)
> a[b]
[1] 25  2  3
```

Accordingly, the command `Rb[link_fb]` returns a vector whose i^{th} element is equal to the element of `Rb` which occupies the position corresponding to the value of the element in the ith position of `link_fb`, i.e. the interest rate offered by the bank selected to the ith firm.

Under the simplifying assumption that firms are able to place all their output at their stochastic price, we can then compute firms' profits, update firms' net worth accordingly, and check whether some firms defaults. The elements of vector `fallf` are then set equal to 0 if the corresponding firm survives, or 1 in case the firm defaults. Finally, we compute the loss given default ratio for each firm which for obvious economic reasons must be defined on the interval [0, 1].

```
# 9)COMPUTE FIRMS' PROFITS
Prf = pf * Yf - Rbf * Bf #Firms profits

# 10)UPDATE FIRMS' NET WORTH AND CHECK WHETER THEY ARE DEFAULTED
Af=Af+Prf
# AND DEFAULT CHECK
fallf[Af>0]=0
fallf[Af<=0]=1 #Firm defaults
```

```
# 11)COMPUTE THE LOSS GIVEN DEFAULT RATIO
LGDf[1:Nf]= -(Af) / (Bf)
LGDf[LGDf>1] = 1
LGDf[LGDf<0] = 0
```

We now switch our focus to banks. We iterate on the banks' population in order to compute individual banks' deposits, bad debt and profits. Deposits are given by the bank's total loans `sum(Bf[link_fb==j])` minus the bank's net worth `Ab[j]`. We introduce an `if` statement to check that deposits are non negative. Bad debts are calculated by summing the products of the loss-given default ratio for the outstanding debt of those firms which have defaulted and have a link with the bank (`LGDf[fallf==1&link_fb==j] * Bf[fallf==1&link_fb==j]`).

Finally, bank's j profits are computed by summing the interest flows on active loans (`Bf[link_fb==j&fallf==0] %*% Rbf[link_fb==j&fallf==0]`)[31] and then subtracting interests on deposits, managerial costs, and the bank's bad debt.

```
# 12)COMPUTE "DEPOSITS"
for (j in 1:Nb) {
  D[j] = sum(Bf[link_fb==j])-Ab[j]
  if (D[j]<0) {
    D[j]=0
  }
  # 13) COMPUTE THE BAD DEBT
  Badb[j] = sum(LGDf[fallf==1&link_fb==j] * Bf[fallf==1&link_fb==j])
  # 14) COMPUTE BANKS' PROFITS
  Prb[j] = Bf[link_fb==j&fallf==0] %*% Rbf[link_fb==j&fallf==0]
   - rCB * D[j] - cB * Ab[j]-Badb[j]
}
```

Finally, banks update their new worth and check whether they default or not.

```
# 15)UPDATE BANKS' NET WORTH AND CHECK WHETHER THEY ARE DEFAULTED
  Ab=Ab+Prb
  fallb[Ab>0] = 0
  fallb[Ab<=0] = 1 #Bank defaults
```

This concludes the timeline of events within a single simulation round. However remember that we kept an empty spot at the beginning of this section related to the implementation of the defaulted agents' replacement procedure. Before moving on, it is convenient to come back and fill this spot.[32]

[31] Notice that the operator `*` in **R**, when applied to two equally long vectors, multiplies each element of the former for the correspondent element of the latter, so that the output is still a vector of the same length. Here instead the operator `%*%` is employed to calculate the internal product between the two vectors whose outcome is a number.

[32] Please notice that we might move the block referring to the replacement procedure to the bottom of the code developed at this stage without altering in any way the execution flow of the program. However, to be consistent with the timeline presented in Sect. 2.2.2.2, we prefer to embed this part on the top of the simulation `for` loop.

The lines displayed below first identify firms and banks which defaulted in the past period - that is the elements of `fallf` and `fallb` equal to 1 - and then initialize the new entrants which replace them.

```
for (t in 1:Time) {

  # 0)REPLACEMENT OF DEFAULTED FIRMS & BANKS
   #FIRMS
  for (i in 1:Nf) {
   if (fallf[i] == 1) {
      #NEW FIRMS INITIALIZATION
     Af[i] = 2*runif(1)
      lev[i] = 1
      pf[i] =  rnorm(1) * varpf + alpha
      link_fb[i]=ceiling(runif(1)*Nb)
      Rbf[i] = rCB + Rb[link_fb[i]] + gamma*(lev[i]) / ((1+Af[i]/max(Af)))
      }
    }
   #BANKS
  for (j in 1:Nb) {
    if (fallb[j] == 1) {
    #NEW BANK INITIALIZATION
      Ab[j] = 2 * runif(1)
      }
  }
  # 1)UPDATE BANK SPECIFIC INTEREST COMPONENT
  ...
```

The previous block concludes the implementation of the body of the simulation part. However, in order to analyze the dynamics of the model, we still have to update the reports initialized at the top of our implementation procedure, filling them with the values generated in each round by the simulation:

```
#REPORTS
  YF[t,mc]=sum(Yf) #Total output
  AB[t,mc]=sum(Ab) #Total banks' wealth
  AF[t,mc]=sum(Af) #Total firms' wealth
  BF[t,mc]=sum(Bf) #Total debt
  RBF[t,mc]=sum(Rbf*Bf)/sum(Bf) #(Weighted) average interest rate
  BAD[t,mc]=sum(Badb) #Total bad debt
  PRF[t,mc]=sum(Prf) #Firms' profits
  PRB[t,mc]=sum(Prb) #Banks' profits
  FALLF[t,mc]=sum(fallf==1) #Number of failures (firms)
  FALLB[t,mc]=sum(fallb==1) #Number of failures (banks)
  LEV[t,mc]=BF[t,mc]/AF[t,mc] #The economy leverage
  #The growth rate
  if (t==1){
    gr[t,mc]=0
  }
  else{
    gr[t,mc]=YF[t,mc]/YF[t-1,mc]-1
  }
  PF[t,mc]= mean(pf) #Average price

  } #CLOSURE OF SIMULATION FOR CYCLE
```

One thing that must be highlighted is that the lines related to the simulation reports update[33] conclude the block of command in the simulation `for` cycle.

2.2.3.4 A First Flavor of the Model Dynamics

Though the code of the simulation would be ready to be executed, we still have to write the code to display graphically the data stored in the reports of the simulation. The code below allows to produce some synthetic plots of our aggregate variables using the `plot` function, and to display them in a 3×3 matrix structure using the `par(mfrow=c(Nrows,Ncolumns))` function. Figure 2.10 displays the outcome of this code. **R** allows to save the plots in various formats, such as PNG, JPEG, PDF, EPS, or PS (as in our example). The figure is saved in the folder "Result", which we have previously created in our working directory to store the outcomes of our simulation experiments. By using the `paste` function of **R**, which concatenates vectors after having converted his elements to characters, we can specify the saving path, name, and extension of the figure. In our example, where we defined `folder` as a string equal to `\Results`, the chosen specification `file=paste(folder,"/SimOverview",mc,".ps",sep="")` for the argument of the `dev.copy2eps` function saves MC figures in the folder "Results", each one characterized by the filename SimOverview, followed by the number of the correspondent Monte Carlo simulation and by the file extension.ps.[34]

```
} #CLOSURE OF SIMULATION FOR CYCLE

#PLOTS SIMULATION REPORTS
folder="Results/"
par(mfrow=c(3,3))
#Output
plot(YF[,mc],type="l",main="Output (YF)",
ylab="",xlab="",lwd=1, lty=1)
#Firms' profit
plot(PRF[,mc],type="l",main="Firms' profits (PRF)",
ylab="",xlab="",lwd=1, lty=1)
#Banks' profit
plot(PRB[,mc],type="l",main="Banks' profits (PRF)",
ylab="",xlab="",lwd=1, lty=1)
#Firms' net worth
plot(AF[,mc],type="l",main="Firms' Net Worth (AF)",
ylab="",xlab="",lwd=1, lty=1)
#Banks' net worth
```

[33]This part of the code should be easily understood by the reader as it does not present any peculiarity, apart from the `if` statement in the growth rate report update by which we assign value 0 to the report in the first period. This is motivated by merely technical reasons: in the first period (`t==1`) of the simulation we would have YF[t-1,mc]=YF[0,mc] which would raise an error message because in **R** indexation of vectors and matrices starts from 1.

[34]The command `dev.off()`, if uncommented, would allow to save the graphs without showing them on the console of **R**.

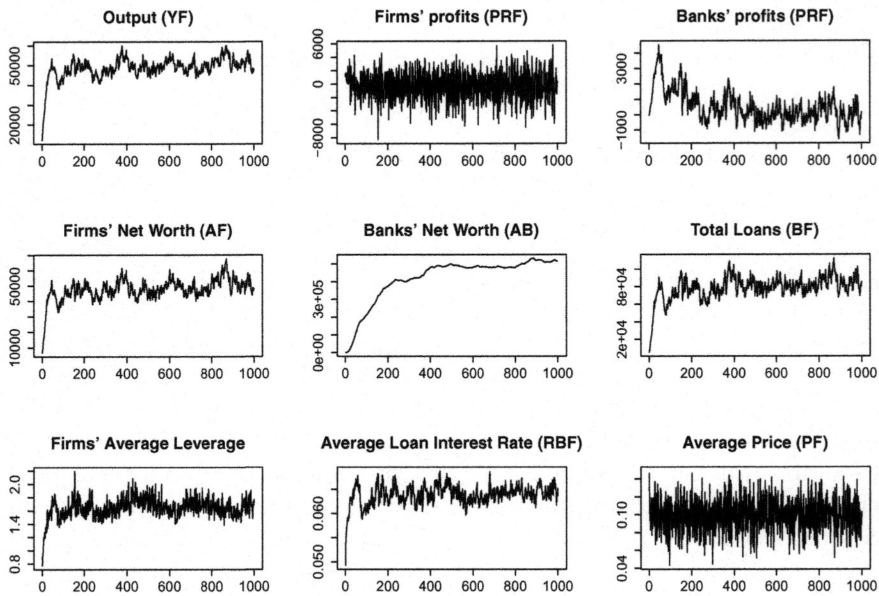

Fig. 2.10 Overview of the results of a single simulation run

```
plot(AB[,mc],type="l",main="Banks' Net Worth (AB)",
ylab="",xlab="",lwd=1, lty=1)
#Loans
plot(BF[,mc],type="l",main="Total Loans (BF)",
ylab="",xlab="",lwd=1, lty=1)
#Average leverage
plot(LEV[,mc],type="l",main="Firms' Average Leverage",
ylab="",xlab="",lwd=1)
#Average interest rate
plot(RBF[,mc],type="l",main="Average Loan Interest Rate (RBF)",
ylab="",xlab="",lwd=1, lty=1)
#Average price
plot(PF[,mc],type="l",main="Average Price (PF)",
ylab="",xlab="",lwd=1, lty=1)
dev.copy2eps(file=paste(folder,"/SimOverview",mc,".ps",sep=""),
width = 10, height= 7)
#dev.off()
```

Another plot which may usually help to get a first flavor on the model dynamics is represented by the time series of firms' and banks' defaults, from which we can get a first insight about the stability, instability, and possible cyclicality of the model. The block of commands below produces the bar plot presented in Fig. 2.11 which highlights a certain degree of cyclicality in both firms' and banks' defaults.

```
#Firms' and banks' defaults
par(mfrow=c(2,1))
barplot(FALLF[,mc], main="Firms' Defaults", names.arg=c(1:Time),
```

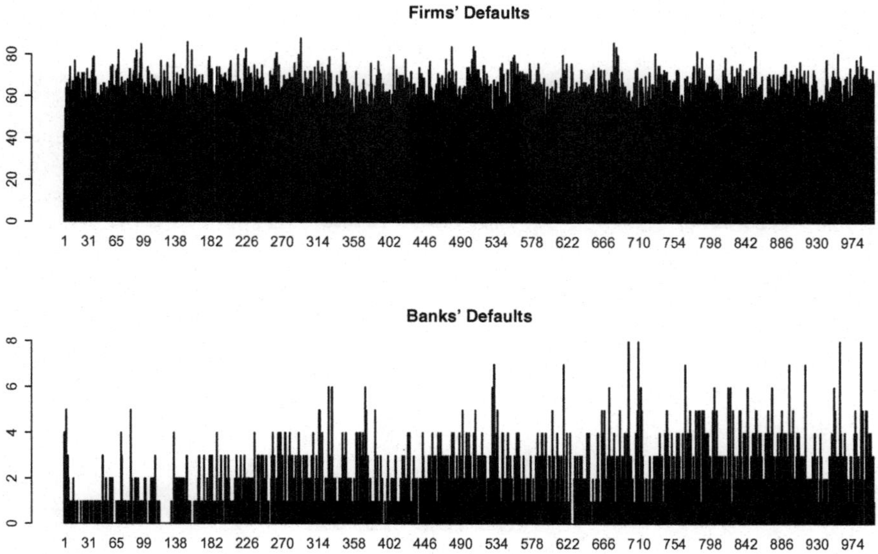

Fig. 2.11 Defaults by banks and firms in a single simulation time span

```
    xlab="")
  barplot(FALLB[,mc], main="Banks' Defaults", names.arg=c(1:Time),
    xlab="")
  #dev.copy2eps(file=paste(folder,"/Defaults",mc,".ps",sep=""),
    width = 15, height= 9.5)
    #dev.off()
```

Finally, a very important set of plots are those displaying cross correlations between macro variables. These graphs, at a first approximation, are useful in at least two respects: first, they provide a guidance to analyze how macro variables impact each other, helping to identify the causal links and feed-backs between variables in the model. Secondly, cross correlations between macro variables (more precisely, between their cyclical components) are often employed in the macro modeling literature to validate models through a comparison of real world and artificial cross correlations properties. In the example hereunder we plot nine cross correlations plots, employing for this sake the function `ccf` of **R**, which computes the cross correlation between two time series. This function allows to specify the maximum lags of the cross correlation (`lag.max=25`) and whether to plot the results (`plot= true`) or not. The plot provides, besides the value of the cross correlations, also the confidence interval (dashed) which is set equal to 95 % by default. However, this value can be modified by specifying the desired level through the argument `ci = desired level` of the `ccf()` function.[35] The output of the code is displayed in Fig. 2.12.

[35]A very similar function in **R** is `acf`, which computes the autocorrelation function for a given variable. The arguments of the `acf` function are very similar to `ccf`.

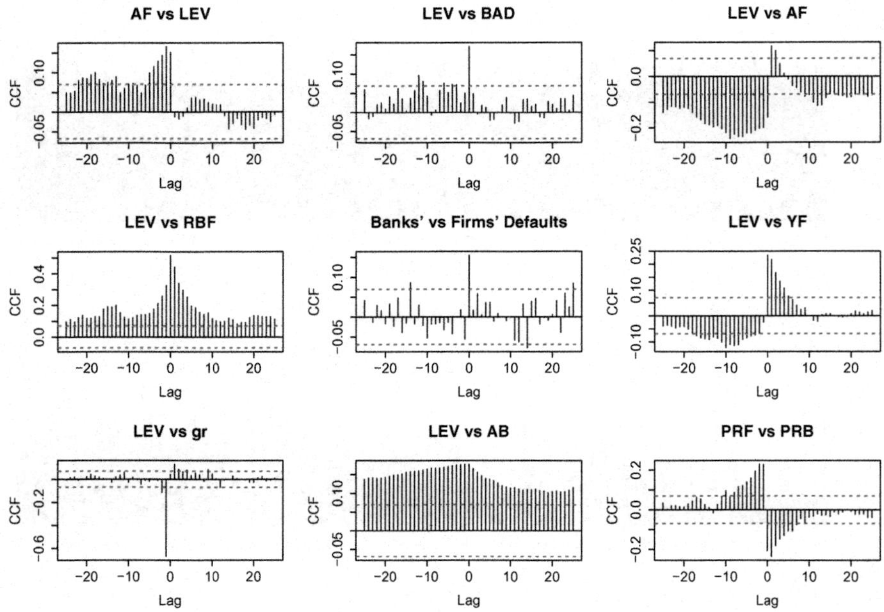

Fig. 2.12 Cross correlations between aggregate variables computed over the time span [200:Time]

```
#CROSS CORRELATIONS
par(mfrow=c(3,3))
ccf(PF[201:Time,mc], AF[201:Time,mc], lag.max = 25, type =
c("correlation"), plot = TRUE, ylab="CCF", main="AF vs LEV")
ccf(LEV[201:Time,mc], BAD[201:Time,mc], lag.max = 25, type =
c("correlation"), plot = TRUE, ylab="CCF", main="LEV vs BAD")
ccf(LEV[201:Time,mc], AF[201:Time,mc], lag.max = 25, type =
c("correlation"), plot = TRUE, ylab="CCF", main="LEV vs AF")
ccf(LEV[201:Time,mc], RBF[201:Time,mc], lag.max = 25, type =
c("correlation"), plot = TRUE,ylab="CCF", main="LEV vs RBF")
ccf(FALLB[201:Time,mc], FALLF[201:Time,mc], lag.max = 25, type =
c("correlation"), plot = TRUE, ylab="CCF", main="FALLB' vs FALLF")
ccf(LEV[201:Time,mc], YF[201:Time,mc], lag.max = 25, type =
c("correlation"), plot = TRUE, ylab="CCF", main="LEV vs YF")
ccf(LEV[201:Time,mc], gr[201:Time,mc], lag.max = 25, type =
c("correlation"), plot = TRUE, ylab="CCF", main="LEV vs gr")
ccf(LEV[201:Time,mc], AB[201:Time,mc], lag.max = 25, type =
c("correlation"), plot = TRUE, ylab="CCF", main="LEV vs AB")
ccf(PRF[201:Time,mc], PRB[201:Time,mc], lag.max = 25, type =
c("correlation"), plot = TRUE, ylab="CCF", main="PRF vs PRB")
dev.copy2eps(file=paste(folder,"/CrossCorrelations",mc,".ps",sep=""),
 width = 10, height = 7)

 } #CLOSURE OF MONTE CARLO FOR CYCLE
```

After the closure of the Monte Carlo `for` cycle, at the end of the block of commands referring to the simulations output graphs, the code is ready to be launched. Its execution, as discussed above, will produce a number of graphs referring to the output of each single simulation run. However, we sill lack reports to analyze in an exhaustive way the across-runs robustness of the dynamics highlighted by each type of graph. Producing these reports is the objective of the next subsection.

2.2.3.5 Monte Carlo Analysis

The simplest way to compare Monte Carlo simulations is to employ synthetic statistics on artificial time series, such as the moments (e.g. the mean, variance, skewness, or kurtosis) of the distribution of some variable of interest. For example, having run MC Monte Carlo, each one over a time span of $Time$ periods, we obtain a set of $MC \cdot Time$ observations for the output growth rates, on which we can compute the mean and standard deviation.[36] An example of this is shown in the following block of commands where we employ the `mean()` and `sd()`[37] functions of **R**.[38]

```
#COMPUTE GLOBAL AVERAGE GROWTH RATE
avGr=mean(gr[201:Time,])
#COMPUTE GLOBAL STANDARD DEVIATION OF GROWTH RATES
stdGr=sd(as.vector(gr[201:Time,]))
print (paste("Growth rate - average:", avGr,"std growth:", stdGr))
```

As an alternative, one might be interested in analyzing the distribution of given simulation properties across the Monte Carlo: we can then compute the moments of the distribution of a synthetic measure characterizing each simulation, such as the average rate of growth over a single simulation time span, across the Monte Carlo. In this case we analyze a distribution of MC elements, each one representing the value of the synthetic measure in a specific Monte Carlo repetition. The code below provides the commands to calculate the average rates of growth for each single simulation, and then their mean and standard deviation across the Monte Carlo runs.

```
#COMPUTE THE MEAN OF SINGLE SIMULATIONS AVERAGE RATES OF GROWTH
avGr=mean(colMeans(gr[201:Time,]))
#COMPUTE THE SD OF THE SINGLE SIMULATIONS AVERAGE RATES OF GROWTH
stdGr=sd(colMeans(gr[201:Time,]))
print (paste("Growth rate - average:", avGr,"std growth:", stdGr))
```

[36] Admittedly, it is common practice to neglect the initial periods of the simulation, which usually represent the transient phase, that is a sort of training of the model, and to focus the attention just on the time span in which the model shows an inherent coherent dynamics. In our examples below we analyze the time span [200:Time].

[37] In the last versions of **R**, we need to force the matrix `gr` to a vector in order to employ the function `sd()` to calculate the standard deviations over all the elements of the matrix.

[38] Similarly, we might compute the kurtosis and skewness of this distribution by employing the `kurtosis()` and `skewness()` functions which require the installation and import of the package "moments" of **R**.

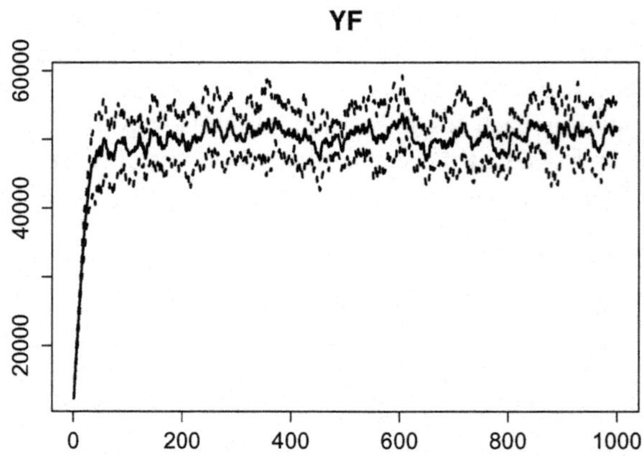

Fig. 2.13 Average output (*continuous line*) and standard deviations (*dashed line*) over the simulations time span

In many cases one might be interested in having some measure which allows to compare Monte Carlo simulations, while making at the same time possible to track its dynamics over the simulation time span, thus also allowing to draw insightful graphs of the type already seen for the simulation time series. The code below, for example, takes the $Time \times MC$ matrix `YF` and compute the average over the rows, that is the average output across simulations for each simulation period. In the same way, we compute the standard deviation of output across Monte Carlo runs, for each simulation period. The time series of the average output is then plotted together with its standard deviations, the output (obtained with 10 Monte Carlo repetitions) being represented in Fig. 2.13. The last line of code presented allows to export and save the data contained in `YF.average` in a .csv format.

```
YF.average=apply(YF,1,mean)
YF.sd=apply(YF,1,sd)
plot(YF.average,ylim=range(YF.average+YF.sd,YF.average-YF.sd),
type="l",main="YF",ylab="",xlab="",lwd=2)
lines(YF.average+YF.sd,lwd=2,lty=2)
lines(YF.average-YF.sd,lwd=2,lty=2)
dev.copy2eps(file=paste(folder,"/YFMonteCarlo.ps",sep=""))
write.csv(YF.average,file=paste(folder,"/YF_average.csv",sep=""))
```

Still, Fig. 2.13 might not be the best solution if one wants to focus on the medium and long term dynamics of the model, as it is affected by the variability related to the short term cyclical components of our raw time series (though this effect should be progressively washed out as the number of Monte Carlo simulation increases). A possible solution to this issue is to "clean" the raw data by using specific filters, such as the Hodrick–Prescott or the Band Pass filters, to separate the cyclical and trend components of our time series. In the following example we employ the Hodrick–Prescott filter provided in the library "mFilter" which we import by writing the code line `library (mFilter)` at the top of our script. Since the filter can be used only on **R** objects of the type "time series" we first force the matrix `YF` to a time series, by declaring for this sake a new variable `YF.TS`. After having declared two matrices

`YF.trend` and `YF.cycle`, we fill their columns with the trend and cyclical components of each artificial time series, obtained by applying the `hpfilter()` function to `YF.TS`, and specifying the arguments `freq=1600,type="lambda"` which correspond to quarterly data. The next lines export the cyclical and trend components that we saved in the `YF.trend` and `YF.cycle` matrices into two separated .csv files.[39]

```
#FILTER THE YF SERIES WITH THE HP FILTER

#FORCE THE YF MATRIX TO A TIME SERIES
YF.TS=as.ts(YF, frequency=1, start=2)

#COMPUTE THE HP FILTER AND STORE RESULTS
YF.trend=matrix(data=NA,nrow=Time, ncol=MC)
YF.cycle=matrix(data=NA,nrow=Time, ncol=MC)
for (i in 1:MC){
YF.HP=hpfilter(YF.TS[,i],freq=1600,type="lambda")
YF.trend[,i]=YF.HP$trend
YF.cycle[,i]=YF.HP$cycle
}

#EXPORT DATA IN A .CSV FILE
write.csv(YF.trend,file=paste(folder,"/YF_Trend.csv",sep=""))
write.csv(YF.cycle,file=paste(folder,"/YF_cycle.csv",sep=""))
```

Again, we can compute moments and other statistics on the distribution of filtered variables in order to highlight the model properties and check across runs variability.

The cyclical and trend components of our filtered variables may be also plotted using the `matplot()` function, as shown in the example below, in order to get a further insight on the short and long term dynamics of the model. However, notice that this type of graph, which plots a line for every single filtered series, becomes less and less intelligible as the the number of Monte Carlo simulations increases. In particular, the cyclical component across Monte Carlo are mostly overlapping, so that different lines are difficult to identify already when we include just 2 or 3 Monte Carlo. Therefore, it is usually convenient to plot just a restricted set of Monte Carlo simulations for the trend components and one or two time series at a time for the cyclical components. Figure 2.14 shows the output of the commands below which plot the trend components of `YF` for the first 3 Monte Carlo (top), and the cycle component for just the first simulation (bottom).

```
#WE PLOT TREND AND CYCLE COMPONENTS OF THE MC SIMULATIONS
par(mfrow=c(2,1))
matplot(YF.trend[,1:3], type ="l", lty = 1, col=1:MC, lwd = 1)
matplot(YF.cycle[,1], type ="l", lty = 1, col=1:MC, lwd = 1)
```

[39] These data files will be subsequently employed in the sensitivity and policy analysis sections, providing a benchmark to assess the impact of different parameterizations or policy changes on the model dynamics. These files can be loaded in our **R** workspace through the command `YF.trend1=read.csv(paste(folder,"/fileName.csv",sep=""))`.

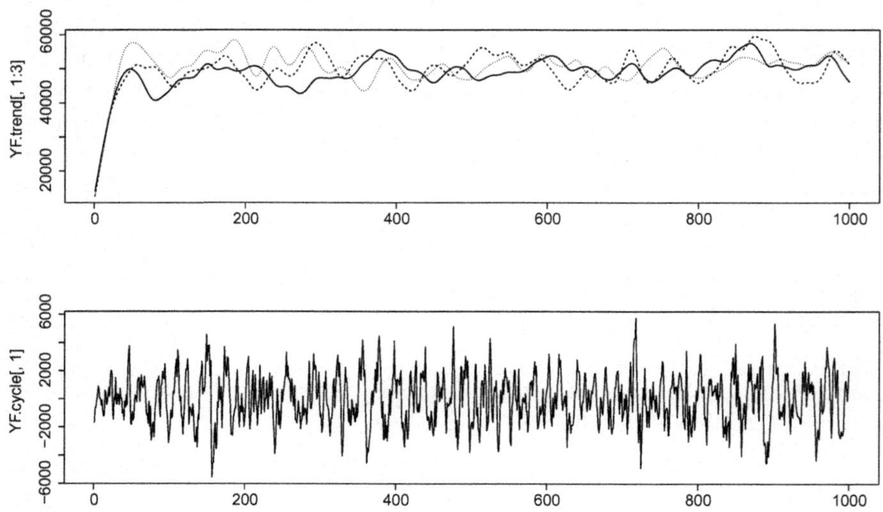

Fig. 2.14 Trend component of three Monte Carlo simulations (*above*) and cyclical component of one Monte Carlo simulation (*below*)

Finally, in order to analyze the long term dynamics of the model, we might want to calculate an average trend across Monte Carlo and its standard deviation. The following lines carry out this task[40]:

```
#COMPUTE AVERAGE TREND AND SD:
YF.avTrend=rowMeans(YF.trend)
YF.trendSD=apply(YF.trend, 1, sd)
```

Then we may plot the average trend an its standard deviation using the following commands.

```
#PLOT AVERAGE TREND WITH TREND SD
par(mfrow=c(1,1))
plot(YF.avTrend,ylim=range(YF.avTrend+YF.trendSD, YF.avTrend-YF.trendSD),
main="Average trend", ylab="", xlab="", na.rm=T, type="l")
#arrows(seq(1:Time), (YF.avTrend-YF.trendSD), seq(1:Time),
(YF.avTrend+YF.trendSD), length=0.05, angle=90, code=3)
lines(YF.avTrend+YF.trendSD,lwd=1,lty=2)
lines(YF.avTrend-YF.trendSD,lwd=1,lty=2)
```

The output of this block is shown in Fig. 2.15.

[40]The first line may be alternatively expressed as `YF.avTrend=apply(YF.trend, 1, mean)`.

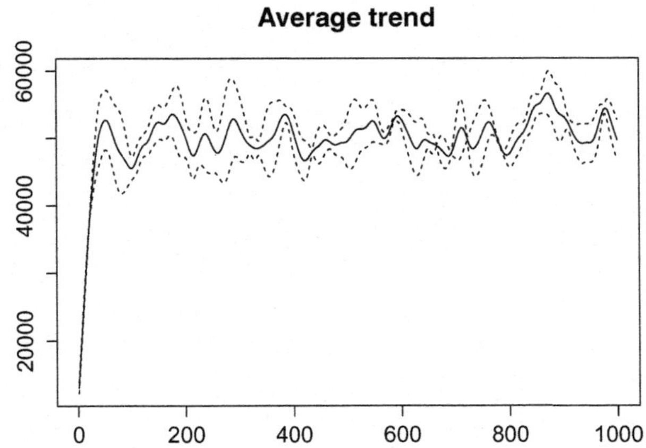

Fig. 2.15 Average trend (*continuous*) and standard deviation (*dashed*)

The above lines conclude the script to analyze the baseline scenario of the model.[41] Before concluding this section, let us point out that the same technique applied above to analyze the dynamics and statistical properties of `YF` over the Monte Carlo experiment, may be employed to analyze a wide variety of other model statistics as well. For example, one may compute the (across Monte Carlo) average cross correlations between some variables of interest, and their standard deviation. This values can then be plotted - as we just did - to assess how much the cross-correlation structure of the model for such variables is robust against the changes in the stochastic component of the Monte Carlo experiments.

2.2.4 Sensitivity

In the present section we carry out a simple example of sensitivity analysis by performing a "parameter sweep" on the parameter adj. The scope of this exercise is to assess how the setup of this parameter affects the results of the model, by repeating the Monte Carlo experiment for different values of the parameter. The implementation of the sensitivity experiment requires a slight integration of the code structure presented in the previous section, as shown in Fig. 2.16. Apart from the blocks referring to the initialization of sensitivity report variables (at the top) and to the computation of sensitivity statistics (bottom), the main differences with respect to Fig. 2.9 are to be

[41]To tell the truth, it is common practice to terminate a script with a code line similar to this: `print(paste("Elapsed time is ",proc.time()[3],"seconds"))`. The function `proc.time()` is called to evaluate how much CPU or real time (as in our example) the currently running process has taken. In this way we can precisely figure out how much time our simulations take to be executed, thus having also a benchmark to assess the efficacy of possible variations of the script intended to speed up the simulations.

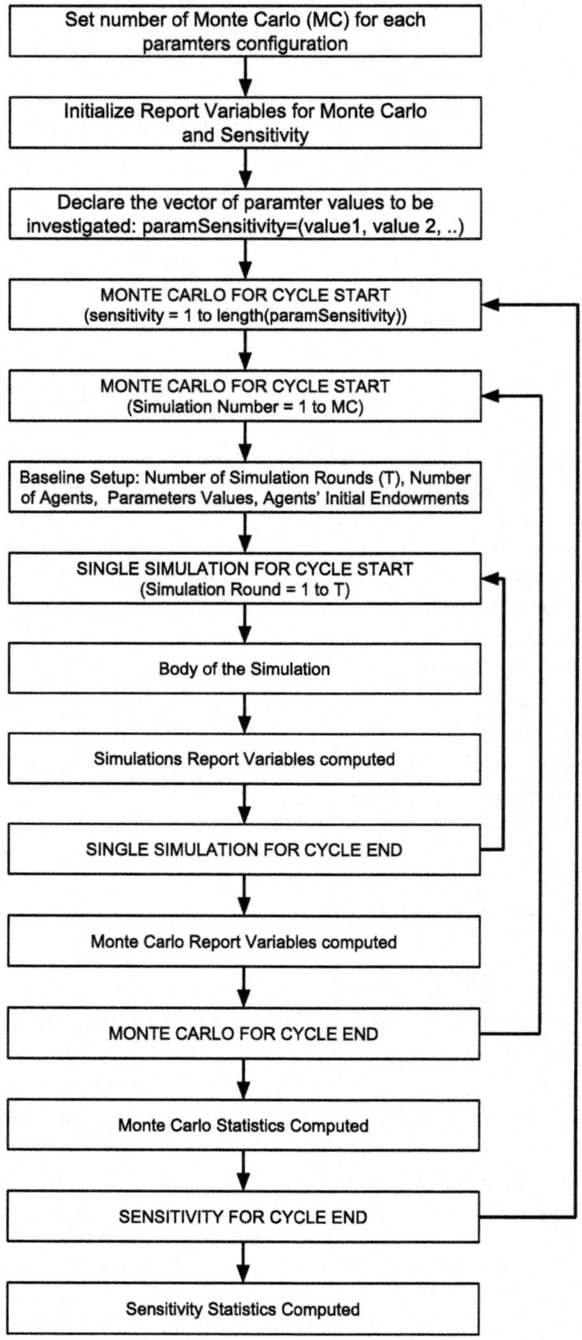

Fig. 2.16 Code structure

found in the inclusion of a third `for` loop encompassing both the Monte Carlo and the single simulations loops. This new loop iterates on the vector of parameter values to test in the sensitivity, by running a Monte Carlo experiment for each parameter value.

The first block of code seen in Sect. 2.2.3.2, in which we defined the Monte Carlo invariant parameters, is to be modified as shown hereunder, where we commented the line of code relative to the setup of the parameter involved in sensitivity (`adj = 0.1`), while adding a new code line declaring the set of values the sensitivity "sweeps". The function `seq(x,y,z)` creates a vector of elements defined as a sequence with starting value equal to `x`, end value equal to `y`, and increment `z`. Therefore, the last line of the block of commands presented here clarifies that we are going to perform a sensitivity experiment on 5 different values of the parameter `adj`: 0.00, 0.05, 0.10, 0.15, 0.20.

```
##############BEGIN OF THE SCRIPT###############

#IMPORT LIBRARIES
library (mFilter) #employed for the Hodrick-Prescott Filter

MC=1 #Number of Monte Carlo Simulations to be executed

#MONTE CARLO INVARIANT PARAMETERS SETTING
#Number of simulation rounds
Time=1000
#Number of firms
Nf = 500
#Number of banks
Nb = 50
#Interest rate parameter
gamma = 0.02
#Number of potential partners on credit market
chi = 5
#Partner choice parameter: intensity of choice
lambda = 4

#Leverage adjustment speed parameter
#adj = 0.1

#Production function parameter
phi = 3
#Production function parameter
beta = 0.7
#Firms' price parameter: mean of Normal Distribution
alpha = 0.1
#Firms' price parameter:variance of Normal Distribution
varpf = 0.4
#Central bank's interest rate
rCB = 0.02
#Banks' costs
cB = 0.01

#DECLARE THE SENSITIVITY VALUES TO BE TESTED
adjS=seq(0.0,0.2,0.05)
```

The next integration needed is the initialization of the reports referring to the sensitivity experiment.

A very simple way to compare the sensitivity experiments is by employing synthetic measures, such as the first and second order moments of some variables of interest. In the block hereunder we thus define a matrix `sensMat` where we are going to store the Monte Carlo averages and standard deviations for the following eight variables: the rate of growth, the leverage, the bad debt ratio, the number of banks' failures (in each period), the average interest rate on loans, banks' net worth, firms' net worth, and firms' failures (in each period). The rows number of the matrix is given by the number of indexes computed (2 for each variable, i.e. 16 in total) plus 1, as in the first row we put the value of the parameters for which the statistics are computed (i.e. the experiment to which the statistics refer). The number of columns is thus given by the number of parameter values tested (five) plus 1, since the first column displays the name of the variable tracked.[42]

```
...
#BANKS' PROBABILITY OF DEFAULT REPORT
PBB= matrix(data = 0, ncol = MC, nrow = 1)

#DECLARE THE SENSITIVITY REPORTS
sensMat = matrix(, nrow=17, ncol=length(adjS)+1)
sensMat[1,2:(length(adjS)+1)] = adjS
sensMat[1:17,1] = c("Parameter value","avGr","stdstdGr","avLEV",
"stdLEV","avBAD","stdBAD","avFALLB","stdFALLB","avRBF","stdRBF",
"avAB","stdAB","avAF","stdAF","avFALLF","stdFALLF")
```

We then create the `for` loop referring to the sensitivity experiment, which iterates on the parameters values. Just after the opening of this loop and before the declaration of the Monte Carlo loop, we assign to the parameter `adj` the value to be employed in the Monte Carlo simulations of the currently running sensitivity.

```
#THE SENSITIVITY EXPERIMENT LOOP
for (sensitivity in 1:length(adjS)){

  #ASSIGN TO adj THE VALUE TO BE TESTED
  adj=adjS[sensitivity]

  #THE MONTE CARLO LOOP
 for (mc in 1:MC) {
   print(paste("Monte Carlo N", mc))
 set.seed (mc)
 ...
```

Now we can appreciate the utility of the choice we made in Sect. 2.2.3.2 of assigning a different seed, equal to the index of the corresponding Monte Carlo repetition,

[42]It should be noticed that by first assigning a vector of string elements to the first column of the `sensMat` matrix, as we have done here, all the elements that will be embedded in the matrix later on, such as the values of the statistics computed for each variable, will be treated by default as strings as well, thus eventually implying the need to coerce them in a different type (e.g. numeric), when needed.

to each simulation run. Since every sensitivity experiment has the same number of Monte Carlo repetitions and each of them has a random seed equal to its index, we can preserve the stochastic variability across Monte Carlo runs while ensuring that differences between the ith runs (with $i = 1, \ldots, MC$) under different sensitivity scenarios are exclusively due to the change in the parameter setup, since they all employ the same random seed.

The remaining of the code shown in the previous section can then be left unaltered since neither the block referring to the simulation body, nor those referring to the simulations reports update are affected by the integrations required for the sensitivity. However, before closing the sensitivity `for` loop, at the bottom of the script, we have to insert the block of commands required to compute the sensitivity statistics and embed them in the `sensMat` matrix declared before.

```
  #SENSITIVITY REPORTS UPDATE

  #Average (std) growth rate
  avGr=mean(gr[201:Time,])
  stdGr=sd(as.vector(gr[201:Time,]))

  #Average (std) leverage
  avLEV=mean(LEV[201:Time,])
  stdLEV=sd(as.vector(LEV[201:Time,]))

  #Average (std) bad debt
  avBAD=mean(BAD[201:Time,]/BF[201:Time,])
  stdBAD=sd(as.vector(BAD[201:Time,]/BF[201:Time,]))

  #Average (std) banks' failures
  avFALLB=mean(FALLB[201:Time,])
  stdFALLB=sd(as.vector(FALLB[201:Time,]))

  #Average interest on loans
  avRBF=mean(RBF[201:Time,])
  stdRBF=sd(as.vector(RBF[201:Time,]))

  #Average (std) banks' net worth
  avAB=mean(AB[201:Time,])
  stdAB=sd(as.vector(AB[201:Time,]))

  #Average (std) firms' net worth
  avAF=mean(AF[201:Time,])
  stdAF=sd(as.vector(AF[201:Time,]))

  #Average (std) firms' defaults
  avFALLF=mean(FALLF[201:Time,])
  stdFALLF=sd(as.vector(FALLF[201:Time,]))

  #UPDATE sensMat
  sensMat[2:17, (sensitivity+1)] = c(avGr, stdGr,
  avLEV, stdLEV, avBAD, stdBAD, avFALLB, stdFALLB,
  avRBF, stdRBF, avAB, stdAB, avAF, stdAF, avFALLF,
  stdFALLF)

} #END OF SENSITIVITY LOOP
```

Alternatively, the results of the sensitivity experiments may be displayed graphically as we do in the following block where, just after the closure of the sensitivity loop, we declare 9 vectors - one containing the parameter values and the other containing the results extracted from the sensMat matrix - and then draw a plot displaying the average and standard deviation of the variables in the various sensitivity scenarios. The results of the experiment for MC=10 and Time=1000 are shown in Figs. 2.17 and 2.18.

```
} #END OF SENSITIVITY LOOP

#PLOT SENSITIVITY STATISTICS
#1)EXTRACT VALUES FROM sensMat
parameterValues=as.numeric(sensMat[1,2:(length(adjS)+1)])
averageGrowth=as.numeric(sensMat[2,2:(length(adjS)+1)])
sdGrowth=as.numeric(sensMat[3,2:(length(adjS)+1)])
averageLeverage=as.numeric((sensMat[4,2:(length(adjS)+1)]))
sdLeverage=as.numeric(sensMat[5,2:(length(adjS)+1)])
averageBAD=as.numeric(sensMat[6,2:(length(adjS)+1)])
sdBAD=as.numeric(sensMat[7,2:(length(adjS)+1)])
averageFALLB=as.numeric(sensMat[8,2:(length(adjS)+1)])
sdFALLB=as.numeric(sensMat[9,2:(length(adjS)+1)])
averageRBF=as.numeric(sensMat[10,2:(length(adjS)+1)])
sdRBF=as.numeric(sensMat[11,2:(length(adjS)+1)])
averageAB=as.numeric(sensMat[12,2:(length(adjS)+1)])
sdAB=as.numeric(sensMat[13,2:(length(adjS)+1)])
averageAF=as.numeric(sensMat[14,2:(length(adjS)+1)])
sdAF=as.numeric(sensMat[15,2:(length(adjS)+1)])
averageFALLF=as.numeric(sensMat[16,2:(length(adjS)+1)])
sdFALLF=as.numeric(sensMat[17,2:(length(adjS)+1)])

#2)PLOT AVERAGE AND STD
par(mfrow=c(2,2))
plot(parameterValues, averageGrowth, ylim=range(averageGrowth
+sdGrowth,averageGrowth-sdGrowth), type="o",pch=1,
main="Average Rate of Growth (SD) ", ylab="", xlab="Parameter Value")
arrows(parameterValues,  averageGrowth+sdGrowth, parameterValues,
averageGrowth-sdGrowth, length=0.05, angle=90, code=3)

plot(parameterValues, averageLeverage, ylim=range(averageLeverage
+sdLeverage,averageLeverage-sdLeverage), type="o",pch=1,
main="Average Leverage (SD)", ylab="",xlab="Parameter Value")
arrows(parameterValues,  averageLeverage+sdLeverage, parameterValues,
averageLeverage-sdLeverage, length=0.05, angle=90, code=3)

plot(parameterValues, averageBAD, ylim=range(averageBAD
+sdBAD,averageBAD-sdBAD), type="o",pch=1,
main="Average Bad Debt Share (SD)", ylab="", xlab="Parameter Value")
arrows(parameterValues,  averageBAD+sdBAD, parameterValues,
averageBAD-sdBAD, length=0.05, angle=90, code=3)

plot(parameterValues, averageFALLB, ylim=range(averageFALLB
+sdFALLB,averageFALLB-sdFALLB), type="o",pch=1,
 main="Average Banks' Failures (SD)", ylab="", xlab="Parameter Value")
arrows(parameterValues,  averageFALLB+sdFALLB, parameterValues,
averageFALLB-sdFALLB, length=0.05, angle=90, code=3)
```

```
plot(parameterValues, averageRBF, ylim=range(averageRBF
+sdRBF,averageRBF-sdRBF), type="o",pch=1,
main="Average RBF (SD)", ylab="", xlab="Parameter Value")
arrows(parameterValues,  averageRBF+sdRBF, parameterValues,
averageRBF-sdRBF, length=0.05, angle=90, code=3)

plot(parameterValues, averageAB, ylim=range(averageAB
+sdAB,averageAB-sdAB), type="o",pch=1,
main="Average Banks' NW (SD)", ylab="", xlab="Parameter Value")
arrows(parameterValues,  averageAB+sdAB, parameterValues,
averageAB-sdAB, length=0.05, angle=90, code=3)

plot(parameterValues, averageAF, ylim=range(averageAF
+sdAF,averageAF-sdAF), type="o",pch=1,
main="Average Firms' NW (SD)", ylab="", xlab="Parameter Value")
arrows(parameterValues,  averageAF+sdAF, parameterValues,
averageAF-sdAF, length=0.05, angle=90, code=3)

plot(parameterValues, averageAF, ylim=range(averageFALLF
+sdFALLF,averageFALLF-sdFALLF), type="o",pch=1,
main="Average Firms' Failures (SD)", ylab="", xlab="Parameter Value")
arrows(parameterValues,  averageFALLF+sdFALLF, parameterValues,
averageFALLF-sdFALLF, length=0.05, angle=90, code=3)
```

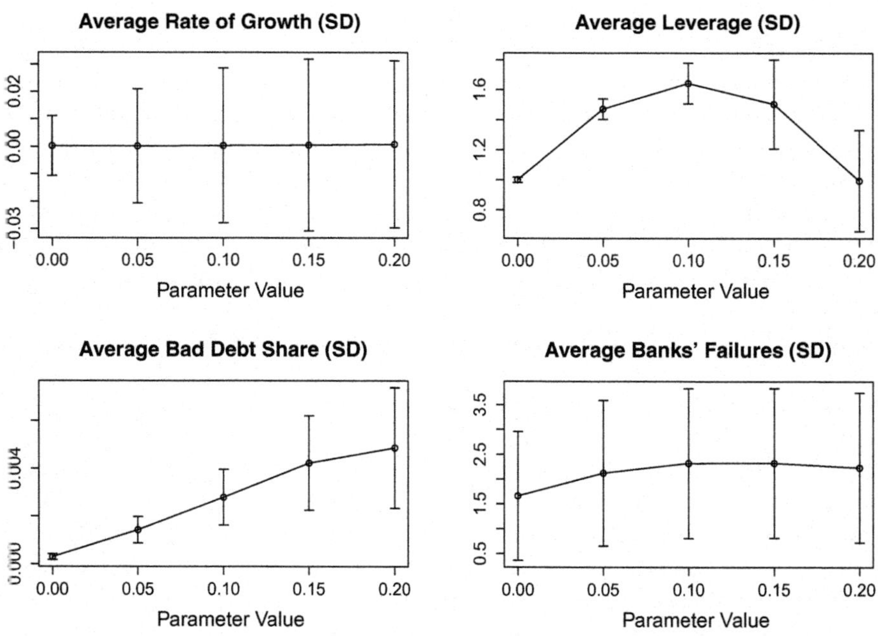

Fig. 2.17 Synthetic statistics for the sensitivity experiment performed on `adj`

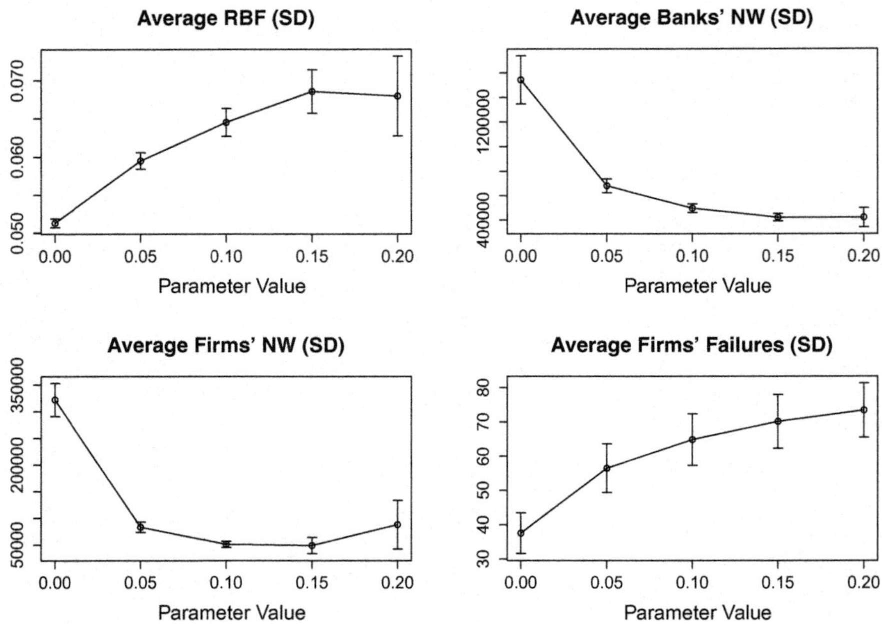

Fig. 2.18 Synthetic statistics for the sensitivity experiment performed on `adj`

The previous pictures shows that a strong adjustment of the leverage level (i.e. `adj` increases) does not affect growth rates which remain on average close to 0, while it significantly increases the volatility of the system, as testified by the rising standard deviations of aggregate production growth rates, which directly reflect the increased volatility of average leverage ratios. The latter seem to be in a non-monotonic relationship with `adj`, first increasing and then decreasing for further increments of the parameter. The higher volatility of firms' leverage directly affects the volatility of several other variables which depend on it, such as the average interest rate on loans, and the bad debt share over total outstanding credit. Both increase for higher values of the parameter, with the only exception of the average interest rate in correspondence to the highest value of `adj` (0.20), which is slightly below the value observed for `adj` $=0.15$, mainly as a consequence of the lower average leverage ratio characterizing this scenario. Banks' and firms' failures volatilities, on the contrary, are not apparently affected in a significant way by the parameter although their average values tend to increase for higher values of `adj`. The rise of firms' defaults and the share of non-performing loans over total credit are one of the possible explanations of the non-monotonic relationship between firms' leverage and `adj`, as defaults and replacements of highly leveraged firms impose a process of de-leveraging on the economy. These first results seem to suggest that cascades of bad debt are more likely to appear for larger values of `adj`. Interestingly, the volatility of firms' and banks' net worth decreases at the beginning and then increases for further increment of `adj`. Firms' and banks' net worth display a marked drop from the scenario with no adjustment to the scenarios with positive adjustment speed, then remaining relatively stable through the remaining sensitivity scenarios.

2.2.5 *Policy Experiment*

In the last exercise, using the simple model developed in the previous sections, we perform a simple policy analysis assuming that the Central Bank increases her interest rate to 4 %. As for previous applications, rather than focusing on the economic content of the experiment, the exercise represents more an expedient to highlight the logical and technical steps required to perform a policy analysis experiment. The same logic and code structure can thus be employed to analyze a wide variety of policies.

Our starting point for this application is represented by the code developed for the baseline scenario, on which we make just a few amendments. Our monetary policy experiment takes the form of a change in the interest rate of the Central Bank in period 400, when the simulated economy has already passed through the transition phase and reached its quasi steady state.

The first integrations to the baseline code are the declaration of a variable `policySwitchPeriod` representing the period in which the policy switching takes place and the removal of the line referring to the Central Bank interest rate parameter setting. The top of our code now looks like this:

```
##############BEGIN OF THE SCRIPT###############

#IMPORT LIBRARIES
#No libraries to be imported for the moment

#Number of Monte Carlo Simulations to be executed
MC=1

#MONTE CARLO INVARIANT PARAMETERS SETTING
#Number of simulation rounds
Time=1000
#Policy switching period
policySwitchPeriod=400
#Number of firms
Nf = 500
#Number of banks
Nb = 50
#Interest rate parameter
gamma = 0.02
#Number of potential partners on credit market
chi = 5
#Partner choice parameter: intensity of choice
lambda = 4
#Leverage adjustment speed parameter
adj = 0.1
#Production function parameter
phi = 3
#Production function parameter
```

```
beta = 0.7
#Firms' price parameter: mean of Normal Distribution
alpha = 0.1
#Firms' price parameter:variance of Normal Distribution
varpf = 0.4
#Banks' costs
cB = 0.01
```

The only other amendment to the baseline code has to be made at the beginning of the `for` loop containing the body of our simulations. Here we insert an `if` statement which assigns to the parameter `rCB` a value equal to either 0.02 or 0.04 according to whether the policy switching period has been reached or not.

```
for (t in 1:Time) {
if (t < policySwitchPeriod) {
    rCB = 0.02
    }
    else{
    rCB = 0.04
    }
```

While these modifications are sufficient to execute the Monte Carlo simulations containing the policy experiment, we still have to find a convenient way to compare the artificial times series obtained for the policy regime switching scenario with the original times series under the baseline. The simplest way is to save the results of the baseline in a .csv file - as we did before for the output - and then import them in the script of the policy experiment. The block of commands presented hereunder, which has to be placed at the bottom of the baseline script, allows to compute some synthetic statistics on the impact of the policy regime switch, and to draw some plots displaying the difference between the baseline and policy scenarios. Remember that, in order to make the time series of each Monte Carlo simulation executed under the policy switching scenario comparable with the correspondent simulation under the benchmark, we need them to start with the exact same initial conditions and, in particular, with the same random seed. Our choice of setting the random seed of each simulation equal to the index identifying it ensures that the sequence of pseudo-random numbers picked up will be exactly the same across pairs of correspondent Monte Carlo simulations. This implies that the dynamics of the system up to the policy regime switching period will be exactly the same, whereas the following divergences eventually observed should be exclusively imputed to the policy switch, rather than to some stochastic component.

Figures 2.19 and 2.20 displays the results of the baseline and policy experiments with 5 Monte Carlo repetitions, each one lasting 1000 periods. The figures highlight that an increase in the policy rate of the Central Bank determines a rapid and significant drop of output levels, which are not recovered as the model converges towards a new quasi steady state. This can be easily explained with the fact that an increase of interest rate by the Central Bank fosters a spur of interest rates paid by firms on

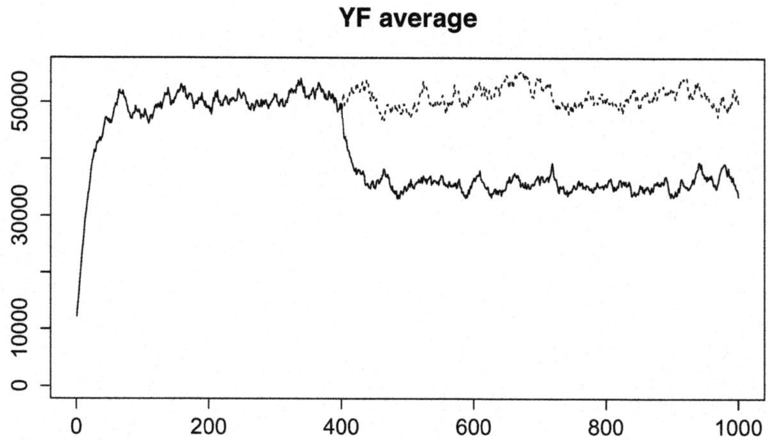

Fig. 2.19 Average output in the baseline and policy scenarios

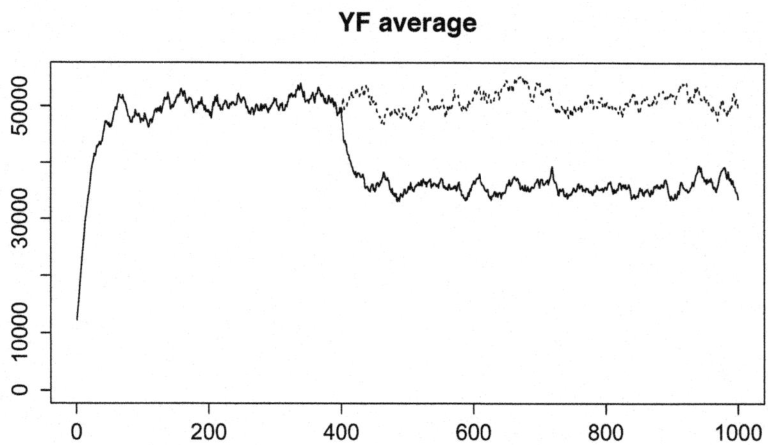

Fig. 2.20 Average trend of output in the baseline and policy scenarios

loans. This translates into a drop of their net worth which in turn reduces the amount of financial capital available for production, thus eventually reducing output levels.

```
######################################################
#POLICY EXPERIMENT SYNTHETIC REPORTS
avGrpre=mean(gr[201:Experiment,1])
avGrpost=mean(gr[(Experiment+1):Time,1])
print (paste("Growth rate - average pre-policy:", avGrpre,
"Growth rate - average post-policy", avGrpost))

stdGrpre=sd(gr[201:Experiment,1])
stdGrpost=sd(gr[(Experiment+1):Time,1])
```

```
print (paste("Growth rate - standard deviation pre-policy:", stdGrpre,
"Growth rate - standard deviation post-policy:", stdGrpost))

avLEVpre=mean(LEV[201:Experiment,1])
avLEVpost=mean(LEV[(Experiment+1):Time,1])
print (paste("Leverage - average pre-policy:", avLEVpre,
"Leverage - average post-policy:", avLEVpost))

avBADpre=mean(BAD[201:Experiment,1]/BF[201:Experiment,1])
avBADpost=mean(BAD[(Experiment+1):Time,]/BF[(Experiment+1):Time,])
print (paste("Bad debt ratio - average pre-policy:", avBADpre,
"Bad debt ratio - average post-policy:", avBADpost))

avFALLBpre=mean(FALLB[201:Experiment,1])
avFALLBpost=mean(FALLB[(Experiment+1):Time,1])
print (paste("Bank defaults - average pre-policy:", avFALLBpre,
"Bank defaults - average post-policy:", avFALLBpost))

#A GRAPHICAL WAY TO COMPARE BASELINE AND POLICY:
#1)USING THE AVERAGE ACROSS MC

#COMPUTE AVERAGE AND SD OF YF UNDER THE POLICY SCENARIO
YF.average=apply(YF,1,mean)
YF.sd=apply(YF,1,sd)

#IMPORT THE BASELINE AVERAGE YF FROM THE .CSV FILE
YF.average_base=read.csv(paste(folder,"/YF_average.csv",sep=""))
#YF.average_base=YF.average_base[-1] #REMOVE THE TIME COLUMN

#DRAW A GRAPH COMPARING THE BASELINE AND POLICY TIME SERIES
par(mfrow=c(1,1))
plot(YF.average, main="YF average", ylab="", xlab="", na.rm=T,
type="l")
lines(YF.average_base,lwd=1,lty=2)


#2)USING AVERAGE TREND ACROSS MC SIMULATIONS

#APPLY THE HP FLTER TO YF IN THE POLICY SCENARIO (AS IN THE BASELINE)
YF.TS=as.ts(YF, frequency=1, start=2)
YF.trend=matrix(data=NA,nrow=Time, ncol=MC)
YF.cycle=matrix(data=NA,nrow=Time, ncol=MC)
for (i in 1:MC){
  YF.HP=hpfilter(YF.TS[,i],freq=1600,type="lambda")
  YF.trend[,i]=YF.HP$trend
  YF.cycle[,i]=YF.HP$cycle
}


#IMPORT THE BASELINE TREND COMPONENT OF YF FROM THE .CSV FILE
YF.trend_base=read.csv(paste(folder,"/YF_Trend.csv",sep=""))
YF.trend_base=YF.trend_base[-1] #REMOVE THE TIME COLUMN

#COMPUTE AVERAGE TRENDS
YF.avtrend=rowMeans(YF.trend)
YF.avtrend_base=rowMeans(YF.trend_base)

#DRAW A COMPARING THE BASELINE AND POLICY TIME SERIES
par(mfrow=c(1,1))
```

```
plot(YF.avtrend, main="YF average trend", ylab="", xlab="",
     na.rm=T, type="l")
lines(YF.avtrend_base,lwd=1,lty=2)
```

Although the didactic model presented in this chapter presents several oversimplifications, the reader can easily guess how the logic followed in its development, the structure of the codes presented, the techniques employed, and the methods adopted to assess the robustness and sensitivity of results can be equally applied for much more complex and realistic models and policy experiments.

2.2.6 *Network Analysis*

After having read the arguments presented so far, the reader should have sensed that the AB models, intended as a tool to support economic analysis, fundamentally aim to explain how the local decentralized interaction of heterogeneous agents endowed with bounded rationality, gives rise to the economic regularities (often referred to as emergent properties of the system) observed in real world economic systems.

The centrality of agents' interactions in shaping both agents' behaviors and system wide properties explains why networks analysis has become a standard tool in the AB field of research.

In order to gives the reader a sense of this important component of the AB methodology, in this section we sketch out a basic analysis of the properties of the credit network generated by the simplified model introduced in the previous sections. Network analysis is facilitated in most programming languages by dedicated libraries. R relies on `igraph`, which is a multi-platform library providing a wide collection of network analysis tools (Csardi and Nepusz 2006). The first step of our exercise is thus to import the library:

```
[language=R]
>library(igraph)
```

The network structure generated by the model is pretty simple, and not particularly realistic. Indeed, firms have a single credit supplier, which means that the credit network is a collection of disjoint star subgraphs, i.e. graphs of n vertices and $n-1$ links in which $n-1$ vertices (firms) are connected with the same (central) vertex (bank). A sample network generated by the model is depicted in Fig. 2.21.

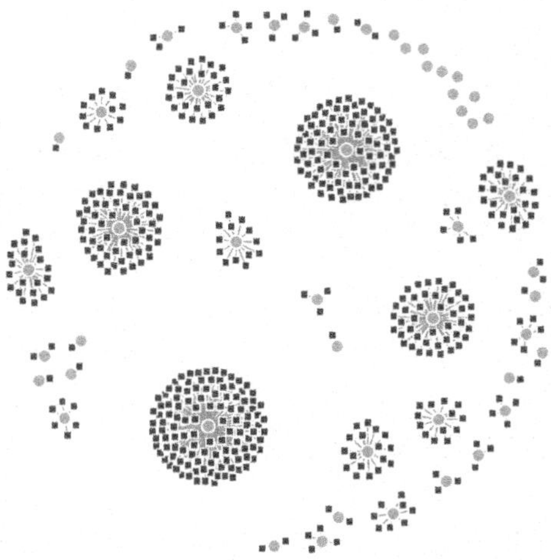

Fig. 2.21 ABM credit network

The code needed to obtain the network representation is the following

```
# SET THE BACKGROUND
V(G)$frame.color <- "white"
# ASSIGN DIFFERENT COLOR, SHAPE AND SIZE TO BANKS AND FIRMS
x <- V(G)$type+1
V(G)$color <- c("steel blue", "orange")[x]
V(G)$shape <- c("square", "circle")[x]
V(G)$size <- c(3, 5)[x]
# SUPPRESS NODE LABELS AND EDGE DIRECTION
E(G)$arrow.mode <- 0
V(G)$label <- ""
plot(G)
```

G is an instance of the basic *igraph* class for graphs, whose construction will be clarified below, while `V(.)` and `E(.)` are methods to access respectively vertices and edges of objects belonging to this class. Since firms and banks are agents of two different types, and there are no links between agents from the same type in our simplified credit market, the credit network is said to be *bipartite* according to the standard terminology. For such networks igraph stores a variable `type` which assigns each node to its type (bank/firm). We can use this variable to assign different properties to the graphical representation of firms and banks in Fig. 2.21.

The statistics that can be collected from a network of this kind are quite limited. For instance, consider the size of the neighborhood of a given node i, called the *degree* of that node and denoted as k_i. This is a basic measure of centrality which has a key role in network theory. Given the preferred partner matching mechanism (Sect. 2.2.3.3), firms in the model have by construction a degree equal to one, and cannot thus resemble real firms which have instead a number of different creditors. This variable is instead meaningful for banks, since it equals the number of their customers in a given period. Thus, the largest the bank, the higher its degree.

2.2.7 Network Statistics

We are interested in understanding the relationship within the model between credit market concentration and economic activity. In order to capture market concentration with a single statistic, we collect the size of the largest component in the credit network and the density of links in the firm projected network. The set of components of a network is populated by the maximal connected subnetworks of the network itself, where the latter is defined as a subnetwork such that there exists a path of links between any two nodes belonging to it. The projected networks associated with a bipartite networks are built in the following way: a link between node i and j from the same type exists if and only if i, j are linked to the same node k of the other type. In our case, two firms i, j are linked if they are clients of the same bank. Thus, if all firms borrow from the same bank, the projected network will be complete, i.e. all firms will be directly connected, while if all firms borrow from a different bank, the projected network will be empty. In the first case, we have that the density $\rho \equiv \frac{2l}{n(n-1)} = 1$, while in the latter of course $\rho = 0$.

In order to collect these statistics from simulations we initialize two matrices:

```
#### NETWORK REPORTS ###

# 1) BIPARTITE CREDIT NETWORK
# largest component share
GC <- matrix( data = NA, ncol = MC, nrow = Time)

# 2) PROJECTED FIRM-FIRM NETWORK
# density of links
DensPr <- matrix( data = NA, ncol = MC, nrow = Time)
```

Then we add to the main simulation cycle the following lines

```
# CREATE AN ADJACENCY MATRIX FOR CREDIT NETWORK
  crednet = matrix(data=0, nrow = Nf, ncol = Nb)
  for (i in 1:Nf) {
    value = Bf[i]
    j=link_fb[i]
    crednet[i,j]=value
  }
  G <- graph_from_incidence_matrix(crednet,weighted = TRUE)
  GC[t,mc] <- max(component_distribution(G))
  Gpr <- bipartite_projection(G,which ="false")
  DensPr[t,mc] <- edge_density(Gpr)
```

After simulation runs we may plot the cross-correlations e.g. of firms' network density with the economic variables of the model:

```
EcVar <- list('YF','AF','AB','BF','FALLF',
              'FALLB','LEV','RBF','PRB')
labels <-list('YF' ="Output (YF)",
```

```
                'PRB' ="Banks profits (PRF)",
               'AF' ="Firms Net Worth (AF)",
               'AB' ="Banks Net Worth (AB)",
               'BF' ="Total Loans (BF)",
                'LEV' ="Firms' Average Leverage",
               'RBF' ="Average Interest Rate (RBF)",
                'FALLF' ="Firms' defaults",
               'FALLB' ="Banks' defaults")
par(mfrow=c(3,3))
mc = 1
for (i in EcVar)
{
  y <- get(i)
  ccf(DensPr[,mc],y[,mc], lag.max = 200,
      cex.lab = 0.8,
      type = c("correlation"),ylab ='CCF',
      main =labels[[i]])
}
```

obtaining the results of Fig. 2.22. These are consistent with financial fragility, indeed higher market concentration is associated with higher production and net worth, as well as with higher leverage, in the short run, but with lower values of the same variables over longer time horizons.

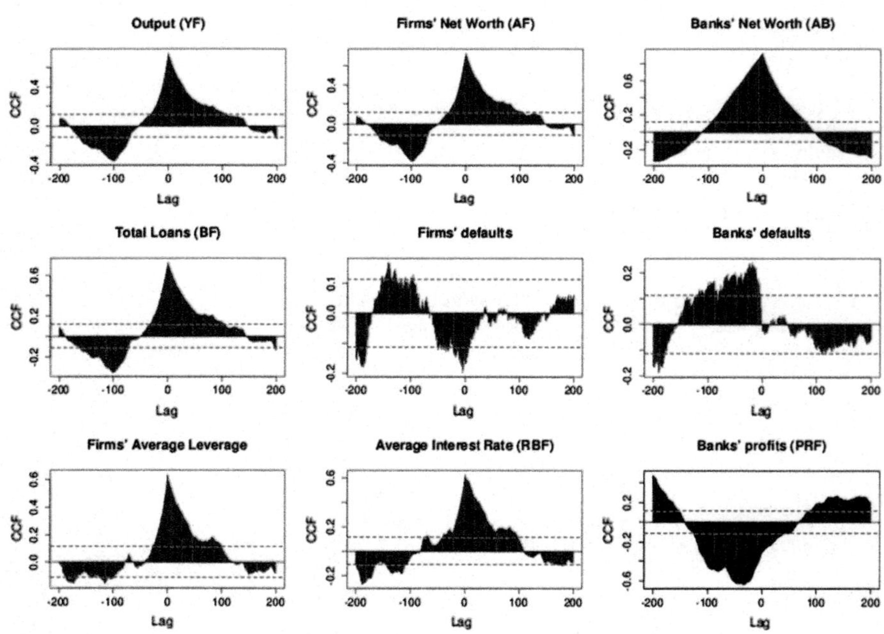

Fig. 2.22 Cross correlations between network density and economic variables

2.3 A Calibration Experiment

In this last section of the chapter we propose a simple example of empirical calibration by performing a sensitivity analysis with respect to the switching parameter λ governing agents' matching mechanism on the credit market, and then comparing the results with available real data concerning banks' degree distribution, credit supply, and credit demand. The calibration exercise, which follows Bargigli et al. (2014), regards the degree distribution of banks as well as their credit supply and the credit demand of firms. In order to obtain a first flavor of the model, we draw the evolution of these distributions over simulation steps. Firstly we initialize/update the following matrices

```
[language=R]
# ALLOCATE MATRICES FOR STORING DATA
#banks' degree distribution
creditDegree = matrix(data = 0, ncol = Nb, nrow = Time)
#Credit demand
Bff = matrix(data = 0, ncol = Nf, nrow = Time)
#Credit supply
Bb = matrix(data = 0, ncol = Nb, nrow = Time)
```

Then we add the following lines to the main simulation loop

```
Bff[t,] = Bf #credit demand at time t

# BANKS' DEGREE AND CREDIT SUPPLY DISTRIBUTION
  for (j in 1:Nb){
    jlinks <- Bf[link_fb==j]
    creditDegree[t,j]=length(jlinks)
    Bb[t,j] <- sum(jlinks)
  }
```

Finally we draw three 3d plots, from which we see that the distributions are pretty stable over simulation steps (Fig. 2.23).

```
distrs <- list('creditDegree','Bb','Bff')

for (i in distrs)
{
  i <- get(i)
  y <- seq(0,max(i),length=200)
  y <- c(-1,y)
  n <- length(y) - 1
  # skip the first 50 simulation steps
  r <- 50
  z <-matrix ( data = NA, ncol = n, nrow = Time - r)
  x <- seq(r + 1,Time)

  for (t in 1:(Time - r))
  {
    q <- i[r + t,]
```

```
    m <- ncol(i)
    q <- cumsum(hist(q[q>0], breaks = y, plot = F)$counts)
    z[t,] <- 1 - q / m
  }

  # THIS IS TO AVOID INF ERRORS WITH LOG-TRANSFARMATION
  y[y == 0] <- 1e-6
  z[z==0]<-1e-6
  y <- log10(y[2:(n+1)])
  z <- log10(z)

  persp(x,y,z, phi = 30, theta = 120,
        xlab = expression(t),
        ylab = expression(x),
        zlab = expression(1 - F(x)))
}
```

In order to characterize the distributions, we estimate the exponent α of the Pareto distribution $p(x) \propto x^{-\alpha}$ generated at each step of the simulation. This is accomplished by means of the Hill estimator (Sects. 3.9 and 4). In **R** the `poweRlaw` package provides a set of functions derived from the work of Clauset et al. (2009), see Gillespie (2015), which we can employ for this purpose. We want to compare the results for simulated data with those obtained with real data from the Japanese dataset described in Bargigli et al. (2014) (Table 2.1).

The code for estimating the α's from the ABM is as follows:

```
# DIFFERENT poweRlaw FUNCTIONS MUST BE USED FOR DISCRETE AND
# CONTINOUS DATA
methods <- list('creditDegree' = displ,
                 'Bb' = conpl,
                  'Bff' = conpl)

# VALUES OF \alpha IN JAPAN (MEAN)
jvalues <- list('creditDegree' = 1.91,
                 'Bb' = 1.50,
                 'Bff' = 1.90)

for (i in distrs)
{
  fit <- methods[[i]]
  jv <-jvalues[[i]]
  i <- get(i)
  r <- 50
  x <- vector(mode = "double", length = Time - r)

  for (t in 1:(Time - r))
  {
    q <- i[r + t,]
    q <- q[q>0]
    #### THESE ARE FUNCTION FROM poweRlaw
    q <- fit$new(q)
    xmin <- estimate_xmin(q)$xmin
    q$setXmin(xmin)
    x[t] <- estimate_pars(q)$pars
    #####
```

```
    }
    breaks <- seq(min(x),max(x,jv)+ 0.05,length = 20)
    hist(x,xlab = expression(alpha), breaks = breaks,
         ylab = '',
         main = '')
    abline(v = jv,lty = 2)
}
```

Table 2.1 Estimation of Pareto exponents from Japanese data (Bargigli et al. 2014)

	2000	2001	2002	2003	2004	2005	Mean
α Banks' degrees	1.81	1.82	1.91	1.96	1.97	1.98	1.91
α Credit supply	1.49	1.47	1.44	1.53	1.56	1.53	1.50
α Credit demand	1.85	1.84	1.83	1.99	1.92	1.94	1.90

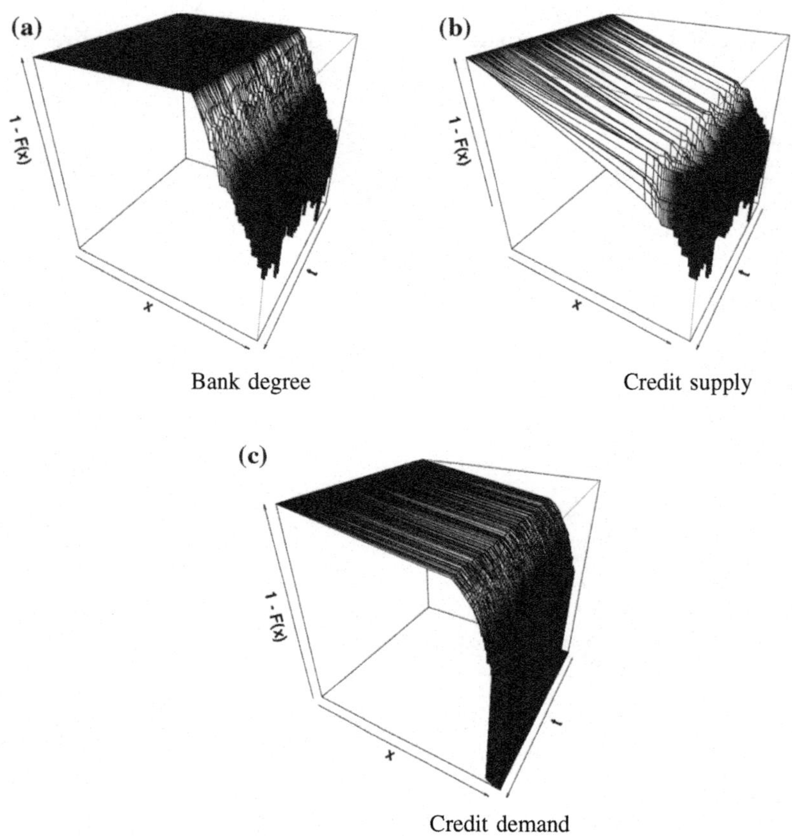

Fig. 2.23 Time evolution of distributions

The results are summarized in Fig. 2.24. We see that the distribution of credit supply is highly misaligned with respect to the observed value. In order to improve the alignment between model and data we perform a sensitivity analysis with respect to the switching parameter λ, which in the baseline configuration is set to $\lambda = 4$. The results are summarized in Table 2.2, along with the average values of the switching rate s_r and of the fraction of bank failures by period F_b. Indeed, we wish to check that the latter variables, which are affected by λ directly, as s_r, and indirectly through the effects of market concentration as F_b, take plausible values in the sensitivity exercise. From the data we see that this is the case for $\lambda \leqslant 2$. The switching rate for the Japanese credit network varies indeed between a minimum of 3.13 % and a maximum of 7.4 % in the period 2000–2005. Under this limit, although we lack data, the default rate is also plausible. The last column reports the absolute value distance between the simulated averages and the mean real values of Table 2.1:

$$\delta = \left|\alpha_{\text{degree}}^{\text{ABM}} - \alpha_{\text{degree}}^{\text{Jp}}\right| + \left|\alpha_{\text{supply}}^{\text{ABM}} - \alpha_{\text{supply}}^{\text{Jp}}\right| \tag{2.21}$$

We see that the best alignment for α_{degree} and α_{supply} is obtained for $\lambda = 2$. Of course, we could obtain a better alignment with a rigorous optimization over the full

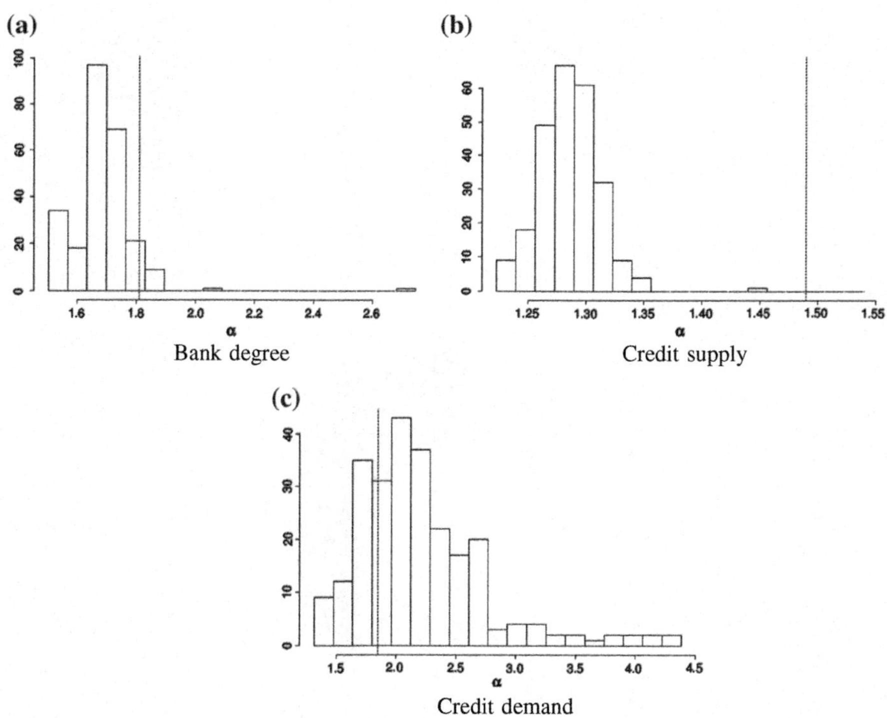

Fig. 2.24 Estimation of α (the *vertical line* is the mean value in the Japanese credit network, Table 2.1)

Table 2.2 Pareto exponents (α_{degree}, α_{supply}), switching rates (s_r), banks' default rates (F_b) for different values of λ. The reported values are averages over 10 replications

λ	α_{degree}	α_{supply}	α_{demand}	s_r	F_b	δ
0.5	4.416	2.566	2.263	0.011	0.000	3.572
1.0	2.672	1.904	2.256	0.039	0.003	1.166
2.0	1.961	1.387	2.278	0.099	0.015	0.164
3.0	1.780	1.309	2.286	0.181	0.025	0.320
4.0	1.696	1.298	2.219	0.279	0.027	0.415
5.0	1.653	1.302	2.265	0.388	0.028	0.454
6.0	1.623	1.307	2.250	0.506	0.028	0.479
8.0	1.600	1.313	2.238	0.638	0.030	0.497
16.0	1.591	1.329	2.225	0.797	0.031	0.491

parameter space, which however is beyond the scope of this book. Credit demand is instead insensitive to this parameter as we might expect from the equations of the ABM. It is also remarkable that an increasing market concentration (i.e. lower Pareto exponents), which on its turn is correlated with higher growth in the short term, goes hand in hand with a higher riskiness of banks. These results, again, are consistent with the financial fragility hypothesis.

2.4 Exercise

Exercises on the Model Presented in Sect. 2.1

Exercise 1

After having set the seed of the random number generation process to 15 in Sect. 2.1.3, plot a measure of financial leverage as the ratio between aggregate debt and aggregate net worth.

Exercise 2

Plot the same measure as in Exercise 1 by setting the investment accelerator parameter equal to 2.

Exercise 3

Based on the model as developed in Sect. 2.1.6, plot the time evolution of the average production (`meanYY`) and the two confidence bars (`YYup` and `YYdown`) around it.

Exercise 4
Within the same framework as in Exercise 2, compute the median (you may call it `medianYY`) and the MAD (`madYY`) across 100 simulations of the model. After that, calculate two confidence bars (`YYup` and `YYdown`) as the median ± two times the MAD. Finally, plot the median production and the two confidence bars.

Exercise 5
Display in a single plot the time evolution of aggregate production in the three simulations of the sensitivity analysis proposed in Sect. 2.1.7.

Exercise 6
Implement the policy experiment as described in Sect. 2.1.8 and plot the results reproducing Fig. 2.8 (hint: Make sure that the random numbers are the same in the two sets of multiple simulations).

***Exercises on the Model Presented in Sect.* 2.1**

Exercise 7
In the block of commands referring to the replacement procedure of defaulted firms and defaulted banks try to change the rule of initialization of the new entrant for $A_{z,t}$, $(z = i, b)$ by assuming that $A_{z,t} = u * \bar{A}_{z,t-1}$, being u a random draw from $U(0, 1)$ distribution and $\bar{A}_{z,t-1}$ the average of firms (banks) net worth in the previous period.

Exercise 8
Revise the script in order to replace the leverage revision adaptive rule, with the new one:

$$\begin{cases} leverage_{i,t+1} = leverage_{i,t}(1 + adj \cdot u) \text{ if } Pr_{i,t-1} > 0 \\ leverage_{i,t+1} = leverage_{i,t}(1 - adj \cdot u) \text{ if } Pr_{i,t-1} \leq 0 \end{cases} \tag{2.22}$$

Exercise 9
Revise the expectation formation mechanism employed to forecast future prices in the leverage revision heuristics with a mechanism which computes future expected prices as the simple mean of past prices over the last 4 periods:

$$p^e_{i,t+1} = \frac{\sum_{j=1}^{4} p_{i,t-j}}{4} \tag{2.23}$$

Exercise 10
Replace in the script the stochastic firms' price determination rule implemented in the chapter with a rule which fixes a homogeneous price as a decreasing function of total output: $\alpha\phi / \sum_i Y_{i,t}$. Then, run the simulations for the following values of ϕ: $\phi = 10000, 50000, 100000, 200000$.

Try to sketch out a brief discursive explanation of how the model dynamics is impacted by these different setup.

Exercise 11
Try to fix the seed to a constant (`set.seed(constant)`) for each Monte Carlo repetition. Compare the time series of different Monte Carlo. On the base of the arguments proposed in the chapter, how do you expect the across run volatility will be affected by this change?

Exercise 12
Try to plot `PRF` and `PRB` in a unique graph, in order to allow for a comparison between firms' and banks' profits. The graph should also provide a legend to distinguish the two lines. Finally, save the figure in a .eps format.

Exercise 13
Try to accomplish the task suggested at the end of the chapter in order to assess how much the cross-correlations between some variables of your interest are robust across Monte Carlo Experiment. In the implementation of the necessary code we suggest you to follow these steps:

- In the `for` cycle of single simulations compute the cross correlation between two variables X, Y of your interest, using the `ccf()` function employed in the text.
- store the values of the cross correlations (with lags ranging in $[-25, +25]$) for each simulation in the rows of a data frame initialized on the top of the script as follows:
  `crossCorrXY=as.data.frame(matrix(NA,ncol=51,nrow=MC))`
- compute the mean and standard deviation across Monte Carlo of each cross-correlation value (`avgCrossCorrXY` and `sdCrossCorrXY`)
- Finally, plot `avgCrossCorrXY` and `sdCrossCorrXY`. For this sake, you might consider to use the following set of commands:

```
lagseq=seq(-25,25)
par(mfrow=c(2,1))
plot(lagseq,avgCrossCorrXY,ylim=range(avgCrossCorrXY+
sdCrossCorrXY, avgCrossCorrXY-sdCrossCorrXY),
main="X vs Y", ylab="CCF", xlab="Lags",
na.rm=T, type="l")
arrows(lagseq, (avgCrossCorrXY-sdCrossCorrXY), lagseq,
(avgCrossCorrXY+sdCrossCorrXY), length=0.05, angle=90,
code=3)
```

Exercise 14
Try to "close" the model by adding labor, employment, and market clearing prices. More precisely:

- Assume that firms require $N_{i,t} = Y_{i,t}/10$ workers to produce the desired amount $Y_{i,t}$ (being determined as before), where 10 is the (fixed) labor productivity.

- Assume that wages w paid by firms to her employees are homogeneous and fixed to 5.
- Assume that prices are homogeneous and market clearing, and that workers consume all their income. Therefore, the price is defined as total wages (i.e. nominal demand) divided by total output: $p = wN_f^{tot} / \sum_i Y_{i,t}$

After the implementation run some simulations to analyze the model dynamics. What does it happen to firms' profits? Try to provide an explanation of the observed dynamics. Try to change wages paid to workers from 5 to 10000. Are firms' profits affected by this change? Why?

Chapter 3
Modeling Financial Markets in an Agent-Based Framework

Ruggero Grilli and Gabriele Tedeschi

3.1 Introduction

In this chapter we present a stylized financial agent-based model able to reproduce some important regularities emerging in financial time series. Following Tedeschi et al. (2009) and Tedeschi et al. (2012c), we show how an expectation feedback system can produce synchronization effects generating large fluctuations in returns. By introducing an endogenous mechanism of imitation, *via* a preferential attachment rule (Barabási and Albert 1999) such that each trader is imitated by others with a probability proportional to its profits, we generate herding that leads to a large excess demand and, consequently, has an obvious and immediate impact on prices. Moreover, this mechanism produces an evolving network structure ranging from the random graph to the scale-free one. This allows us to analyze how the endogenous evolution in the network topology impacts on market prices *via* the imitation of traders' strategies. We show how the transition from periods of network centralization, corresponding to high synchronization in agents' expectations, to periods of decentralization, when traders play randomly, is the key ingredient to reproduce fat tailed distributions (see Chap. 4 for details) and volatility clustering in our artificial stock market.

From the point of view of traders' microfoundations, the model proposed in this chapter must be considered as a toy model that relies on a number of exogenous

R. Grilli (✉)
Dipartimento di Scienze Economiche e Sociali, Università Politecnica delle Marche,
Piazzale Martelli 8, 60121 Ancona, Italy
e-mail: r.grilli@univpm.it

G. Tedeschi
Departament d'Economia, Universitat Jaume I de Castellon,
Avenida de Vicent Sos Baynat, s/n, 12071 Castellón, Spain
e-mail: gabriele.tedeschi@gmail.com

A. Caiani et al. (eds.), *Economics with Heterogeneous Interacting Agents*,
New Economic Windows, DOI 10.1007/978-3-319-44058-3_3

rules whose purpose is not to describe the behaviour of real agents in real markets, but to identifying the main conditions under which imitation leads to fat tails and volatility clustering. In contrast with other models where sophisticated strategies are implemented (see, for instance, Brock and Hommes 1998; Lux and Marchesi 2000; Chiarella et al. 2009), our traders are unsophisticated noise traders. Specifically we assume that agents have random expectations about future returns and a random demand function. Twofold is the reason for this choice. First, this allows us to focus on the impact of imitation on prices dynamics. In fact, by keeping as simple as possible the agents' microfondations, the network dynamics appears more clearly. Second, the presence of noise traders and their impact on prices' movement is well documented. Some authors (see for instance, Figlewski 1979; Shiller et al. 1984; Campbell and Kyle 1993; De Long et al. 1990) show that if "rational agents" are risk averse, then their ability to take positions against noise traders, who drive prices away from their fundamental value, is limited. All these works show that "irrational" noise traders, if sufficiently aggressive, can destabilize prices and earn larger returns. Moreover, "zero intelligence agents" have a long tradition in Economics and Sociology, closely related to the idea of animal spirits of Keynes and of boundedly-rational agents of Simon, Kahneman and Tversky.

Whether from the microfoundations point of view this model is parsimonious, it can be considered a rigorous market microstructure model. To this end, we implement a realistic mechanism of price formation. Specifically, following the working mechanism of the Euronext and the London Stock Exchange, here the price dynamic is determined by the structure of the exchange process without using any ad hoc mechanism. We develop an order-driven market where traders can either place limit or market orders. On the one hand, an investor is usually allowed to place a so-called "market order to sell (buy)", which is an instruction to automatically sell (buy) a particular amount of stock, if its selling price (buying price), called ask (called bid), is lower (higher) than the market price. On the other hand, a trader placing an ask (bid) higher (lower) than the market price is allowed to place a so-called "limit order to sell (buy)". Limit orders are stored in the exchange's book and eventually executed whether, in a short time horizon, match with an appropriate counterpart. Limit orders still unmatched after a predetermined time horizon, are removed from the book. Clearly, only market orders form the market price which readjusts itself whenever a new transaction occurs.

3.2 The Model

3.2.1 The Market Microstructure

We start the description of the model by explaining the trading mechanism which characterizes our stock market.

Following Tedeschi et al. (2009), in our model a population of N agents trade on an order-driven market. All investors display, in an order book, the prices at which they wish to buy or sell securities, as well as the amount of securities they desire to bargain. Specifically, our traders can either place market orders, which are immediately executed at the current best listed price, or they can place limit orders. Limit orders are stored in the exchange's book and executed using time priority at a given price and price priority across prices. A transaction occurs when a market order hits a quote on the opposite side of the market.

Trading happens over a number of periods (days) t_k, with $k = 1, \ldots, T$. Each trading day is divided into τ intra day operations; it means that we have τ transactions each trading day.

At the beginning of each day, traders make expectations about the price at the end of the time horizon τ. The future price expected by agent i at time $t_k + \tau$ is given by

$$\hat{p}^i_{t_k,t_k+\tau} = p_{t_k} e^{\sqrt{\tau}\hat{r}^i_{t_k,t_k+\tau}} \tag{3.1}$$

where $\hat{r}^i_{t_k,t_k+\tau}$ is the agent's expectation on the spot return which, as we will see later, depends on the communication network among traders, and p_{t_k} is the reference price observed by all agents at the beginning of each period. Equation 3.1 reproduces a geometric Brownian motion. This process, for its simple properties, has many applications in many asset-pricing models[1] (see Merton and Samuelson 1992).

After expectations are made, agents enter the market, sequentially and in a random order and place a buy or a sell order of a certain size. Traders expecting a future price to increase (decrease) decide to buy (sell) at a price b^i_t (a^i_t) lower (higher) than their expected future price $\hat{p}^i_{t_k,t_k+\tau}$. The purchase and sale price, namely bid and ask, are uniformly distributed around the current price and calculated according to the following rule:

$$\begin{aligned} b^i_t &\sim U(p^b_{\min}, \hat{p}^i_{t_k,t_k+\tau}),\ p^b_{\min} = p_t(1-\gamma^1_t), \\ a^i_t &\sim U(\hat{p}^i_{t_k,t_k+\tau}, p^a_{\max}),\ p^a_{max} = p_t(1+\gamma^2_t) \end{aligned} \tag{3.2}$$

where $\gamma^{1,2}_t$ are random variables uniformly distributed in the interval (0, 1) and p_t is the price at the time the order is submitted. As trading goes on the price is recalculated as follows: p_t is given by the price at which a transaction occurs, if any. If no new transaction occurs, a proxy for the price is given by the average of the quoted ask a^q_t (the lowest ask listed in the book) and the quoted bid b^q_t (the highest bid listed in the book): $p_t = \frac{(a^q_t + b^q_t)}{2}$. If no bids or asks are listed in the book a proxy for the price is given by the previous traded or quoted price.

If $b^i_t \geq a^q_t$, then, agents place market orders for a purchasing stock at a current quoted ask a^q_t. If the supply available on the book at a price a^q_t is not sufficiently large, they buy only stocks they can afford; otherwise, they buy all the quantities

[1] A geometric Brownian motion (also known as exponential Brownian motion) is a continuous-time stochastic process in which the logarithm of the randomly varying quantity follows a Brownian motion (also called a Wiener process) with drift.

Table 3.1 Summary of the trading mechanism of a typical trader i

	Position	Type of order	Volume
$b_t^q \geq a_t^i > \hat{p}^i_{t_k,t_k+\mathcal{T}}$	SELL	Market order	$s_t^i = \xi_t S_t^i$
$a_t^i > \hat{p}^i_{t_k,t_k+\mathcal{T}} > b_t^q$	SELL	Limit order	$s_t^i = \xi_t S_t^i$
$a_q^t \leq b_t^i < \hat{p}^i_{t_k,t_k+\mathcal{T}}$	BUY	Market order	$s_t^i = \xi_t C_t^i / a_q^t$
$b_t^i < \hat{p}^i_{t_k,t_k+\mathcal{T}} < a_q^t$	BUY	Limit order	$s_t^i = \xi_t C_t^i / b_t^i$

available and, then, move on to check the second best ask price, iterating the process until they have no more stocks to buy or there are no more sell orders in the book at a price smaller than b_t^i. If $b_t^i < a_t^q$ traders submit limit orders at b_t^i.

Symmetrically, if $a_t^i < b_t^q$, then, investors place market orders for selling stock at a price b_t^q. If the demand available on the book at this price is sufficiently large, they sell only the stocks they own; otherwise, they fill the available demand and, then, move on to check the second best bid price, iterating the process until they have no more stocks or cannot find a nth level bid price on the book greater than a_t^i. If the second condition occurs, investors place limit orders. If limit orders are still unmatched at time $t + \tau$, they are removed from the book.

For the sake of simplicity, we assume investors to have a random demand function and that the size of their order is bounded by budget constraints.[2] Agents hold a finite amount of cash C_t^i and stocks S_t^i in their portfolio. When agents place a market order, their cash and stocks decrease by an amount equal to their market order. Similarly, when agents place a limit order, their cash and stocks decrease by an amount equal to the limit order stored in the book. Even if a limit order does not comport any real transaction, we assume that cash and stocks placed in the book by traders are held there until they do not become market orders. This hypothesis implies that agents can not spend money or sell stocks which they have already tied down in the book.

The size s_t^i of agents' order is determined as follows:

- Traders expecting a decreasing price sell a random fraction of their assets $s_t^i = \xi_t S_t^i$
- Traders expecting an increasing price invest a random fraction of their cash in the assets according to the rule

  $s_t^i = \xi_t C_t^i / b_t^i$ if limit order
  $s_t^i = \xi_t C_t^i / a_q^t$ if market order (agents buy at the current ask)

with ξ_t to be a random variable uniformly distributed on the interval (0, 1). Table 3.1 summarizes the essential details of the trading mechanism.

[2] An interesting modification is in Tedeschi et al. (2012c). Authors model their agents as risk averse maximizing an exponential CARA utility function. Consequently, the number of stocks investors are willing to hold in their portfolio at a given price level depends on the choice of the utility function.

3.2.2 The Communication Network

At the beginning of each day t_k, traders have idiosyncratic expectations about the spot return, $r^i_{t_k,t_k+\tau}$ in the interval $(t_k, t_k+\tau)$. We assume that agents are noise traders and have random expectations of future returns. We also assume that agents are heterogeneous in that they have different forecasts of the returns' volatility, σ^i_t. Expected returns are thus given by

$$r^i_{t_k,t_k+\tau} = \sigma^i_{t_k}\epsilon_{t_k}, \tag{3.3}$$

where $\sigma^i_{t_k}$ is a positive, agent specific, constant and $\epsilon_t \sim N(0,1)$ is a normal noise. Before negotiations start, traders ask opinions of their neighbours; in this way each agent can revise its expectation and, consequently, its future price (see Eq. 3.1). Specifically, we model an imitation mechanism such that the investor i imitates the opinion of its neighbour j. Therefore, trader i's revised expected return becomes that of trader j to which i is linked to, i.e. $\hat{r}^i_{t_k,t_k+\tau} = r^j_{t_k,t_k+\tau}$.

To model how agents' decision are influenced by their mutual interaction we introduce a communication structure in which nodes represents agents and the hedges are the connective links between them. Links are directional and go from the agent that requests advice to the agent that provides advice. Specifically, we introduce an endogenous mechanism of imitation, by implementing a preferential attachment rule (Barabási and Albert 1999) such that each trader is imitated by others with a probability proportional to its wealth. This mechanism of links formation allows us to study how imitation affects the asset price and the distribution of agents wealth.

Agents start with the same amount of cash $C_{t=0}$ and stocks $S_{t=0}$, so that all agents have the same initial wealth $W_{t=0} = C_{t=0} + p_{t=0}S_{t=0}$. As time goes by, some traders may become richer than others. As a measure of agents' success we define their fitness at time t as their wealth relative to the wealth $W^{\max}_t$ of the richest agent $i_{\max}$:

$$f^i_t = \frac{W^i_t}{W^{\max}_t}. \tag{3.4}$$

Each agent i starts with one outgoing link with a random agent j, and possibly with some incoming links from other agents. Links are rewinded at the beginning of each period, in the following way: each agent i cuts his outgoing link, with agent k, and forms a new link, with a randomly chosen agent j, with a probability:

$$p^i_t = \frac{1}{1+e^{-\beta_t(f^j_t - f^k_t)}}, \tag{3.5}$$

while he keeps his existing link with probability $1 - p^i_t$.

The rewind algorithm is designed so that successful traders, here called gurus, gain a higher number of incoming links and thus have a higher probability of being imitated. Nonetheless the algorithm introduces a certain amount of randomness, and links with more successful agents have a finite probability to be cut in favor of links with less successful agents. In this way we model imperfect information and bounded rationality of agents. The randomness also helps unlocking the system from the situation where all agents link to the same guru. The parameter β_t in Eq. (3.5) represents the *intensity of choice* and answers the question how much traders trust on the information (expectation) about other agents' performances. In some sense, β_t measures the "imitative behavior". In fact, the most profitable strategy has more followers. This means agents tend to synchronize (or coordinate) their own expectations. Specifically, when β_t is zero, agents act independently from each other, however, increasing β_t, agents behave similarly and their faith increases. This parameter, therefore, amplifies the fitness signal and generates different network topologies. In this model, the intensity of choice, β_t, endogenously evolves over the time. Specifically, we link this parameter to the guru life: the longer the period the guru survives the higher is his signal credibility. We set β_t equal to 1 and increase it by more than 1 every day the guru survives. When the guru is replaced, the new β_t is set again to the value of 1.

3.3 Implementing the Financial Model: Preliminary Steps

Whenever a modeler approaches the step of the implementation of its set of equations, fatally he/she has to face the issue of the execution time. At the end, once you have written down the equations that rule the behavior of your artificial system, you need to translate them into a language that can be read and executed by a machine. If the reader does not have a background in computer science (as the authors of this chapter) there might be many variables—some of which also random—that can bring he/she to learn a programming language instead of another. However, eliminating all the factors due to chance (i.e. the language used by your supervisor or by most of your colleagues), the solution to this choice problem is often a good compromise between (i) the time you need to become a ''good enough'' programmer in your language, (ii) the time that your program needs in order to execute the block of instructions composing your code and (iii) how the features of the software fit the features of the model. In this fashion, if we consider the point (i) as a sort of fixed cost—and therefore, equal and uniform across agents and programming languages—what really differs the programming languages is their execution time.[3] The source of this diversity depends on the way in which a source code is translated into machine language. The simple idea is that different languages (with different syntaxes) have different translation processes which imply a different execution time. Generally speaking, this translation process is called *compiling* and it can happen in three ways:

[3]Obviously, when we talk about different time of execution we refer to the implementation of the same set of equation in different programming languages.

- the instructions of the source code are translated *run-time* by an *interpreter* which takes care of the conversion into machine language,
- firstly a *compiler* translates all the instruction into machine language, generating an executable file, then the executable can be run,
- a mixture of the two previous approach: a compiler can translate the instructions of the source code into an intermediate form (*bytecode*) and then pass it to an interpreter for the execution.

Even if this classification is not considered very rigorous by computer scientists, for our purpose it is convenient to refer to *interpreted languages* for those languages belonging to the first type and to *compiled languages* for those within the second group.[4] It is broadly acknowledged that compiled languages tend to be quicker than those interpreted, due to the run-time translation process which is generally more CPU and RAM intensive.

As the reader may have recognized from the previous chapter, **R** is an example of an interpreted language, since you can check run-time the execution of your code: by simply prompting on terminal the name of a variable, it will return you the value(s) stored in that variable until that time. On the other hand, C is a typical case of compiled language: a *filename.c* is the source code whose instructions are passed to a compiler (*gcc* for Unix and Unix-like systems, *MinGW* for Windows system) which returns an executable file (sometimes with extension *.exe*) ready to be run. The separation between the compiling and execution ensures a faster processing, mainly because (i) it does not need an interpreter and (ii) it eliminates any dependency on additional libraries during the execution.

To sum up this discussion, there is not a general solution—good for every model—in the choice between interpreted and compiled languages; nevertheless, the modeler should be aware of this kind of problems, before starting the implementation. A good way to face this issue is to know at least one language of both type, in order to be able to switch when the implementation of the model requires an intensive calculus capacity.

This is exactly the approach we have followed, in the implementation of our Financial Model. That is the reason why we have switched from **R** to C in order to speed up its execution. In this way, we give the reader the possibility to learn the principles of a compiled language and to store them into his/her own toolbox.

The rest of the chapter is organized as follows: we list the sequence of the events in our artificial order driven market, then we briefly introduce the basic structure of a C source code, we browse through the main functions which implement the code and finally we propose some exercises.

[4]It is indeed the existence of a third mixed group of languages which reduces the rigorousness of this classification.

3.4 Order of Events in the Simplified Financial Model

In the previous chapter, we have learnt that, once you have mathematically formalized your model, the following step is to order the sequence of events that happens in every iteration. Therefore, let us try to list what traders do in our artificial order driven market. The sequence of events we propose below, is just one of the possible solution to the problem of implementation of our simplified financial model. Maybe the reader has already acquired the skills to detect some possible permutations of the sequence's items which produce the same results. Nevertheless, the list we propose is the one followed by the C source code. In this way, we hope to ease the understanding of this different language. Since the model reproduces a high frequency trading market, it is important to acknowledge that within a certain iteration (say a day) t, many operations take place many times. We may summarize by saying that the core of tradings happens on an intra-day time span, while the communication structure among agents is rewinded with daily frequence.

Before starting with the sequence of events, a brief recall on the mathematical notation we are going to employ. As in the previous chapter, we have tried to recall the variables of the mathematical description of the model, and to express the functions in implicit form. However, some additional definitions are required in order to enhance both the description and the comprehension of what follows.

We define the communication network through which agents imitate the expectation of their neighbours as $\mathbf{C} = (V, E)$. V is the set of nodes (each of whom is a trader) and E is the set of links which join the different agents. Alternatively, the graph $\mathbf{C}$ can be represented by its adjacency matrix A, whose $a^{i,k}$ entry is equal to 1 if there is a link between i and k.[5] In each period, the connections of $\mathbf{C}$ are rewinded according to Eq. (3.5). The probability that agent i stops to imitate k in favor of j, depends positively by:

(i) how much j is wealthier than k
(ii) the intensity of choice, β_t.

The first item is expressed by the difference between the fitness of j and the one of k, $(f^j_{t-1} - f^k_{t-1})$. The second item mirrors how much traders rely on the information about other agents' performances. Therefore, β_t measures the imitative behavior within the network and its time evolution depends on the life span of a guru g_t.[6] Since β_t evolves according to the number of periods that a certain trader is durably a guru, we define $\Theta_t = \{\tau_g \subset T | g_t = g_{t-\tau_g}, 1 \leq \tau_g \leq t-1\}$ as the set of consecutive days in which a certain trader is the guru. Therefore, its cardinality $|\Theta_t|$ mirrors how long a guru survives. The higher the cardinality, the longer is the guru's life, the stronger is the preference of all others traders to link with him (increasing β_t).

---

[5]Since the communication network is directed, generally $a^{i,k} \neq a^{k,i}$. Therefore, $a^{i,k} = 1$ is a link from i to k that means that agent i imitates k's expectation on future price.

[6]The rationale behind this algorithm is: the longer the time in which the richest trader (namely the guru) has been imitated by others, the higher is his signal's credibility and the higher is the incentive to further imitate him.

Each trader can imitate the strategy of just one another player. In terms of network representation, this means that each node has just one outgoing link per day. On the contrary, nodes can acquire multiple incoming links, in particular, when their strategies are successful and they have been imitated by other players. We define the indegree of the i-th node at day t as $\deg(i)_t$. Now we can formally define the guru at time t, $g_t = \{i \mid \max_{\forall i \in V} \deg(i)_{t-1}\}$, as the node that in $t-1$ had the maximum number of incoming links.[7]

Now we got all the definitions that allow us to compile our sequence of the events. We split the enumeration between daily and intra-daily operations, to highlight the different time horizons of these actions. As we have already pointed out, the reader can easily note that the daily operations deal with the formation of the communication network, which is essentially a network of expectations. Whilst the pure market trading mechanism is repeated within intra-day loops.

Daily operations:

1. Traders randomly select a new possible neighbour, j
2. Traders calculate the probability of switching from the old neighbour, k, to the new selected one, j, $Pr(a_t^{i,k} = 1 | a_{t-1}^{i,j} = 1) = f(\beta_{t-1}, f_{t-1}^j, f_{t-1}^k)$
3. Traders choose their neighbours (filling the communication network adjacency matrix), $a_t^{i,j} = (0||1), \forall i, j \in V$
4. Traders update their fitness, $f_t^i = f(W_t^i, W_t^{max})$
5. The trader with the maximum in degree at day $t-1$ is the guru at time t, $g_t = f(\max_{\forall i \in V} \deg(i)_{t-1})$
6. Traders form their expectation on the volatility of returns, $\sigma_{t_k}^i = f(\deg(i)_{t_k})$
7. Traders intensity of choice is updated according to the guru's life span, $\beta_t = f(|\Theta_t|)$
8. Traders calculate their expectation on returns, $r_{t_k,t_k+\tau}^i = f(\sigma_{t_k}^i, \epsilon_{t_k}), \epsilon_{t_k} \sim N(0,1)$

Intra-daily operations:

(i) Checking of orders already written in the book (if any) before the matching
(ii) Each intra-day, a trader has been randomly selected, to play in the financial market.[8]
(iii) Traders update their expectation according to the one of their neighbours (imitation), $\hat{r}_{t_k,t_k+\tau}^i = r_{t_k,t_k+\tau}^j$. Only the guru keeps its own expectation
(iv) If trader i expects returns to rise, $\hat{r}_{t_k,t_k+\tau}^i > 0$, it becomes a buyer, otherwise a seller
(v) Traders calculate the expected price at time $t_k + \tau$, $\hat{p}_{t_k,t_k+\tau}^i = f(p_{t_k}, \hat{r}_{t_k,t_k+\tau}^i, \tau)$
(vi) Buyers calculate their minimum price, $p_{\min}^b = f(p_t, \gamma_t^1)$ and their bid, $b_t^i \sim U(p_{\min}^b, \hat{p}_{t_k,t_k+\tau}^i)$

[7]The careful reader will have noticed that the guru not only has the maximum in degree but with probability tending to one it is also the wealthiest agent and thus the one with the highest fitness.
[8]Traders put orders following a random sequence. On average, each agent makes $n = \frac{N_t}{N}$ intra-day operations, where N_t is the number of intra-days and N is the number of traders.

(vii) Sellers calculate their maximum price, $p^a_{max} = f(p_t, \gamma^2_t)$ and their ask,[9] $a^i_t \sim U(\hat{p}^i_{t_k,t_k+T}, p^a_{\max})$
(viii) Buyers calculate the size of their orders, $s^i_t \sim U(0, \frac{C^i_t}{b^i_t})$
(ix) Sellers calculate the size of their orders, $s^i_t \sim U(0, S^i_t)$
(x) If $b^i_t \geq a^q_t$, the buyer i places market orders for a purchasing stock at current quoted ask a^q_t[10]
(xi) If $b^i_t < a^q_t$, the buyer i submits limit orders at b^i_t
(xii) If $a^i_t \leq b^q_t$, seller i places market orders for selling stock at price b^q_t
(xiii) If $a^i_t > b^q_t$, seller i submits limit orders at a^i_t
(xiv) The price p_t is given by the price at which a transaction occurs, $p_t = f(a^i_t, b^i_t)$
(xv) If limit orders are still unmatched after $t + \tau$ periods, they are deleted from the book.

3.5 Implementing the Model in C

3.5.1 Basic Structure of a C Source Code

In a very general way, there are at least five basic elements we must include in our C source code, in order to run it. Listing 3.1 reproduces the skeleton of the Financial Model's source code. In particular, we have highlighted the five essential elements that cannot be omitted in order to compile it. By scrolling it, our aim is to comment these essential features and also to explain the basic syntax of the C language.

Listing 3.1 The five basic elements that compose a C source code.

```
/* 1 LIBRARIES */
#include <stdio.h>
#include <stdlib.h>
#include "ran2.h"
...
/*2 DEFINES*/
#define VOL 100
#define NDAY 2000
#define TOT_SIM 100
...
/*3 GLOBAL VARIABLES*/
long idum;
...
int dMarketMatrix[VOL][VOL];
...
float wealth[VOL];
...
double profit[VOL];
...
```

[9]We remind from the mathematical description of the model that $\gamma^{1,2}_t \sim U(0, 1)$.

[10]Let us remind to the reader that a^q_t and b^q_t are respectively the lowest ask and the highest bid listed in the book.

```
char file_name[100];
...
FILE *out;
...

/*4 FUNCTIONS DECLARATION*/
void InitializeMatrix(void);
...
void check_book(int tt);
...

/*5 MAIN*/
int main()
{
    int i;
    idum = -123456789;
    ...
    //File printing
    sprintf(file_name,"df_vol_NG_%d_p%.2f_w%.2f",NGURU,prob,
        w);
    ...
    //File writing
    out=fopen(file_name,"w");
    ...

    InitializeMatrix();

    // Monte Carlo Simulations Loop.

    for (n_sim = 0; n_sim < TOT_SIM; n_sim++)
    {
        /*List of function to execute each run*/
        Init_all();

        Trade();
    }

    return 0;
}
```

Libraries

When the `C` code is still a blank page, the reader must be aware that the first item he/she has to include it is the list of *libraries*. Basically, the libraries contain useful functions for many different tasks. The range of functions goes from the managing of the input/output files to the loading of most mathematical operators. The typical argument of the directive `include` is a *header file*—which has an extension `.h`. A header file is a file that collects all the prototypes of the functions stored in a certain library.[11] For what concerns the most standard libraries, both header and source files are usually placed in a folder of the file system. In this case, the header file name must be included within `<...>`, since this is the syntax for absolute path files. However,

[11] Usually the extension of the library is `.c`.

it is allowed to load external libraries also from local path.[12] In this latter case, the header file name must be included within "...", as shown in Listing 3.2.

Listing 3.2 Include examples

```
#include <filename_abs.h>
#include "filename_local.h"
```

Therefore, Listing 3.3 is the first piece of our Financial model code, where we include all the libraries which allow us to run it. The reader may notice that four out of five of them have an absolute path, while only `ran2.h` is local. This latter library holds the functions to generate pseudo-random numbers Press et al. (1992).

Listing 3.3 Libraries included in the Financial Model source code

```
#include <stdio.h>
#include <stdlib.h>
#include <math.h>
#include <string.h>
#include "ran2.h"
```

Defines

Once the set of libraries has been included, the next step is to define the set of basic parameters of the model. This operation uses the directive `#define` in the following way:

Listing 3.4 Define examples

```
#define PARAM_NAME PARAM_VALUE
```

where `PARAM_NAME` is the name of the parameter and `PARAM_VALUE` its value. Usually, this operation is applied to all those parameters which are invariant within the system's runs. For instance, we can set in this way the number of Monte Carlo loops we want to perform (as in Listing 3.1, line 9), or we can define the values for the initial conditions of the system. Another class of parameters that must be defined at this stage is those which sets the number of agents who populate the system. This is particularly important, since it is going to be employed in the next step, when we define the arrays. In Listing 3.1 line 7 we have set the number of traders, `VOL`, to 100. Thus, `VOL` will be the size of those arrays which are going to collect the micro data of agents' performances.

Below, we show the set of parameters that we have defined in our Financial Model

Listing 3.5 Set of parameters defined in our Financial Model

```
#define VOL   100
#define DAY   300
#define TOT_SIM 100
#define GDAY 10
#define NDAY  2000
#define NTIMES  200000

```

[12]Obviously, loading a library from local path implies to include that library and its header file within the same folder of the source code you are working on. Alternatively, you must specify the full local path.

```
#define STEP_TOT (NDAY * DAY)
#define DIMENSION (NDAY * DAY + THERM)
#define MAX_O (50000*VOL)
#define BOOK_MAX 5000000
#define DIST_MAX 20000
#define TIME_MAX 5000
#define AVE_MAX 5000
#define book_bin 1

#define NGURU 1
```

Global Variables

In C language it is possible to define two family of variables: *globals* and *locals*. A global variable is defined immediately after the call of `#define` or generally outside of any particular function. On the contrary, a local variable is called for the first time within a block of code which composes a specific function. Therefore, the different placement of a variable definition assigns different properties to that variable. A global variable occupies a memory space that it is accessible from every point of the source code. A local variable can be used only within the function where it is defined.

Both global and local variables may differ according to their type. The C language presents many basic type but all of them can be obtained by combining the four basic arithmetic type specifiers—`int`, `float`, `double` and `char`—with the optional specifiers—`signed`, `unsigned`, `short` and `long`. For the purpose of our dissertation, we are going to employ just five out of the available types of variables. For what concern the integer variables, we use:

- `char`, an integer type, which allows to manage basic character set. Its size is `CHAR_BIT` per bits[13]
- `int`, basic integer type, 16 bits
- `long`, long integer type, 32 bits

while for the floating point type variables, we use:

- `float`, single precision floating point, 32 bits
- `double`, double precision floating point, 64 bits.

Below we propose the part of the Listing 3.1 which defines the global variables in our source code

Listing 3.6 An example of global variable definition

```
long idum;
...
int dMarketMatrix[VOL][VOL];
...
float wealth[VOL];
...
double profit[VOL];
...
```

[13]The number of bits depends on the length of the string.

```
char file_name[100];
...
FILE *out;
...
```

As the reader may notice, this example employs all the five types of variables we have just described, plus a sixth type that is a *pointer*. A pointer is basically an address to a memory allocation. Kernighan (1988) have provided a better definition of a pointer as "a variable that contains the address of (another) variable." If also this definition may sound a bit cryptic to the reader, the Listing 3.7 provides an example of pointers functioning.

Listing 3.7 An example of how pointers work

```
1 int a = 1, b = 2;
2 int *p; /*p is a pointer to int*/
3
4 p = &a; /*p points to a*/
5 b = *p; /*b is now 1*/
6 *p = 10;     /*a is now 10*/
```

At line 4, we assign the address of `a` to the variable `p`, by means of the unary operator `&`. Thus we can state that `p` "points to" `a`. Then, by using another unary operator `*`, we can modify the value of `a` by assigning a new value to `*p` (line 6). This is allowed because a pointer accesses the memory space of the object it points to (Kernighan 1988). Now the reader have surely recognized that pointers are a very powerful programming object, whose use it is as much tricky as their definition. Therefore, despite we have recalled them for completeness, for the sake of simplicity, we have tried to limit their usage.[14] Herein we have just used pointers to address those memory spaces where we have stored the data we want to write in the output files.

If we go back to the Listing 3.6, we can note different definitions of global variables. Independently on their type, `idum` represents the definition of a *scalar*. The variable `dMarketMatrix` defines an array with `VOL` rows and `VOL` columns. The variables `profit` and `wealth` are arrays of `VOL` rows and just 1 column. Even if in principle it is allowed to dynamically resize the arrays, here we keep their dimension as fixed. This is quite a crucial point: in `C` you must declare in advance if a certain variable is a scalar or an array. In general, shrinking an array to a scalar is allowed but it is not a trivial operation that requires the use of pointers. Therefore, this topic exceeds our purpose. A careful definition of variables will prevent the occurrence of memory allocation errors (the infamous Segmentation Fault).

Listing 3.8 List of global variable in our Financial Model

```
long    idum;
int     dMarketMatrix[VOL][VOL];
float   n[VOL], cash[VOL];
float   al[MAX_O], bl[MAX_O], p[DIMENSION], p0[DIMENSION];
float   al_0[MAX_O], bl_0[MAX_O], sigma_f;
float   book_stat_a[BOOK_MAX], book_stat_b[BOOK_MAX], prob;
float   distribution_time_a[TIME_MAX];
```

[14]The reader must bear in mind that our aim is just to provide the basic principles of `C` programming. The interested reader may refer to more advanced and specific texts as Kernighan (1988).

```
float     distribution_time_b[TIME_MAX];
float     td, tot_cash[VOL], cash0[VOL];
int       count_stat, distance2, distance1, stocks[VOL];
int       stocks0[VOL], ilambda, time;
int       count_time_a, count_time_b, limit_stock[VOL];
int       ao_t_entry[MAX_O], a_trader[MAX_O];
int       bo_t_entry[MAX_O], b_trader[MAX_O];
int       b_t_trade[VOL],a_t_trade[VOL], execution_time;
int b_t_entry[VOL], a_t_entry[VOL], neighbour[VOL];
int       dayc, N_a, N_b, T_max, L_max, L[VOL], status[VOL] ;
int       n_sim, gurut,gurut_old,tot_stocks[VOL];
float     wealth0[VOL][DIMENSION], wealth[VOL];
double    profit[VOL], profit0[VOL];
float     sigma, k_max, sigma_g1, sigma_g2;
float     sigma_d, n00, n0, Delta, lambda;
float     Wi, scale,  tau, pf, T[VOL];
float     instvol[DIMENSION];
FILE      *out, *out1, *out2, *out3, *out4, *out5;
char      file_name[100], file_name1[100],file_name2[100];
char      file_name3[100]file_name4[100], file_name5[100];
int       mean_size, size, tot_h, connected[VOL];
float     r_long[NDAY],r_per[DIMENSION], limit_cash[VOL];
float     sig_size, fact_book, w;
int       NMAX, NMIN, START, NSTEP, DIM, iT_inv;
float     expectation[VOL], T_inv;
```

Function Declaration

In this part of the code, the programmer must declare the functions that he/she is going to use in the source code. Herein, with the term *function*, we refer to a set of instructions that implement the model's behaviors into the source code. Generally, those functions represent the core of the model's implementation since they are often written by the programmer for each specific model. However, the full block of instructions that compose a certain function should be written later; now the modeler has just to define the name and the arguments of the function.

Listing 3.9 An example of functions declaration

```
1 void FunctionName(void)
2 ...
3 int FunctionName1(int x, int y)
4 ...
5 float FunctionName2(float z)
```

The Listing 3.9 displays two different ways to declare a function. The first one—line 1—makes use of the `void` function, and define an empty function whose arguments are empties as well. This is the most flexible and general case of function declaration. This statement is useful whenever a function performs several operations, also very heterogeneous across them. Then the function's arguments might be so many that it is easier to do not list them. The second way to declare a function is more canonical. It requires the definition of the type of the function's outcome—integer, float, etc.—as well as the type of the arguments employed. Below, we list the functions employed in our Financial Model.

Listing 3.10 The list of function declaration in our Financial Model

```
void InitializeMatrix(void);
void Matrix1(void);
void Matrix3(void);
void Init_all(void);
void Trade(void);
void check_book(int tt);
float gasdev(long *idum);
```

The `main()` function

As the name may suggest, the `main` function is the core of every program. Each `C` source code must at least include it and only the items that are called or defined inside the `main` will be compiled and executed by the machine. Whenever a `C` source code is executed, the first call is for the `main` function and only what lies within its curly braces `{}` it is run. A good practice is to keep the `main` as clean as possible. Typical operations that are included into the `main` are:

- set the seed for pseudo-random number generator (`idum`),
- instructions for output files printing and writing,
- Monte Carlo simulation loop,
- within the Monte Carlo loop, call all the functions which implement the model.

An example of the syntax which implements this list of tasks is given by the Listing 3.11.

Listing 3.11 A stylized example of included elements into the `main` function, in our Financial Model.

```
 int main()
{
    int i;
    idum = -123456789;
    ...
    //File printing
    sprintf(file_name,"df_vol_NG_%d_p%.2f_w%.2f",NGURU,prob,
        w);
    ...
    //File writing
    out=fopen(file_name,"w");
    ...

    // Monte Carlo Simulations Loop.

    for (n_sim = 0; n_sim < TOT_SIM; n_sim++)
    {
        /*List of function to execute each run*/
        Init_all();

        InitializeMatrix();

        Trade();
    }

    return 0;
}
```

Just some few remarks before concluding this section. According to Press et al. (1992), the value of `idum` must be negative.[15] The syntax to call a function is

Listing 3.12 A function call example

```
FunctionName();
```

where the name of the function is followed by a pair of blank parenthesis and by a semicolon. In general, each instruction must be closed by a semicolon, otherwise the execution will be stopped in the point in which it lacks. Each variable—either a scalar or an array—must be initialized after they have been defined. In this fashion, it is useful to create an *ad hoc* function, which takes care of this task.[16] As the reader can see at line 17 of Listing 3.11, the `for` loop syntax is very intuitive. There are three expressions within the parenthesis: the first and the last define respectively the starting and the increment of the loop's index. The second is a relational expression which basically defines the length of the loop. In our example, the length of the Monte Carlo loop is equal to `TOT_SIM`, while `n_sim` ranges between `[0,(TOT_SIM-1)]`.

Finally the `return 0;` expression, identifies the successful outcome of the `main` execution. Therefore, a `0` value of the `main` function means that no errors have occured during its execution. On the contrary, when the `main` function returns a value of `1`, it signals that something has gone wrong during the execution of the program.

3.6 Implementing the C Source Code

3.6.1 Introduction

Once we know how to build the elementary structure of a `C` source code, we can start to implement the functions that will shape the interaction in our artificial financial market. Of course, after the few pages that the reader has just read, probably he/she has still a vague idea of how a `C` program works. However, we would like to say that the best way to learn and practice a programming language is "to put the hands on codes." On our side, we will try to comment step by step the basic functions which compose the source code.

In Sect. 3.5 we have underlined that only the functions included in the `main` are executed when you run the program. Figure 3.1 describes the structure of the `main` function. The reader may notice the nested architecture: we have three functions, the last of which comprises other three functions. The rest of this section will review each function in order to show how to build a simple program to simulate a financial market. First of all, we analyze the functions that take care of the initialization of global variables. Then we describe the functions which create the structure of

[15]We refer to Press et al. (1992) for a more detailed explanation of the `ran2` algorithm.

[16]Since this operation is needed just once for each execution, the initialization function can be placed outside the Monte Carlo loop.

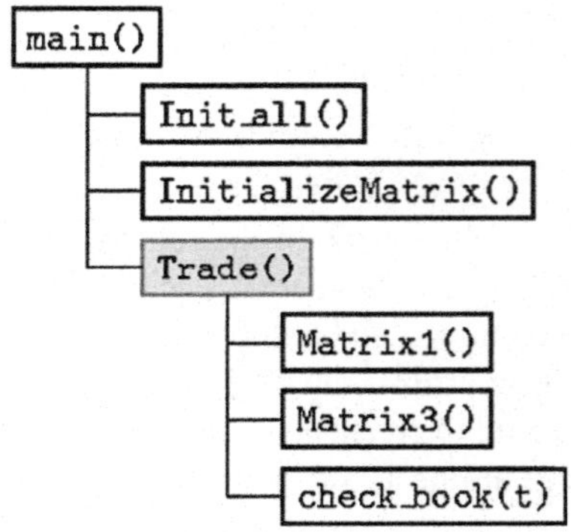

Fig. 3.1 The nested architecture of the `main` function of the financial model source code

the communication network and finally we illustrate the two functions—`Trade` and `check_book`—which govern the mechanism of financial transactions in our artificial market.

Only a final remark before starting with the description of the code implementation. In our code, the time—day and intra-day loops—is running only within the `Trade` function. In other words, each simulation run provides: one call to the `main` function which, in turn, calls only once the functions `Init_all`, `InitializeMatrix` and `Trade`. Then, within the `Trade` function, we find the time loops, which execute the instructions and the functions—`Matrix1`, `Matrix3` and `check_book`—for the whole length of our simulation.[17]

3.6.2 *Initialize Variables*

In C programming, once you have defined all your variables—both global and local—it is a good practice—as well as highly recommended—to set all of them at zero.[18] This process is called *initialization*. Whenever a new variable is defined, this corresponds to an allocation of a void memory space (whose size depends on the variable type, as stated in Sect. 3.5.1). Therefore, this space is not filled with a zero by default, unlike to what happens in some others interpreted languages, such as **R**. Hence, it is better to take care of this task, by defining one (or more) *ad hoc* function which initializes at zero the whole set of arrays and scalars. To perform this duty we have employed two functions:

[17]Obviously, the design of this code's architecture is a particular choice of the programmers. It is just one of the possible solution of the implementation problem, given the sequence of the events described in Sect. 3.4.

[18]It is always better to populate a new variable with its initial condition, either a zero or another value, before use it for the first time.

(i) Init_all, a generic function which initializes globally defined arrays
(ii) InitializeMatrix, a specific function which initializes the network's adjacency matrix.

Let us give a look to the coding of these functions.

Init_all()

This function is composed by a sequence of loops, which initialize globally defined arrays. The loops have different length, and variables are clustered within them according to their dimensions. The first loop sets at zero the individual variables of traders. The others loops take care of the book's variables initialization. Finally, we initialize the price at intra-day 0, p[0], by assigning the value of pf and we set at zero all the time counters. It is worth to highlight again that only those variables which are globally defined can be included in this function.

Listing 3.13 The Init_all function source code

```
void Init_all(void)
{
  int  site, t,max_t, try;

  long k;
  max_t =0;

  for (site=0; site<VOL; site++){
    status[site] = 0;
    limit_stock[site]=0;
    limit_cash[site]=0.;
    tot_stocks[site] =0;
    tot_cash[site]=0.;
    expectation[site]=0.;
    T[site] = (int)(tau);
  }

  for(k=0; k < BOOK_MAX; k++){
    book_stat_a[k]=0;
    book_stat2_a[k]=0;
  }

  for(k=0; k < BOOK_MAX; k++){
    book_stat_b[k]=0;
    book_stat2_b[k]=0;
  }

  for(k=0; k < DIST_MAX; k++){
    distribution_dist[k]=0;
    distribution_dist1[k] =0;
    distribution_dist_a[k] =0;
    distribution_dist_b[k] =0;
  }

  for(k=0; k < TIME_MAX; k++){
    distribution_time_a[k]=0;
    distribution_time_b[k]=0;
  }
```

```
    dayc=0;
    t=0;
    p[t] = pf;
}
```

InitializeMatrix()

This function initializes at zero the entries of the adjacency matrix—`dMarketMatrix`- of the communication network. `dMarketMatrix` is a square matrix of `VOL` rows and `VOL` columns, whose elements can be either `1` when there exists or `0` when there isn't an edge between traders `i` and `j`. Herein, a third variable is initialized, whose name is `neighbour`. This is an array of `VOL` dimension, which keeps in memory, for each trader `i`, the id of the trader whose `i` had a link with, in the previous period (namely its neighbour). Since each element of `neighbour` can assume values in the interval `[0,(VOL-1)]`, we initialize `neighbour` at `-1`, to avoid wrong linkages with the trader whose id is equals to `0`.

Listing 3.14 The `InitializeMatrix` function source code

```
void InitializeMatrix()
{
    double value;
    int i;
    int j;

    for( i=0;i<VOL;i++){
        neighbour[i]=-1;
        for( j=0;j<VOL;j++){
            dMarketMatrix[i][j]=0;
            dMarketMatrix[j][i]=0;
        }
    }
}
```

3.6.3 The **`Matrix`** *Functions*

Once we have initialized the adjacency matrix of our communication network, we face the problem of how we can populate it, in order to reproduce the mechanism we have described in Sect. 3.4.

To implement this task, we make use of two different functions, `Matrix1` and `Matrix3`. The two functions differ for the attachment mechanism they provide.

Matrix1

This function implements a random attachment among traders. We make use of this function to ''initialize'' the network structure (i.e. the interactions among agents). In other words, at the beginning of each simulation run, when we have no connections between nodes, which kind of network structure should we assume? In most cases, a reasonable and convenient answer is to assume a random interaction as the initial configuration of an evolving network. This step essentially creates a "history" in the connection structure of agents.[19] Here we have slightly modified the mechanism of attachment in order to allow a set of topologies, ranging from a pure random network to a star one.[20] For the temporary nature of its task, the `Matrix1` function is called just for few periods at the beginning of each run. Let us give a look to Listing 3.15 which implements the function `Matrix1`.

Listing 3.15 The `Matrix1` function source code

```
1  void Matrix1()
2  {
3    double value;
4    int i;
5    int j;
6  
7    for( i=0;i<VOL;i++){
8      j = 30;
9      if(i!=j){
10       dMarketMatrix[i][j]=1;
11       neighbour[i]=j;
12       value=ran2(&idum);
13       if (value>=prob){
14         dMarketMatrix[i][j]=0;
15         j= ran2(&idum)*VOL;
16         dMarketMatrix[i][j]=1;
17         neighbour[i]=j;
18       }
19     }
20   }
21 }
```

At line 7 we start to populate our adjacency matrix. We choose a certain trader and we treat it as a fixed guru (line 8). For each trader that is not the guru we create a link with it (lines 10, 11). Now, the trader `i` has a link with the fixed guru, but, with a probability equals to `prob`, it can cut this link and establish a new one with a random selected trader `j` (lines 13–17). Thus, as `prob` tends to `1`, it is much likely that most of the nodes will keep their linkages with the guru. Namely, the network tends to be a star. To manage this probabilistic process, we employ two variables. `prob` defines the probability to link with the guru and it is a fixed scalar. `value` is pseudo-random scalar, drawn from an uniform distribution with support `[0,1]`. Once `prob` is assigned, each trader extracts a random `value` (line 12) and if it is not lower than `prob` (line 13), the trader breaks up the link with the guru.

`Matrix3`

Once we have fulfilled all the preliminary tasks concerning the initialization of our program, we can start to implement the operations we have listed in Sect. 3.4. In

[19]For instance, each trader selects at random the neighbour to link with (i.e. the variable `neighbour`).

[20]However, we have to say that the model's results are not affected by the set up of different topologies.

particular, Matrix3 translates into C language the first three point of the daily operation sequence.

Here the goal is to create a fitness network, where links are rewinded in each period according to the probabilistic rule expressed by Eq. 3.5. Along this chapter, we have already discussed the rationale behind a fitness network, thus we don't want to repeat it. The first step is to assume the traders' profits as their fitness measure. Then with a for loop on agents, we find the traders with the highest fitness.[21] This procedure is a way to identify the guru, by selecting the id of the agent which has realized the maximum profit (lines 10–18).

Listing 3.16 The Matrix3 function source code

```
1  void Matrix3()
2  {
3     double value;
4     int i;
5     int j,k;
6     float neew;
7     int imax1;
8     float max1 ref, fact;
9
10    max1=-10000;
11    imax1=-1;
12
13    for(i = 0; i< VOL; i++){
14       if( max1< profit[i]){
15          max1 = profit[i];
16          imax1=i;
17          }
18    }
19
20    for(i=0; i<VOL; i++){
21       j= ran2(&idum)*VOL;
22       k=neighbour[i];
23       value= ran2(&idum);
24       ref =   prob*(profit[j]- profit[k]);
25       fact = 1./(1.+   exp(-ref));
26       if(value< fact && i!=j){
27          dMarketMatrix[i][j]=1;
28          dMarketMatrix[i][k]=0;
29          neighbour[i]=j;
30       }
31    }
32 }
```

From line 20 to 29 we implement the algorithm that updates the network linkages according to the traders' fitness. For each trader, a new potential neighbour j is randomly selected,[22] as well as the old neighbour is assigned to the variable k. In

[21] Since this happens at the beginning of each period, the values of profits refer to the previous period.

[22] A quick remark on the functioning of ran2. By default, it returns uniform random numbers in the interval [0,1]. Those numbers are obviously floating point. But, if you multiply ran2 by an integer, the result will be an integer too.

line 24 we write down the argument of the exponential of the Boltzmann equation and, in the following line, we pass it to Eq. 3.5. Let us notice that here `prob` is our β, that is the level of intensity of choice of traders.[23] `ref` mirrors the comparison between the new and the old neighbour's fitness. `fact` returns the value of the probability that agent `i` stop to imitate `k` and starts to follow `j`. To mimic the probabilistic behaviour, we extract a random number from a (0, 1) uniform distribution and we assign it to the flag `value`. If `fact` is bigger than `value`, `i` breaks up the link with `k` and creates a new one with `j` (lines 27–29). Otherwise, it keeps its existing relationship.

Once this operation has been repeated for each trader, the network's adjacency matrix has been filled. The reader can verify that the trader with the highest fitness—namely the guru—will have acquired the highest amount of incoming links.[24]

Finally, we want to stress that the calls of `Matrix1` and `Matrix3` are dichotomous, since they perform the same task in different ways. We run `Matrix1` in the first steps of the simulation and then only `Matrix3` is executed.

3.6.4 *The* `Trade` *Function*

This function is the real core of the model's implementation. Almost all of the tasks depicted in the sequence of the events, have been designed here—from the detection of the guru, to the execution of tradings, passing by the filling of the book. As we have already mentioned, the stream of the simulation's time is running within this function. Since the block of instructions of this function is quite rich, we are going to split it into different parts. Our idea is to scroll down the lines of code and to comment the blocks which perform different duties.

At the beginning of the `Trade` function we find a block of definitions of local variables, followed by different loops to set up the initial condition of both traders and book's variables.

Listing 3.17 The `Trade` function source code: local variables, and initial set up

```
void Trade()
{
  int        j, site,  fact, i, temp, t;
  int        kk, k_trade, k_insert, t_trade;
  float      spread, spread_ave, b[VOL], a[VOL];
  int        tr,  vol_ask_market, vol_ask_limit;
  int        vol_bid_market, vol_bid_limit, count;
  double     r_i, r_j, bid, ask,exp_p;
  int        try, depth_bid, depth_ask, k_last;
  float      a_gap1, b_gap1;
  int        maximum, n_trades;
  int        neighbours[VOL], friends[VOL];
  long       k, trading_volume;
  int        sign_limit,  sign_market, trader[VOL];
```

[23] See Sect. 3.2.2 for a deeper explanation of the meaning of β and of the entire Eq. 3.5.

[24] To be more rigorous, we need to rephrase this sentence in a probabilistic fashion. The guru will have the higher probability to acquire the highest amount of incoming links.

```
int         depth_ask_old, depth_bid_old;
int         id, tot_link, total_s;
float       p_ref, prof_max, pmin, pmax;
float       ave_wealth, wealth_max;
double      ave_profit;
int         stock_max, delta0, i_max;


/*Intra-days counter*/
t =0;

N_a = 0;        /*Number of asks*/
N_b = 0;        /*Number of bids*/

spread_ave = 0.;
count = 0;

gurut= 30;          /*Fixed guru*/
gurut_old=gurut;    /*Keep in memory the (t-1) guru*/

int stock_tot = 0;

/*Initialization of agents' variables: bids and asks*/
for (site=0; site < VOL; site++){
  a[site]=0.; /*asks*/
  b[site]=0.; /*bids*/
  /*Storing the intra-day at which each trader inserts a
      bid/ask*/
  b_t_trade[site]=0;
  a_t_trade[site]=0;
  b_t_entry[site]=0;
  a_t_entry[site]=0;
/*Initialization of agents' variables: cash, stocks,
    profits, wealth, and expectations*/
  expectation[site]=0;
  cash0[site] = Wi * p[t];
  stocks0[site] =(int) (Wi);
  cash[site] = Wi * p[t];
  stocks[site] =(int) (Wi);
  profit[site]=0.;
  wealth0[site][0]= cash0[site] + stocks0[site]*p[t] ;
  wealth[site]= cash0[site] + stocks0[site]*p[t] ;
  stock_tot += stocks[site];
  tot_stocks[site]=stocks[site];
  tot_cash[site]=cash[site];
  limit_stock[site] =0;
  limit_cash[site]=0.;
}
stock_max = stock_tot/100.;

/*Inizialization of book's variables*/
for (k=0; k < MAX_O; k++){
  bl[k]=0.;    /*List of bids written in the book*/
  al[k]=0.;    /*List of asks written in the book*/
  b_trader[k]=0;  /*Buyer's id*/
  bo_t_entry[k]=0;     /*Bids timing*/
  a_trader[k]=0;  /*Seller's id*/
```

```
        ao_t_entry[k]=0;      /*Asks timing*/
        book_stat_a[k]=0;
        book_stat_b[k]=0;
        book_stat2_a[k]=0;
        book_stat2_b[k]=0;
    }

    count_stat=0;
    count_time_a=0;
    count_time_b=0;
    int num=0;
    dayc =0;          /*Day 0*/
    delta0 = GDAY*DAY;

    /*...*/

    }
```

We have tried to richly comment the Listing 3.17, in order to explain the reader those variables whose names may not immediately recall their economic counterpart. For what concerns the book's operation, we have already dealt with it in Sect. 3.2.1, therefore we will not repeat it. Nevertheless, we need to illustrate few key variables—both agents and book's specifics—that can hinder our route towards the model's implementation. The reader acknowledges that the trading mechanism is focused on bids and asks. However, looking to the Listing 3.17, there are more than one variable that stored their values. This is due to the fact that we need to save the information on bids/asks in the agents memory space, as well as in the book. Thus it is better to clearly review these key variables, to avoid problems in the following steps of the implementation.

Agent's specific variables

- `N_a` is the number of asks written in the book
- `N_b` is the number of bids written in the book
- `a[VOL]` is the array that collects the traders asks, coming from Eq. 3.2. Those are the prices at which traders want to sell their stocks
- `b[VOL]` is the array that collects the traders bids, coming from Eq. 3.2. Those are the prices at which traders want to buy stocks
- `a_t_trade[VOL]` is the array that collects the intra-day at which traders insert their order to sell
- `b_t_trade[VOL]` is the array that collects the intra-day at which traders insert their order to buy
- `stocks[VOL]` is the array that collects the amount of stocks that traders are going to buy/sell

Book's specific variables

- `al[MAX_O]` is the array that stores all the asks written in the book. This is the ask side of the book. In each period, the asks still written in the book are sorted from the highest to the lowest, such that `al[N_a-1]` it is always the best ask in the book.[25]

- `bl[MAX_O]` is the array that stores all the bids written in the book. This is essentially the bid side of the book. In each period, the bids still written in the book are sorted from the lowest to the highest, such that `bl[N_b-1]` it is always the best bid in the book.
- `a_trader[MAX_O]` is the array that keeps trace of the sellers id associated to the different asks listed in the book. Even the elements of this array follow the same sorting of `al[MAX_O]`.
- `b_trader[MAX_O]` is the array that keeps trace of the buyers id associated to the different bids listed in the book. Even the elements of this array follow the same sorting of `bl[MAX_O]`.
- `ao_t_entry[MAX_O]` is the array that saves the intra-day in which a certain ask has been written in the book. Obviously, also the elements of this array have been sorted as `al[MAX_O]`
- `bo_t_entry[MAX_O]` is the array that saves the intra-day in which a certain bid has been written in the book. Obviously, also the elements of this array have been sorted as `bl[MAX_O]`.

The next step is to write down the loops which govern the passage of time. We should be careful because even time has a multiple dimensions—i.e. days and inta-days. The nested structure of time's loops makes use of three different counters:

- `dayc` is the counter of days and it ranges from `0` to `NDAY`
- `try` is the counter of intra-days. For each `dayc`, `try` runs from `0` to `DAY`. In other words, each day of the simulation is composed by `DAY` subperiods.[26]
- `t` is the cumulative counter of intra-days. Differently from `try`, `t` has not been resetted to `0` at the beginning of each `dayc`. Thus, it keeps on counting along all the simulation span, reaching its maximum at `DAY`×`NDAY`. `t` is the total number of intra-days along the whole simulation as well as the total number of operations performed. Accordingly, `t` is also the length of the time series of prices and returns.

Once the timing structure is clear, we can give a look at coding to check the implementation of such a mechanism. Listing 3.18 proposes the higher time loop which, of course, starts to scroll the first element of its hierarchical structure: `dayc`.

Listing 3.18 The `Trade` function source code: the higher time loop on `dayc`

```
/*...*/
while (dayc < NDAY){
   dayc ++;
   td = (float)t/(float)DAY;
   id = (int)td;
   if(td>=GDAY){
      r_long[id]= log(p[t])- log(p[t-DAY]);
    }
```

[25]The reader should keep in mind this sentence, because it will be useful later to understand the matching of orders.

[26]This is equivalent to say that each day of the simulations, `DAY` operations take place.

```
tot_link=0;
total_s=0;

if(dayc<2*GDAY)
  Matrix1();
else
  Matrix3();

for(i = 0; i < VOL; i++){
  neighbours[i] =0;
  friends[i] =0;
  neighbour[i]=-1;
  total_s +=(stocks[i]-limit_stock[i]);
  if (total_s> stock_tot)
    printf("ERRORSTOCK %d \n", total_s);
  }

for (j=0;j<VOL; j++){
  for(i=0; i<VOL; i++){
    if(dMarketMatrix[j][i]==1 && i!=j){
  friends[j] +=1; // out-going links
  neighbours[i]+=1; // incoming links
  tot_link += 1;
  neighbour[j]=i; // name of neighbour
  }
    }
  }

maximum=0;
gurut_old=gurut;
for (j=0;j<VOL; j++){
  n[j] = n0*(ran2(&idum) + (1.-w)* (float)neighbours[j]/
      VOL);// Agents expectation before interaction
  if(neighbours[j]>maximum){
    gurut=j;
    maximum=neighbours[j];
    }
  }

if (gurut==gurut_old)
  num+=1;
else
  num=ran2(&idum)*2;
prob= (float)num;
ave_wealth = 0;
wealth_max = 0.;

for(i = 0; i< VOL; i++){
  wealth0[i][t]= cash[i] + stocks[i] *p[t];
  if(wealth_max < wealth0[i][t])
    wealth_max = wealth0[i][t];
  if(i != gurut)
    ave_wealth += (wealth0[i][t]);
  }

for(i = 0; i< VOL; i++){
```

```
64        fprintf(out3, "%d %d %d %f %f %d\n", n_sim, dayc, i,
              wealth0[i][t], cash[i], stocks[i]);
65        fflush(out3);
66      }
67
68      if(t>=delta0 ){
69        ave_profit = 0.;
70        prof_max = -10000.;
71        i_max = -1;
72
73        for(i = 0; i< VOL; i++){
74          profit[i] = wealth0[i][t]/wealth_max;
75          if(prof_max < profit[i]){
76        prof_max = profit[i];
77        i_max = i;
78          }
79          ave_profit += (profit[i]);
80        }
81      fprintf(out2, "%d %d  %lf %lf %f %f %lf %f %f  %d %d %d %d
            %f\n",n_sim,
82        dayc,  profit[gurut],
83        ave_profit/(float)(VOL-1), wealth0[gurut][t],
84        ave_wealth/((float)(VOL-1)), prof_max, wealth_max,
85        prof_max/ave_profit,
86        i_max, neighbours[i_max], neighbours[gurut], gurut, prob
            );
87      fflush(out2);
88      }
89
90      for(i = 0; i < VOL; i++){
91        expectation[i]= n[i]*  gasdev(&idum) ; // Agents
              expectation before interaction
92      }
93      p_ref = p[t];
94    /*...*/
95    }
```

The `while` loop ensures that all the instructions that follow are executed until `dayc` does not reach the value of `NDAY`. Differently from a `for` loop, we need to increment "by hand" our daily counter (line 3). This block of instructions takes care of the implementation of the whole set of daily operations we have listed in Sect. 3.4. In lines 12–15, we call the functions which create the structure of our communication network. The `if-else` statement provides a different function call, according to the time of the execution. In the first `GDAY` days of the simulation, we call the `Matrix1` function to initialize our interaction structure.[27] Then we pass to load the fitness network, by employing `Matrix3` for the rest of the simulation. Once the matrix functions have filled the adjacency matrix, `dMarketMatrix`, we can count the number of each node's outgoing links—`friends`—of incoming links—`neighbours`—the total number of links—`tot_link`—and finally storing the id of the neighbour that each node is going to imitate—`neighbour` (lines 17–35). These informations will be useful to understand how imitation spreads among

[27] See Sect. 3.6.3 for a detailed explanation.

traders within the network, as well as to detect which agent will be the guru in that day. Indeed, the next step is to write a `for` loop on traders that elects as guru the agent with the maximum value of `neighbours`.[28] A subtle passage here, needs to be commented. We have stated that the intensity of imitation—i.e. the β parameter—is an increasing function of how long a certain agent survives as a guru. Therefore, we need to count the consecutive days in which this happens. We perform this operation in the following way:

- at line 38 we store in `gurut_old` the name of the previous day guru, just before calculating which is the new one
- at line 42 we assign to `gurut` the id of the trader which has the maximum indegree in the current day
- with an `if-else` statement, we check if the guru of today is indeed the same of yesterday. If this is true, we increment our guru's life span counter `num` (line 48). Otherwise, we pick up at random a value for the imitation's intensity (line 50).
- Finally we assign `num` to `prob`.

This corresponds exactly to the implementation of the point 7 of our sequence of the events. Going one step backward in our list, line 40 translates the point 6, that is the equation through which traders form their expectation on the volatility of returns. The instructions in lines 52–66 provide a ranking of traders according to their wealth. It is worth to note here an example of `fprintf`, the function employed to write the output files (lines 63–66). This function needs three type of arguments: (i) a pointer to the resource we are using to write the file, `out`, (ii) the type of the variable we want to print out and (iii) its name. The call `fflush(out)` allows to check the file writing process, of the variables we want to print out, during the simulation running. The block of instruction within the `if` statement at line 68, performs a task similar to the one of the wealth ranking. The main differences are: (i) the ranking is applied to profits and (ii) this computation starts only after `delta 0` intra-days. In practice, we are delaying the detection of the trader with the highest profits, until we start to call the fitness network. At this point the reader may asks why we are so interested to rank wealth and profits of traders. We can answer that these are equivalent ways to check if the program has correctly selected the guru. Indeed, `out5` collects the main data on performances of both agents and the guru. Finally, the last daily operation, before starting the intra-day analysis, is the computation of expected returns by the traders (point 8 of the event's sequence and line 91 of the Listing 3.18), stored in the array `expectation`.

Listing 3.19 The `Trade` function source code: the intra-day time loop, `try` and `t`

```
/*...*/
for(try = 0; try < DAY; try++){
  check_book(t);

  sign_limit=0;
  sign_market=0;
  vol_bid_limit=0;
```

[28] In other words, the guru is the trader with the maximum number of incoming links.

```
vol_ask_limit=0;
vol_bid_market=0;
vol_ask_market=0;
trading_volume=0;
depth_ask_old = depth_ask;
depth_bid_old = depth_bid;
count ++;
t  ++;
p[t] = p[t-1];
if(p[t] <= 0){
  printf("ERROR 1 negative price %d\n", n_sim);
 }
td = (float)t/(float)DAY;
i = ran2(&idum)*VOL; // RANDOM PLAYER
while(i==j)
  i = ran2(&idum)*VOL;
r_i = expectation[i];

if(i == gurut) {
  exp_p = p_ref * exp(r_i*sqrt(T[i]));
  if (r_i> 0) { // if the agent expects prices to increase buys
    pmin= p[t]*(1.-ran2(&idum));
    bid = pmin  + ran2(&idum)* ( exp_p - pmin);
    fact = (int)round(bid/Delta);
    if(fact==0)
    fact=1;
    b[i] = (fact * Delta);
    distance1= (int)((al[N_a-1] - b[i])/book_bin);
    distance2= (int)((p_ref - b[i])/book_bin);
  }
  if (r_i < 0) { // if the agent expects prices to decrease sells
    pmax = p[t]*(1+ran2(&idum));
    ask = exp_p + ran2(&idum)* (pmax-exp_p );
    fact = (int)round(ask/Delta);
    if(fact==0)
    fact=1;
    a[i] = (fact * Delta);
    distance1=(int)((a[i]-bl[N_b-1])/book_bin);
    distance2=(int)((a[i]- p_ref)/book_bin);
  }
}
if(i != gurut) {
  j = neighbour[i];
  if(j>0){
    r_j = expectation[j];
    r_i = w* expectation[i] + (1. - w)* r_j; // expectation after imitation
  }
  expectation[i]=r_i;
  exp_p = p_ref * exp(r_i*sqrt(T[i]));
  /*buy*/
  if (r_i> 0.) {
    pmin= p[t]*(1.-ran2(&idum));
    bid = pmin  + ran2(&idum)* ( exp_p - pmin);
    fact = (int)round(bid/Delta);
```

```
        if(fact==0)
        fact=1;
        b[i] = (fact * Delta);
        distance1= (int)((al[N_a-1] - b[i])/book_bin);
        distance2= (int)((p_ref- b[i])/book_bin);
      }
      /*sell*/
      if (r_i < 0.) {
        pmax = p[t]*(1. + ran2(&idum));
        ask = exp_p + ran2(&idum)* (pmax - exp_p );
        fact = (int)round(ask/Delta);
        if(fact==0)
        fact=1;
        a[i] = (fact * Delta);
        distance1=(int)((a[i]-bl[N_b-1])/book_bin); //positive distance means limit orders
        distance2=(int)((a[i]-p_ref)/book_bin); //positive distance means limit orders
      }
    }
  /*...*/
}
```

The `for` cycle on `try` gives rise to the intra-day management of our source code. The Listing 3.19 reproduces the beginning of this loop and stop immediately before traders start to submit orders of buying and selling. As a whole, the block of instructions included here computes the price expectation of traders, by implementing Eq. 3.1 of the mathematical model. It is precisely at this stage that the imitation process takes place. Indeed, except for the guru, all the other traders embed the expectation of their neighbour in their own. This is the point where the communication structure plays its role. The network affects the formation of price expectations. When traders have formed their price expectations, they become buyer(seller) if they foresee price to rise(fall). This is a very brief description of the what happens in Listing 3.19. Let us give a more detailed look at it.

The first instruction of this block is a call for the `check_book` function, which we are going to analyze in the next subsection. For the moment we just need to know that it helps to keep the book in order. Then, we start to increment `t` and, before a new market price has been recorded, we assign the previous one to `p[t]`, to fill this memory space (lines 15, 26).

We assume that in each intra-day there is just one trader that can insert just one order. Therefore, each `t`, a random trader `i` is selected (line 21) to play in the financial market.[29] At this point, we have a pair of nested binary options, that we can summarize as follow:

1. the random player is the guru
    a. the guru wants to buy stocks
    b. the guru wants to sell stocks

[29]On average, each agent plays $\frac{DAY}{VOL}$ times per day.

2. The random player is NOT the guru
   a. the random player wants to buy stocks
   b. the random player wants to sell stocks

The feature that discriminates the guru from all the other traders, is that the guru does not imitate anybody, when it forms its expectation on future price (line 27). On the contrary, all the other agents consider not only their expectation but also the one of their neighbour, `r_j` (lines 50–54). Then, regardless if you are the guru or not, if a trader expects the price to rise—`(r_i > 0)`—it becomes a buyer, otherwise a seller. The instructions performed by buyers or sellers do not distinguish if the trader is the guru or not.[30] Each buyer (seller) calculates its minimum (maximum) price and then extracts its bid, `b[i]` (ask, `a[i]`) from a uniform distribution according to Eq. 3.2.

Thus, at the end of this block of code, each trader selects the side of the book where it wants to insert its order. Now it needs to explore the other side of the book to match it. This is the focus of the next branch of code.

Listing 3.20 The `Trade` function source code: Submission of orders to buy

```
/*...*/
/* Submission of Order to buy: BID */
    if (r_i> 0){
      tot_cash[i]=cash[i]-limit_cash[i];
      tot_stocks[i]=stocks[i]-limit_stock[i];
      size = (int)(ran2(&idum)*(tot_cash[i]/b[i])) ;
      if(size<0){
        printf("ERROR 2a negative size %d %d %d %d %d %f \n"
            ,i,tot_stocks[i], stocks[i],limit_stock[i],size,
            b[i]);
        fflush(stdout);
        size=0;
        }
      if(size > stock_max) {
        size = stock_max;
        }
      for(n_trades=0; n_trades < size; n_trades++){
      /* Non marketable buy limit order */
        if ( N_a == 0){
        temp=1;
        tr =0;
        sign_limit=1;
        vol_bid_limit ++;
        limit_cash[i]+=b[i];
        status[i] ++;
        k=-1;
        while( k < N_b){ /*k can be at max equals to (N_b-1)
            */
            k++;
            if(b[i] < bl[k]) break;
         }
        k_insert=k;/*number of bids lower or equal to mine
            */
```

[30] Indeed, we have just repeated them twice in the source code.

```
        for(k = N_b - 1; k > k_insert - 1 ; k--){ /*create space in the book to insert a limitable bid*/
           bl[k+1]=bl[k];
           b_trader[k+1] = b_trader[k] ;
           bo_t_entry[k+1] =  bo_t_entry[k];
        }
        bl[k_insert]= b[i];
        b_trader[k_insert] = i;
        bo_t_entry[k_insert] = t;
        b_t_entry[i] = t;
        N_b ++;
      }
     else  if ( N_a > 0 && b[i] <  al[N_a-1] ){
       temp=1;
       tr =0;
       sign_limit=1;
       vol_bid_limit ++;
       limit_cash[i]+=b[i];
       status[i] ++;
       k=-1;
       while( k < N_b){
         k++;
         if(b[i] < bl[k]) break;
       }
       k_insert=k;/*number of bids lower or equal to mine */
       for(k = N_b - 1; k > k_insert - 1 ; k--){ /*create space in the book to insert a limitable bid*/
        bl[k+1]=bl[k];
        b_trader[k+1] = b_trader[k] ;
        bo_t_entry[k+1] =  bo_t_entry[k];
       }
      bl[k_insert]= b[i]; /*insert my bid which is the k_insert-th*/
      b_trader[k_insert] = i;
      bo_t_entry[k_insert] = t;
      b_t_entry[i] = t;
      N_b ++;
     }
   /* Marketable buy limit order */
    else if (N_a >=1 && b[i] >= al[N_a-1] ){
      sign_market=1;
      vol_bid_market ++;
      trading_volume ++;
      p[t]=al[N_a-1];
      execution_time = t- ao_t_entry[N_a-1];
      execution_time=1;
      if(execution_time < TIME_MAX){
        distribution_time_a[execution_time]++;
        count_time_a++;
      }
      b_t_trade[i] = t;
      b_t_entry[i] = t;
      status[a_trader[N_a-1]] --;
      a_t_trade[a_trader[N_a-1]] = t;
      stocks[i]++;
      stocks[a_trader[N_a-1]]--;
      limit_stock[a_trader[N_a-1]]--;
```

```
        cash[a_trader[N_a-1]]+= al[N_a-1];
        cash[i] -=al[N_a-1];
        if(cash[i]< 0.) {
          printf("ERROR no cash %d %f %f %f %f %f %d\n",i,
              tot_cash[i],cash[i],limit_cash[i], a[i], b[i],
              size);
        }
        if( stocks[a_trader[N_a-1]]<0 ){
          printf("ERROR no stock1\n");
        }
        N_a --;
      }
    }
  }
/*...*/
```

The Listings 3.20 and 3.21 show the implementation of the algorithms which govern the submission and the execution of orders to buy and sell, respectively. As the reader may notice, this two blocks of code seem to look in the mirror. They perform the same tasks, in the same order but in a different side of the book. A buyer explores the ask side, and it looks for the best price—`al[N_a-1]`—in order to match it with its bid, `b[i]`. A seller does the same on the other side of the book, and it searches for the best bid—`bl[N_b-1]`—to combine with its ask, `a[i]`. Thus, the trading takes place essentially as a matching between bids/asks—`b[i],a[i]`—of the random player `i` and those already written in the book—respectively `al[N_a-1], bl[N_b-1]`. It is essential to remind that these latter—called sell or buy limit orders—are always sorted in opposite directions: from the higher to the lower the limit asks, and from the lower to the higher the limit bids.

After this premise, let us try to go deep into coding in order to show what probably is the most challenging part of our source code. A last remark from our side: since the description of buyer and seller operations are really specular, we will not repeat them twice. We think it is better to avoid an excessive repetition of mechanic instructions which perform the same tasks. Therefore, we are going to comment only the Listing 3.20, which implements the buyer's behaviour. The reader may try to copy this part and then substituting the words: buyer with seller, bid with ask and increasing with decreasing. He/she probably will come out with a description of the sellers behaviour as exhaustive as the one we propose below.

Whenever a player expects an increase of the market price, it decides to buy stocks (line 3). First of all, the trader has to check the total amount of available cash and the stocks it owns in its portfolio (lines 4, 5). Now, it can decide the size of the order to buy it wants to submit (line 6). We plug this information into the variable `size`. To keep the framework as simple as possible, we assume that the size of an order is a random variable, uniformly distributed between `0` and the maximum amount of stocks the trader can buy, given its `tot_cash` and its `bid`. Once defined the size, the buyer needs to explore all the selling orders—written in the other side of the book—whose prices are not greater than the one of its order. Therefore, we employ a `for` loop of length `size`, which browses all the asks that can be matched

Table 3.2 Trading example: the buyer's behaviour

Example n.1		
Buyer	Seller 1	Action
`size` 4 `bid` 2 `tot_cash` 10	`size` 3 `ask` 2	Buy all and spend $3 \times 2 = 6$
	Seller 2	
`size` 1 `bid` 2 `tot_cash` 4	`size` 3 `ask` 1	Buy 1 stock at price 1, $1 \times 1 = 2$

potentially. Let us explain this mechanism with a brief example, because once you got the rationale behind it, the implementation is almost straightforward.

Suppose we have a buyer which inserts an order of size equals to 4 and bid equals to 2. When it searches in the book for an ask to match it finds the seller 1 which offers 3 stocks at price equals to 2. This is of course the best selling price[31] and thus it buys all the 3 stocks at that price. Then, the buyer is still looking for another stock to totally fulfill its request of 4. The second seller—that is the seller with the second best selling price—offers 3 stocks at a price of 1 and the buyer can purchase the last stock at that price. Now, the buyer is completely satisfied and no limit order are written in the bid side of the book. On the ask side, a selling order of size 2 and price 1 remains written in the book, for what concerns the seller 2. This is exactly what happens in Table 3.2. The two rows of this table depicts a case of marketable orders from the buyer side that are immediately executed. The only case in which the buyer is not fully satisfied—and therefore it puts a limit order to buy—happens when the size of its order is greater than the number of asks written in the book, that it can afford to purchase. Except for this particular case, the buyer will meet its request, by purchasing stocks from different sellers. The sellers are always sorted according to their selling price in a decreasing way. Hence, from this consideration follows that:

1. the buyer purchases stocks at different prices
2. all these prices enter the definition of the market price, `p[t]`.

Turning back to the branch of code in Listing 3.20, we note that the `for` loop on `size` is divided into 3 `if-else if` statements. The first two represent cases of non marketable order, since:

1. `N_a == 0` means there are not any selling orders written in the book at that moment. Thus, no match can take place, and the buyer submits a limit order to buy,
2. `N_a > 0 && b[i] < al[N_a-1]` means that even if there are selling orders for the matching, this can not take place because the bid is lower than the best selling price. Again, the buyer can only submits a limit order.

[31] Again that side of the book is sorted in increasing way.

Only the third condition gives rise to marketable orders

1. `N_a` $\geq$ `1 && b[i]` $\geq$ `al[N_a-1]` means that not only there are selling orders for matching but the buyer's bid is greater than the best ask. Thus the order to buy can be matched and executed.

The procedure to insert limit orders is the same in both the non marketable conditions. The `limit_cash` of the buyer is incremented by the amount of its bid[32] (line 22, 46) as well as the variable `status`, which counts the total size of limit orders submitted by each trader. When a new limit order must be inserted, we need to create the space in the book to add it. The next block of instructions performs this task. We set to -1 a counter `k`. Then we write a `while` loop of variable length, that can not exceed `N_b-1`. Within this loop, we increment `k` until we find a limit bid greater than the one we are going to insert (lines 27, 51). In this way, `k` represents the number of bids lower than the one we want to insert. We do not need to move these bids. Instead, we must rearrange all the bids ranging from the `k`-th to the `N_b-1`-th. Indeed, the new bid will occupy precisely the `k`-th entry of the book's array. Firstly, we assign `k` to `k_insert`. Then, in a `for` loop we scan the higher part of the book, that goes from `k_insert` to `N_b-1`. In order to free the `k_insert`-th space, we must move forward all the entries within this interval, by the assignation `bl[k+1]=bl[k]` (lines 31, 59). We repeat the same operation for the id of the buyer which submits the limit order, `b_trader`, and for the variable which stores the time at which orders are written in the book, `bo_t_entry` (lines 32, 33, 56, 57). At the end of this `for` loop we can insert our limit bid as we show in lines 35–38 and 59–62. Finally, before exit the non marketable orders loop, we must increment the number of limit orders to buy, `N_b` (lines 39, 63).

Let us now consider the marketable order case, which brings to an immediate execution of the buy order. Since the bid is not lower than the best ask, `al[N_a-1]`, the latter will be the price at which the purchase happens, and therefore, this will be recorded in the market price time series, `p[t]` (line 70). The size of limit orders of the seller—`a_trader[N_a-1]`—is decremented (line 79) as well as its `stocks` and `limit_stocks`. On the contrary, the seller `cash` increases (line 84). For what concerns the buyer, the reader may notice the same variations but with different sign (`stocks` increase and `cash` decreases). Finally, since an ask written in the book has been matched, we must remove it from the book, and so we decrement the appropriate counter, `N_a`.

Listing 3.21 The `Trade` function source code: Submission of orders to sell

```
/*...*/
/* Submission of Order to sell: ASK */
  if (r_i < 0) {
    tot_stocks[i]=stocks[i]-limit_stock[i];
    tot_cash[i]=cash[i]-limit_cash[i];
    size =(int) (ran2(&idum)*tot_stocks[i]) ;
    if (size<0){
```

[32]Since the order will last in the book for at maximum $t + \tau$ periods, that amount of cash will not be available until the period $(t + \tau) + 1$.

```
          printf("ERROR 2b negative size %d %d %d %d %d %f \n",i
              ,tot_stocks[i], stocks[i],limit_stock[i],size, a[i
              ]);
          fflush(stdout);
          size=0;
        }
        if(size>stock_max){
          size = stock_max;
        }
        for(n_trades=0; n_trades < size; n_trades++){
        /* Non marketable sell limit order */
          if ( N_b == 0){
        sign_limit=-1;
        vol_ask_limit++;
        temp =-1;
        tr =0;
        limit_stock[i]++;
        status[i] ++;
        k=-1;
        while( k < N_a){
          k++;
          if(a[i] > al[k]) break;
        }
        k_insert=k;
        for(k=N_a-1; k > k_insert-1 ; k--){
          al[k+1]=al[k];
          a_trader[k+1] = a_trader[k] ;
          ao_t_entry[k+1] = ao_t_entry[k];
        }
        al[k_insert]= a[i];
        a_trader[k_insert]=i;
        ao_t_entry[k_insert] = t;
        a_t_entry[i] = t;
        N_a ++;
      }
      else if ( N_b >= 1 && a[i] > bl[N_b-1] ){
        temp =-1;
        tr =0;
        sign_limit=-1;
        vol_ask_limit++;
        limit_stock[i]++;
        status[i] ++;
        k=-1;
        while( k < N_a){
          k++;
          if(a[i] > al[k]) break;
        }
        k_insert=k;
        for(k=N_a-1; k > k_insert-1 ; k--){
          al[k+1]=al[k];
          a_trader[k+1] = a_trader[k] ;
          ao_t_entry[k+1] = ao_t_entry[k];
        }
        al[k_insert]= a[i];
        a_trader[k_insert]=i;
        ao_t_entry[k_insert] = t;
        a_t_entry[i] = t;
```

```
      N_a ++;
         }
       /* Marketable sell limit order */
    else if ( N_b >=1 && a[i] <= bl[N_b-1]){
      sign_market=-1;
      vol_ask_market++;
      temp = -1;
      tr = 1;
      trading_volume ++;
      /************************/
      p[t]=bl[N_b-1];
      /************************/
      execution_time = t- bo_t_entry[N_b-1];
      if(execution_time < TIME_MAX){
        distribution_time_b[execution_time]++;
        count_time_b ++;
       }
      a_t_trade[i] = t;
      a_t_entry[i] = t;
      b_t_trade[b_trader[N_b-1]] = t;
      status[b_trader[N_b-1]] --;
      stocks[i]--;
      stocks[b_trader[N_b-1]] ++;
      if(stocks[i]<0){
        printf("ERROR 3 no stock3\n");
       }
      cash[i] +=bl[N_b-1];
      cash[b_trader[N_b-1]] -=bl[N_b-1];
      limit_cash[b_trader[N_b-1]] -=bl[N_b-1];
      if(cash[b_trader[N_b-1]] <0.){
        printf("ERROR 4 no cash \n");
       }
      N_b --;
        }
     }
  }
/*...*/
```

Just before concluding the description of the `Trade` function, we have to show the lines of code that defines two fundamental variables of our model: the market price and the returns.

Listing 3.22 The `Trade` function source code: market price and returns

```
/*...*/
if(N_a>1 && N_b>1)
  p[t] = 0.5 * (bl[N_b-1] + al[N_a -1]);
r_per[t] = log(p[t]/p[t-1]);
/*...*/
```

This is really one of the last tasks performed within each intra-day period (`try` loop), after the randomly selected trader `i` has ended its trading activity. The market price definition makes use of an `if` condition, since we need to discern two possible cases:

1. The book is empty, as a whole or just in one side—`(N_a ==0 || N_b==0)`—after the trading: in this case the market price `p[t]` will be equals to the last buying (selling) price—`bl[N_b-1] (al[N_a-1])`—at which the last transaction has occurred

2. There are still orders in both sides of the book—`N_a > 1 && N_b>1`—after the trading: in this case, the market price is given by the average of the best quoted bid and the best quoted ask.

Finally, the variable `r_per` stores the values of returns which are defined as the log difference of `p[t]` and `p[t-1]`.

3.6.5 The `Check_Book` Function

Now that we have deeply analyzed the trading mechanism, it is easier to illustrate how the function `check_book` works. Essentially, this function takes care of the book's management, before the happening of each bargaining. It performs three tasks:

1. it checks that the number of written orders do not exceed the maximum length of the book's array (lines 7–9)
2. it deletes all the limit orders that last for more than $t + \tau$ periods
3. it sorts the bids and the asks listed in both sides of the book.

At a first glance, the reader will notice that Listing 3.23 reproduces the same operations we have broadly commented in Sect. 3.6.4, when we have faced the submission of limit orders. In particular, we refer to the procedure of freeing the space to insert a new limit bid or ask (the `for` loop on `k_insert`). The `check_book` function replicates the same block of instructions, just substituting `k_insert` with `k_del`. Indeed, here the goal is to delete all the limit bids and asks which have overcome the time threshold defined in lines 13 and 29. As a consequence, the function browses all the limit orders and when the (over)time condition is met, the position of the order to delete is assigned to `k_del`. The `k_del`-th order is eliminated from the book and all the others are moved forward or backward, depending on the book's side involved. Let us remark that the direction of prices movement in this case is opposite respect to the one we have described in Sect. 3.6.4. Herein, bids move backward—lines 18–20—and asks move forward—lines 34–36. The `check_book` function takes as input the variable `t`, the cumulative intra-periods counter, since it has to compute the time window $t + \tau$. After each `check_book` call, the book is reorganized and ready for the trading of agents.

Listing 3.23 The `check_book` function source code

```
1  void check_book(int tt)
2  {
3     int k,k_del,kk,hh,trader;
4
5     count_stat ++;
6     if(N_a > MAX_O || N_b > MAX_O){
7       {printf("ERROR 4 \n");exit(0);}
8     }
9     /*Buyers*/
10    for(k=0; k < N_b; k++){
11      trader= b_trader[k];
```

```
        if(tt > (bo_t_entry[k] + T[trader])){
          k_del = k;
          status[b_trader[k_del]]--;
          limit_cash[b_trader[k_del]]-=bl[k_del];
          for(kk= k_del; kk < N_b-1; kk++){
          bl[kk] = bl[kk+1];
          b_trader[kk] = b_trader[kk+1] ;
          bo_t_entry[kk] = bo_t_entry[kk+1];
           }
          k--;
          N_b --;
        }
      }
      /*Sellers*/
      for(k=0; k < N_a; k++){
        trader=a_trader[k];
        if(tt > (ao_t_entry[k] + T[trader])){
          k_del = k;
          status[a_trader[k_del]]--;
          limit_stock[a_trader[k_del]]--;
          for(kk= k_del; kk < N_a-1; kk++){
          al[kk] = al[kk+1];
          a_trader[kk] = a_trader[kk+1] ;
          ao_t_entry[kk] = ao_t_entry[kk+1];
           }
          k--;
          N_a --;
        }
      }
}
```

3.7 Simulations and Results

In the simulations the number of traders is set at $N = 100$. Each agent is initially given an amount of stock equal to $S_0 = 100$ and an amount of cash equal to $C_0 = 1000$. The initial stock price is chosen at $p_0 = 1000$. We also fix $\tau = 300$.

The results reported here are the outcome of simulations of $T = 2000$ periods and $N_t = 300$ trades per periods. Simulations are repeated $M = 10$ times with a different random seed.

We focus on the statistical properties of the probability distribution of stock returns and on the auto-correlation of market volatility.

We also analyze some properties of the order submission strategies such as the spread, the distance between best price (bid/ask) and the trading volume.

In the last part we focus the analysis on some properties of the network such as the in-degree, the fitness and the signal credibility distribution. Then, we analyze the probability distribution of wealth and stocks and the positive feedback on prices.

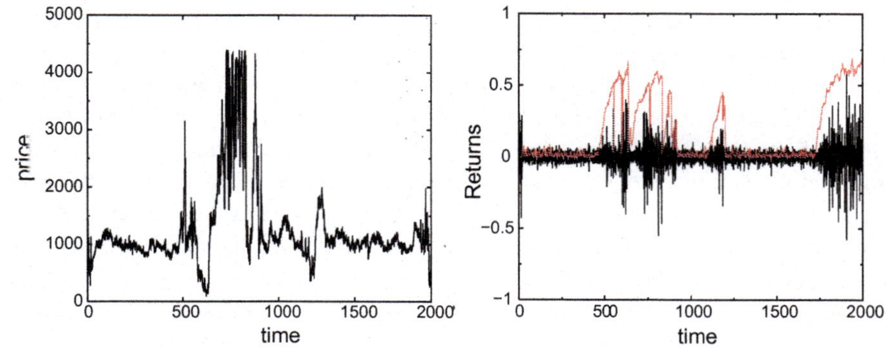

Fig. 3.2 *Left panel* price time series. *Right panel* return time series (*black solid line*) and percentage of guru in-coming link (*red dotted line*)

All our simulated results are compared with the main stylized facts of the financial time series via a descriptive output validation.[33]

3.7.1 Returns and Volatility

We first analyze the returns' statistical properties and the imitation network effect in generating them.

Figure 3.2 displays a sample path of price and return time series. As the left panel of Fig. 3.2 shows, the model is able to generate large excursions in prices. Further, we observe that price bubbles cause volatility in the returns' time series (see right side of Fig. 3.2). The reason lies in the communication network. Our fitness mechanism is able to generate phases of coordination in traders' strategies. In this case, traders are influenced by the behaviour of others, thus generating the well-known "herd behaviour". What can happen in such a case is that a trader considers the information/actions of others more decisive than his own and, thus, follows them. When, via Eq. 3.5, a good percentage of agents detects the most successful trader, called the guru, and imitates his strategy, then coordination emerges. The ability of the model in creating coordination is shown in the right side of Fig. 3.2 where the percentage of incoming link to the guru is displayed. Figure 3.2 shows that there are alternating periods of synchronization and desynchronization. Specifically, the model generates times when the guru is imitated by a large fraction of investors and

[33] As Tesfatsion (2013) points out in her website on the validation of ACE models, there are three different ways of validating computational models: (a) Descriptive output validation, which matches computationally generated output against already-acquired system data; (b) Input validation, which ensures that the structural conditions, institutional arrangements and behavioral dispositions incorporated into the model capture the salient aspects of the actual system; (c) Predictive output validation, which matches computationally generated output against yet-to-be-acquired system data.

periods when just few investors follow him. Furthermore, as the figure shows, there is a strong correlation between coordination, on the one hand, and price bubbles and volatility in the returns, on the other hand. In fact, the guru ability in attracting followers, endogenously generated via the fitness mechanism, creates "information cascade". Traders, seeing the guru becomes richer, think that he has some private information on future stock prices. They, therefore, follow his information although their expectations are different. This leads to the fulfillment of the guru expectation and, consequently, drives prices towards the guru expectation. An intuition of how the expectations feedback system (from guru to followers) works is as follows. If the guru has a pessimistic expectation about an asset, he will start to sell it frantically, driving down its price. A trader, who may want to buy the asset will update his expectations recognizing that in the near future the guru might become even more pessimistic and drive price down even further. The trader may eventually conclude that it is not convenient for him to buy now, but it is better to sell. Conversely, if the trader wants to sell an asset about which the guru has an optimistic expectation, that would drive the price up, he may decide not to sell but to buy. Thus convergence to the rational equilibrium price becomes unlikely. In fact, because of herding, prices can fluctuate significantly even when the fundamental price is stable.

We now investigate the statistical properties of simulated returns shown in the right panel of Fig. 3.2. Specifically, we want to prove that our model is able to reproduce the standard stylized facts emerging in financial markets (see Cont 2001). We begin by showing that the model reproduces some of the most important properties emerging in the returns' time series: returns have a leptokurtic and asymmetric distribution and display fat-tails. Leptokurtosis and fat-tails identify distributions where the mass of probability on the tails is higher than that present in the case of a Gaussian pdf. It is well documented that the unconditional distribution of returns displays a power-law, with a tail index which is finite, higher than two and less than five. A good proxy to quantify the deviation from the Normal distribution is the excess kurtosis. In line with the empirical analysis (see Cont 2001) the simulated returns exhibit an average excess kurtosis, over simulations, equal to 123.54 (st.dev. 4.73). Moreover, we analyze the rate of decay of probability mass in the tails of the distribution (i.e. the presence of fat-tails). Low values of the tail index correspond to relatively slow decay of probability mass in the tail and, in the context of financial returns, relatively high expected loss conditional on a return in the lower $\alpha\%$ tail of the distribution (see Galbraith and Zernov 2009). In stock markets, thus, the tail index is a measure of risk. A precise measure to estimate fat tails is provided by the Hill exponent (see Sect. 3.9). Our simulations generate value for the Hill exponent in the same range of the empirical analysis. Specifically, the average tail exponent, over simulations, approaches the value of 2.21 (st.dev 0.91). It is clear from the analysis that the introduction of a dynamic fitness mechanism in the model leads to fat tails. This is due to the fact that coordination endogenously increases and decreases over time generating transitions from relatively quite trading periods to more turbulent ones.

Another important stylized fact correlated to fat tails is the gain/loss asymmetry. Stock markets, where the returns' left tail is heavier than the right one, exhibit a higher likelihood of losses and, thus, a strong asymmetry (see Chap. 4 for details).

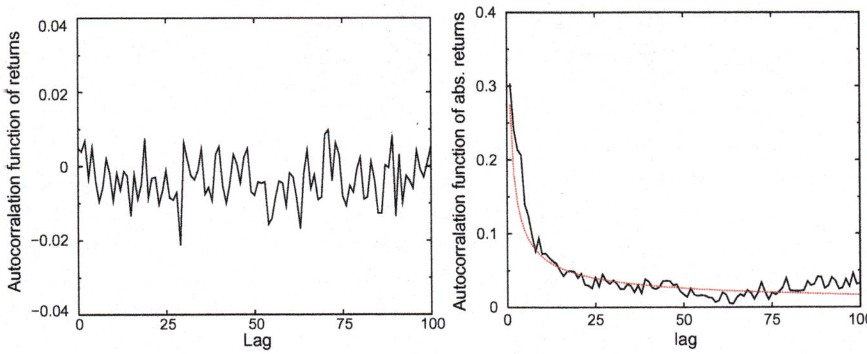

Fig. 3.3 *Left side* Autocorrelation of returns. *Right side* Autocorrelation of absolute returns and the power law best fit (*red line*)

This fact is detected by a negative skewness. In line with the empirical evidence, the average skewness, over simulations, of our simulated returns is -4.54 (st.dev -0.0044).

It is generally accepted in the study of financial time series that prices are not predictable. In line with the efficient market hypothesis and the no-arbitrage condition, it means that asset returns are often non-autocorrelated (see Malkiel and Fama 1970; Pagan 1996). To this end, Cont (2001) writes: "if price changes exhibit significant correlation, this correlation may be used to conceive a simple strategy with positive expected earnings; such strategies, termed statistical arbitrage, will therefore tend to reduce correlations except for very short time scales, which represent the time the market takes to react to new information". In the left panel of Fig. 3.3, we show the autocorrelation function of simulated returns, $C(\tau) = corr(r(t, \delta t), r(t + \tau, \delta t))$,[34] which rapidly decays to zero in a few lags. By contrast, as shown in the right panel of Fig. 3.3, the autocorrelation function of absolute returns remains positive over lags of several weeks and decays slowly to zero. This dependence on the prices' increment is the well-known phenomenon of volatility clustering (see, for instance, Ding et al. 1993). The positive autocorrelation of absolute returns, sometimes called persistence, implies some predictability for the amplitude of returns. As Mandelbrot (1963) notes "large changes tend to be followed by large changes, of either sign, and small changes tend to be followed by small changes". In this stylized market model, it is the dynamic fitness measure which generates clusters of volatility. Specifically, our traders, although fairly unsophisticated, exhibit a kind of herding behaviour. The endogenous attachment mechanism, in fact, is able to create, sustain, destroy and substitute the guru gradually, thus reproducing waves of coordination. On the one hand, during periods of coordination (i.e. of guru stability) traders group into larger dependent "communities", which place sequences of market orders in the same direction of the guru. In this circumstance, imitation creates price bubbles. On the other hand, during periods of no-coordination (i.e. of competition among agents in order

[34] corr is the sample correlation.

to become guru) investors act as noise traders and place trading orders randomly. In these periods price bubbles burst and the market moves to a quiet period. It is the transition from relatively quite trading period to more turbulent ones which creates volatility clustering.

An important issue in the statistical analysis of the returns' time series is determining whether the observations or a transformation of them have short or long memory. A short memory process has autocorrelation decaying to zero exponentially as the lag increases. In contrast, the autocorrelation of the long memory process decays to zero at a hyperbolic rate. Hyperbolic decay rates for the absolute value of asset returns were first shown by Taylor (2007) and are now well documented stylized facts of financial time series (see Ding et al. 1993; Granger and Ding 1994 and Ding and Granger 1996; Dacorogna et al. 1993, for evidence). Specifically, several authors (see Cont et al. 1997; Cont 1998; Liu et al. 1997) show that the autocorrelation function of absolute returns, by increasing the time lag τ, decreases like a power law $|C(\tau)| \sim \frac{A}{\tau^{\beta}}$ with $\beta \in [0.2, 0.4]$ and a positive constant called the tail or scale parameter. The slow decline of the power law shows the presence of long memory in the movements of absolute returns. Our simulated data are consistent with this empirical evidence. The autocorrelation function of absolute returns (see right panel of Fig. 3.3) is well fitted by a power law (dotted line) with $\beta = 0.29$.

A more precise measure of long term memory is provided by the modified R/S statistics (see Sect. 3.10). In the modified R/S analysis the parameter that allows to discriminate between short and long term memory is the exponent β.[35] If only short memory is present β converges to $1/2$ while with long memory, it converges to a value larger than $1/2$. The average modified R/S exponent β, over simulations, for simulated absolute returns becomes significantly larger that 0.5 (i.e. it is 0.82, with st.dev 0.21), proving, thus, that herding generates long memory.

3.7.2 Book and Order Flows

In this part of our study we investigate the correlation between price dynamics and "order book".

The order book is the list of all buy and sell limit orders, with their corresponding price and volume, at a given instant of time. When an order appears (say a buy order), it either adds to the book if it is below the ask price (we call these "limit orders"), or generates a trade at the ask if it is above (or equal to) the ask price (we call these "market orders"). The price dynamics is, therefore, the result of the interplay between the order book and the order flow. The study of the order book is very interesting from several points of view. Firstly, it provides intimate information on the processes of trading and price formation, and reveals not trivial details on the formation of agents' expectation. In this regards it is important to test some

[35]The β estimates the slope of the log of the Lo's modified R/S statistic versus the log of the sample size.

hypotheses on agents' bevaviour (i.e. microfoundations). Secondly, an auction market allows us to determinate the price through the trading mechanism itself, therefore without using ad-hoc pricing rules based on the equilibrium price, such as the supply-demand in-balance. In fact, the mechanism of price formation following the supply demand in-balance requires the presence of a market maker. If in the market there is a market maker there is no explicit mechanism of trading. The market maker is risk neutral and endowed with unbounded liquidity, which is used to absorb excess demand and makes trading always viable, regardless of its size. In each period, the market maker adjusts the price to reduce the excess demand. Inspired by the metaphor of the Walrasian tatonnement, this price-adjusting rule fails to recognize that, in a real market, trade occurs whenever two agents can match their requests at a given price. The supply demand in-balance approach shortcuts the study of the out-of-the-equilibrium price dynamics by jumping to the stationary points. An order driven, instead, enables us to understand how the economy behaves out of equilibrium.

The statistics of the order book has attracted considerable attention, both from an empirical (see Lillo and Farmer 2004; Potters and Bouchaud 2003) and theoretical (see LiCalzi and Pellizzari 2003; Chiarella et al. 2009) point of view. Specifically, empirical analysis has showed fat tails in the distribution of limit order arrivals (Bouchaud et al. 2002; Potters and Bouchaud 2003) and fat tail decay of order distribution in the limit order book. Moreover, some authors (see Gabaix et al. 2003) have also shown that fat tails in the distribution of returns emerge when large market orders arrive. We show that our model is capable of reproducing these stylized facts. The left panel of Fig. 3.4 displays the decumulative distribution function (DDF) of the limit order placement distance from the midpoint. We observe that herding drives limit orders away from the midpoint. Also the bid-ask spread, shown in the central panel of Fig. 3.4, increases with imitation. Specifically, both DDF are power-law, in agreement with the empirical observation that spread and volatility are positively correlated. These results are consistent with the empirical analyses of Potters and Bouchaud (2003) and Zovko et al. (2002).

We now study the correlation between fat-tailed fluctuations in asset prices and trading volume. Gabaix et al. (2003) show empirically that order submission typically results in a large price change when the order is large. Accordingly, power-law tails in

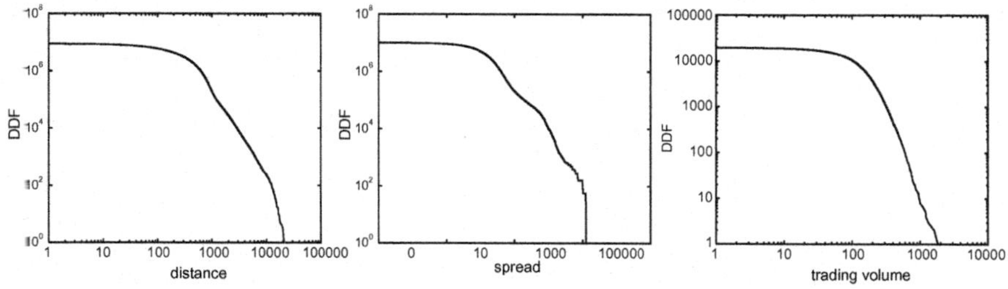

Fig. 3.4 *Left panel* DDF of limit order placement distance from the midpoint. *Central panel* DDF of bid-ask spread. *Right panel* DDF of trading volume

price fluctuation are driven by power-low fluctuations in the volume of transactions. The right hand side of Fig. 3.4 displays the DDF of the trading volume which is fat tailed, thus confirming the argument of Gabaix et al. (2003).

3.7.3 Discussion: The Network Analysis

To explain the above results we analyze the evolution of the imitation network. As already pointed out, it is the transition from coordination periods to non-coordination ones to generate price bubbles and volatility clustering. To better quantify this observation we need to investigate the network topology and its dynamics over time. Figure 3.5 shows one shot of the configuration of the endogenous network in different time horizons. The graphs show how the network architecture changes during the time. Specifically, we observe alternating periods: times when few gurus co-exist and compete for popularity, and times when a single leader emerges and the network becomes more and more centralized.

We now investigate some important statistical properties identifying the network topology. Specifically, the degree distribution (see left panel of Fig. 3.6) analyzes the level of traders' connectivity within network, as measured by their degree k. The degree is defined as the number of agents (in our model imitators) connected to each trader: $k_i = \sum_{j \in \Omega} l_{i,j}$, where Ω is the neighborhood if i and $l_{i,j}$ the number of links pointed to investor i. The left panel of Fig. 3.6 shows that the topology of our network is different from that of the random graph studied extensively by Erdős and Rényi (1960). While in an Erdos-Reny random graph the degree has a Binomial (or Poisson) distribution, in our network some agents have a disproportionately large number of links while others have very few. This characteristic allows us to classify the imitation network as scale-free whose degree distribution follows a power law. This is supported by the Kolmogorov–Smirnov test which does not reject the null hypothesis (K-S = 0.105, p-value = 0.71 and the exponent of the power law is 2.3).

The central panel of Fig. 3.6 displays the distribution of the intensity of choice, β_t, in Eq. (3.5). It is well documented (see Lenzu and Tedeschi 2012; Tedeschi et al. 2014; Grilli et al. 2014) that the network architecture crucially depends on the intensity of choice. This parameter shapes the network topology by amplifying the

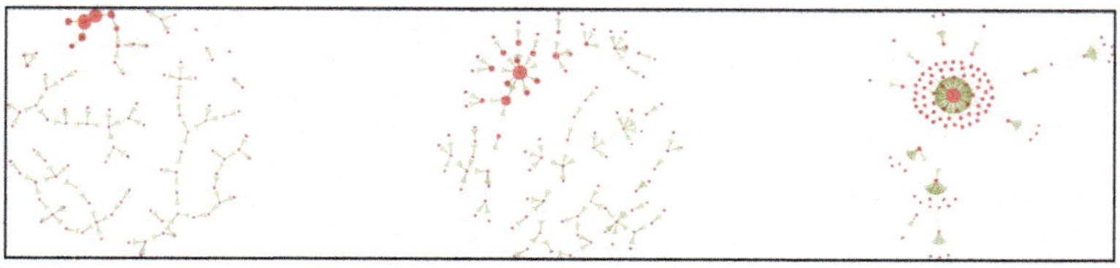

Fig. 3.5 Network configuration in different time. In the time step 939, traders 38 and 10 compete to become guru (*left side*). In the time step 973, trader 38 is the guru (*central side*). In the time step 1500, agent 26 is the new guru (*right side*)

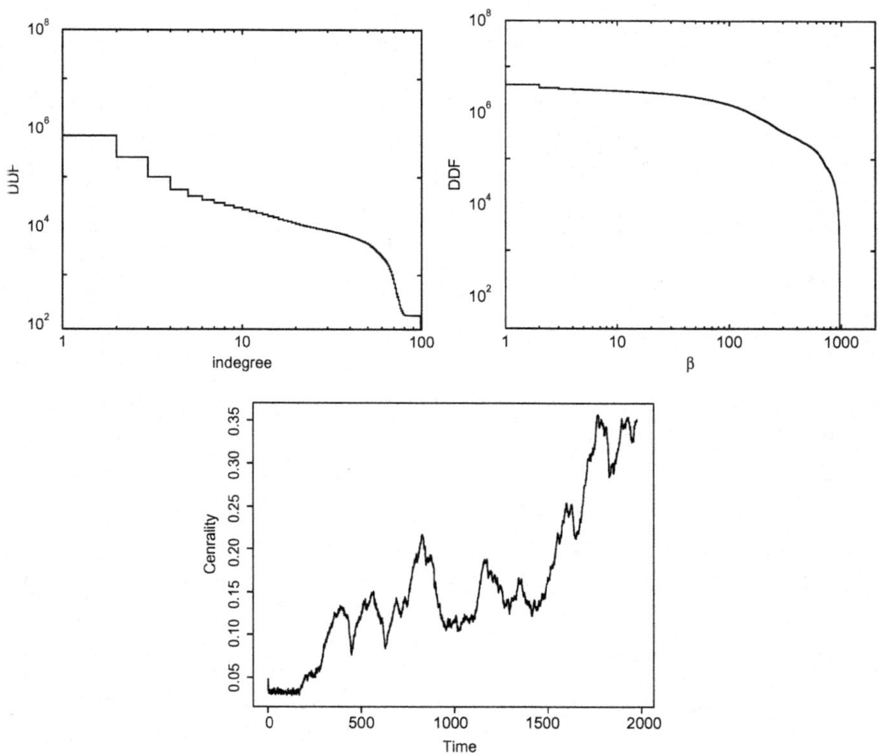

Fig. 3.6 The decumulative distribution (DDF) of the in-degree and of the intensity of choice β_t (*left* and *central panel*, respectively). Average network centrality over simulation (*right panel*)

signal on traders' attractiveness. Low values of β_t characterize random graphs with a Binomial (or Poisson) in-degree distribution, exponential and scale-free topologies emerge for intermediate values of the parameter while the market self-organizes into a pseudo-star for high values of β_t. The originality of this work respect to previous studies is in the endogenous evolution of the intensity of choice. While in the previous models, in fact, was the exogenous modification in the agent's trust on its neighbor's performance to self-organize linkages into very different network architectures, ranging from random to scale-free topologies, here we implement an endogenous feedback mechanism. Specifically, the intensity of choice, β_t, depends on the guru's life, which in turn is function of the guru fitness. Higher is the guru fitness higher his possibility of survive and, consequently, higher his intensity of choice. As Fig. 3.6 (central panel) shows this mechanism generates a heterogenous distribution in the time horizons of the guru life, which indicates an alternation of periods, ranging from stable times, in which the guru is stable and the network centralized, to unstable ones, in which traders compete and the network is decentralized. To better quantify this observation, the right panel of Fig. 3.6 shows the average degree

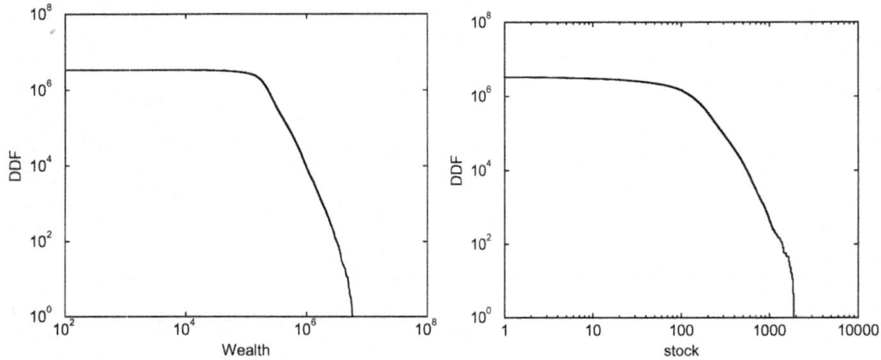

Fig. 3.7 The decumulative distribution (DDF) of the wealth (*left side*) and the decumulative distribution (DDF) of the stocks (*right side*)

network centrality[36] which identifies the most important agents within the network. As already anticipated, the figure shows transition phenomena in which the network switches from decentralized periods where traders act independently to centralized ones where investors coordinate their expectations.

Although traders, in our model, initially start with the same amount of stock and cash, herding generates a fat tail distribution in individuals' wealth and stocks (see Fig. 3.7), in accordance with the empirical evidence that market participants are very heterogeneous in size (see, for example, Pareto 1897b; Zipf 1949; Ijiri and Simon 1977; Axtell 2001; Pushkin and Aref 2004; Gabaix et al. 2006). Moreover, in contrast with the prevailing economic view that informed agents need to hide their private informations in order to profit from it (see Benabou and Laroque 1992; Caldentey and Stacchetti 2007; Chakraborty and Yilmaz 2008), our uninformed gurus gain the highest profits when they reveal their expectations to the highest number of followers. Furthermore, we also show that followers, on average, gain higher profit than non followers, thus providing a justification for herding to occur. Specifically, the average wealth, over time and simulation, of the guru, of the followers and of the non-followers is 598280 (st.dev 5629), 36637 (st.dev 2543) and 2563 (st.dev 1067) respectively.

Next we explain the mechanism driving the evolution of the imitation network and its impact on prices. As already stressed, traders start with the same amount of wealth. However, as time goes by, a trader may become richer than others. Thanks to the fitness measure, this investor enlarges his number of followers and consequently his wealth. Let us assume, for example, that the guru expects the price to rise and, therefore, decides to buy at a price of 10. If the guru is able to place a market order and his followers imitate his strategy, the price increases. Consequently, the guru who had bought at the price of 10, now holds a share whose value is, for example, 15.

[36] Several different measures of centrality exist, such as degree, closeness, betweenness and eigenvector centrality (see Newman (2003)). Readers can find a detailed discussion of network properties applied to economic system in Bargigli and Tedeschi (2014).

This, clearly, increases the guru wealth and via Eq. 3.4 his number of imitators. The increased wealth of the guru, furthermore, increases the likelihood that he remains the guru in the aftermath. This, in turn, increases the intensity of choice, β_t, which farther strengthens the guru fitness and his chances to persist over time. The mechanism of the guru replacement is also very simple. On the one hand, it can happen that the guru places a limit order which is not immediately executable. In this circumstance, one of his followers may be able to exploit the guru strategy and places a market order, thus increasing its wealth at the expense of the Guru. This will decrease the guru fitness and perhaps will determine his replacement. On the other hand, it can happen that, even if the guru places a market order the size of his order is less than the size of imitators. This increases the wealth of the guru but by an amount less than that of the imitator, thus generating a replacement dynamics similar to that described above.

In order to analyze the competition and replacement dynamics driving the "guru life cycle", we run one Monte Carlo simulation of $T = 10000$ periods.

In the top panel[37] of Fig. 3.8 we plot the index of the current guru (black solid line), the percentage of incoming links to the current guru (red dotted line) and the fitness of the current guru (green dashed line). The figure shows that agents alternate as the guru during the simulation (black solid line). In fact, as the guru acquires an increasing number of links (red dotted line), one or more of his followers may become richer than the guru himself, as signaled by the fact that the fitness (green dashed line) of the guru becomes, at times, smaller than 1. As other agents become rich they start to be imitated more and more and eventually one of them becomes the new guru.

We now investigate the correlation between the network dynamics and the return time series. As the bottom panel of Fig. 3.8 shows there is a strong co-movement between volatility clustering (black solid line) and indegree (red dotted line). As already stressed is the mechanism of creation, destruction and replacement of the guru to generate stock return volatility. Moreover, the figure shows the correlation between the life of the guru, the in-degree and the intensity of choice (green dashed line): longest the life of the guru, the greater the number of his imitators, the higher the parameter β_t. By dividing the time series plotted in Fig. 3.8 in two subsets, that is times of coordination in which the guru is stable (i.e. the index of current guru is a continuous line) and periods of non- coordination in which the guru is unstable (i.e. the index of current guru is a fragmented line) we can better quantify the co-movement between the "guru evolution" and the returns' time series. Specifically, we observe that the moments of the return time series associated to coordination periods are far away from those observed in the Normal distribution, while those associated to non-coordination periods better approach the Gaussian distribution (see Table 3.3).

[37]The figure has been divided in two sub-graph in order to be clearer.

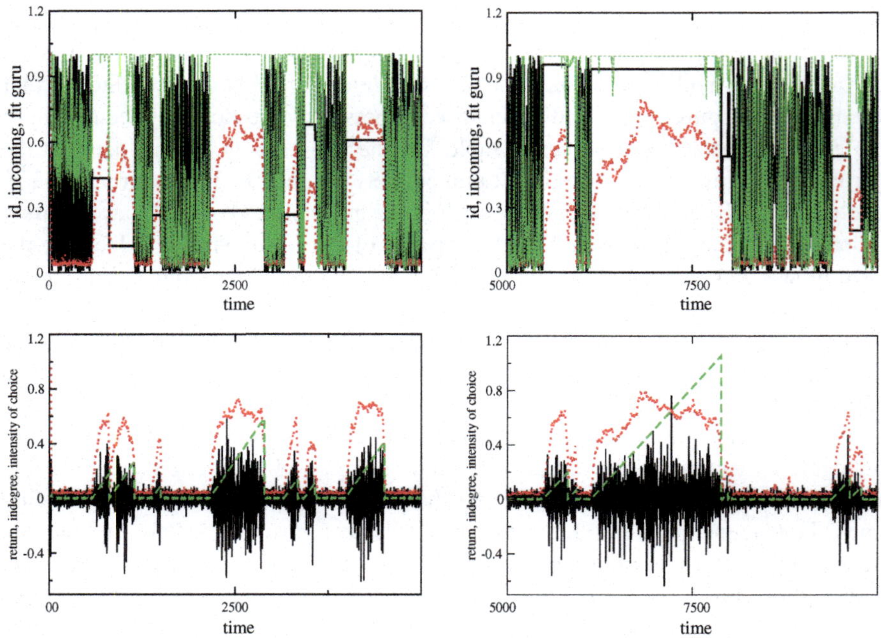

Fig. 3.8 *Top panel* The index of current guru (*black solid line*), the percentage of incoming link to current guru (*red dotted line*) and fitness of current guru (*green dashed line*). *Bottom panel* return time series (*black solid line*), the percentage of incoming link to current guru (*red dotted line*) and the intensity of choice β_t (*green dashed line*)

Table 3.3 Moments of returns in coordination and non-coordination periods

	Mean	Median	Min.	Max.	Skewness	Ex. Kurtosi
Coordination	$-5.57e^{-07}$	0.0	−0.63	0.76	−3.18	796.73
Non-coordination	$1.57e^{-07}$	0.0	−0.12	0.12	−0.14	2.86

3.8 Exercises

Exercise 1

As explained in the session Sect. 3.2.2 "The communication network", the agent i, which is a noise trader, forms its expected returns according to $r^i_{t_k,t_k+T} = \sigma^i_{t_k}\epsilon_{t_k}$. Agent expectation is then revised *via* an imitation mechanism such that the trader completely imitates the opinion of its neighbour j. How should you change the formula in case of a partial imitation? Specifically, what happen if the investor i assigns a weight equal to 0.5 to the expectation of j?

What is the consequence of the decreasing imitation on the simulated return time series?

Repeat the analysis by considering the case of non-imitation. What happen to volatility clustering? Why?

Exercise 2
Equation 3.5 introduces a certain amount of randomness. What happens if we rewrite the algorithm in a deterministic way? Specifically what happens to the guru life, its incoming links and fitness?

Exercise 3
Equation 3.5 implies an endogenous intensity of choice β. Let us assume that the β parameter is exogenous, for instance uniform between 0 and 100, what happen to the network topology, i.e. to the in degree distribution? What is the effect on the return time series?

Exercise 4
What happens if we change the network topology? Specifically, if we implement a random communication network, Erdos Reni, with a probability of attachment equals to 1, what happens to the returns' time series? Moreover, what happen if you decrease the probability of attachment of the random network to the volatility?

3.9 Appendix: Hill Estimator

We want to quantify the fat tail of our distribution of returns. What we do is to estimate the Hill tail index. The Hill estimator is a maximum likelihood estimator of the parameter α of the Pareto law $F(x) \sim 1/x^{\alpha}$ for large x. Because of its simplicity it has become the standard tool in most studies of tail behaviour of economic data.

To compute the Hill tail index, the sample elements are put in descending order: $x_n \geq x_{n-1} \geq \cdots \geq x_{n-k} \geq \cdots \geq x_1$ where n is the length of our data sample and k is precisely the number of observations located in the tail of our distribution. Hence, the Hill estimate obtains the inverse of α as follows:

$$\hat{\gamma}_H(n,k) = 1/\hat{\alpha}_H(n,k) = \frac{1}{k}\sum_{i=1}^{k}\left[\ln x_{n-i+1} - \ln x_{n-k}\right]. \tag{3.6}$$

The main difficulty of this procedure is to choose the optimal threshold $k^{\star}$. If we take a small k we have few statistics while if we include a large data set inside the tail the estimator increases because of a contamination with entries from more central parts of the distribution. There are many techniques aiming to find this optimal cut-off (see for instance Lux and Marchesi 2000). All of them agree that the optimal $k^{\star}$ is defined as the number of order statistics minimizing the mean squared error of $\hat{\gamma}_H(n,k)$. However, the optimal sample fraction is not easy to infer from this assertment and one of the more usual ways to perform the estimation in the literature is by a bootstrapping technique (see for instance Lux and Marchesi 2000).

In our case, we have evaluated the Hill tail index for a fixed threshold taking 5 % of the data. Perhaps, we do not get the optimal cut-off but in any case we give a reasonable one. We have done it for estimating the right and the left tails exponent of the return but also with the absolute return time series.

The estimated tail index $\hat{\gamma} = 1/\hat{\alpha}$ is obtained for every simulation we ran. It can be shown that $(\hat{\gamma} - \gamma)\sqrt{k}$ is asymptotically normal with zero mean and variance γ^2 where $\gamma = 1/\alpha$ (Lux and Marchesi 2000). The confidence level of being inside the interval of one unit of mean squared error is 67 %, being inside the interval of two units of mean squared error is 95 %, and being inside the interval of three units of mean squared error is 99.7 %.

All these properties will allow us to give the error of our measurement and its degree of confidence. The output of our simulations is now giving the average of the Hill tail index over all the path simulations and its standard deviation. The estimation should converge to the "true" Hill tail index in accordance to the Central Limit Theorem. Hence,

$$\langle \hat{\gamma} \rangle = \frac{1}{N} \sum_{i=1}^{N} \hat{\gamma}_i \rightarrow \gamma \qquad \text{as number of simulations is increasing,} \tag{3.7}$$

$$\sigma_\gamma^2 = \frac{1}{N(N-1)} \sum_{i=1}^{N} \left(\hat{\gamma}_i - \langle \hat{\gamma} \rangle\right)^2, \tag{3.8}$$

where N is the total number of simulations and i is the label of each simulation. So that, our result is

$$\langle \hat{\gamma} \rangle \pm \frac{\sigma_\gamma}{\sqrt{N}} \tag{3.9}$$

and if one wants to derive the tail index this reads

$$\frac{1}{\langle \hat{\gamma} \rangle} \pm \frac{\sigma_\gamma}{\langle \hat{\gamma} \rangle^2 \sqrt{N}}. \tag{3.10}$$

3.10 Appendix: Modified R/S and Long Memory

The importance of long range dependence in asset markets was first studied by Mandelbrot (1963), who proposed using the range over standard deviation, or R/S statistic to detect long range dependence in economic time series. Lo (1991) has gone a bit further in this statistical measure in order to distinguish between short-range and long-range dependence. To do so, Lo proposed the modified R/S statistic

$$Q_n = \frac{1}{\hat{\sigma}_n(q)} \left[\max_{1 \le k \le n} \sum_{j=1}^{k} (X_j - \bar{X}_n) - \min_{1 \le k \le n} \sum_{j=1}^{k} (X_j - \bar{X}_n) \right], \tag{3.11}$$

where

$$\hat{\sigma}_n^2(q) = \hat{\sigma}_x^2 + 2 \sum_{j=1}^{q} \omega_j(q) \hat{\gamma}_j, \tag{3.12}$$

with

$$\hat{\sigma}_x^2 = \frac{1}{n} \sum_{j=1}^{n} (X_j - \bar{X}_n)^2 \tag{3.13}$$

$$\hat{\gamma}_j = \frac{1}{n} \sum_{i=j+1}^{n} (X_i - \bar{X}_n)(X_{i-j} - \bar{X}_n) \tag{3.14}$$

and

$$\omega_j(q) = 1 - \frac{j}{q+1}, \qquad q < n. \tag{3.15}$$

The term $\bar{X}_n$ appearing in Eqs. (3.11), (3.13) and (3.14) is the sample mean $(1/n) \sum_{j=1}^{n} X_j$. Also note that $\hat{\sigma}_x^2$ and $\hat{\gamma}_j$ are the usual sample of variance and autocovariance estimators of X. The original estimator is recovered setting $q = 0$. Introducing a $q > 0$ the modified Lo estimator allows to subtract the effects of short range correlations up to the level q and thus focuses on long memory effects in the data.

Chapter 4
Heavy-Tailed Distributions for Agent-Based Economic Modelling

Fabio Clementi

4.1 Introduction

This chapter is devoted to the parametric statistical distributions of economic size phenomena of various types.

Probability distributions of size variables are usually taken as the first quantitative characterization of complex systems, allowing one to detect the possible occurrence of regularities and to identify the underlying mechanisms at their origin—and thus at the origin of the behaviour of the complex system under study.

A rapid survey covers the class of "heavy-tailed" distributions decreasing slower than exponentially at infinity. The fascination for "power laws" is then explained, starting from the statistical approaches for quantifying and testing a power-law distribution from your data, and ending with a (not exhaustive) list of mechanisms leading to power-law distributions. The description of distributions is ultimately enlarged by proposing the Laplace distribution, which has both tails—the upper and the lower—heavier than a standard Gaussian.

Exposition is conveyed by means of computer-based examples designed to assist the reader in understanding of the broad topics that are touched on in other parts of this book. Full code for examples using the R software environment (R Core Team 2015) can be found on the book's website.

Here are some notations and vocabulary that will be useful in the remainder of the chapter.

- *Probability density function*. Consider a random variable X whose outcome is a real number x. The probability density function (PDF) of X, $p(x)$, is such that the probability that X is found in a small interval Δ around x is $p(x)\,\Delta$. The

F. Clementi (✉)
Dipartimento di Scienze politiche, della comunicazione e delle relazioni internazionali, Università di Macerata, Piazza Strambi 1, 62100 Macerata, Italy
e-mail: fabio.clementi@unimc.it

A. Caiani et al. (eds.), *Economics with Heterogeneous Interacting Agents*, New Economic Windows, DOI 10.1007/978-3-319-44058-3_4

probability that X is between x and $x + \Delta$ is therefore given by the integral of $p(x)$ between x and $x + \Delta$, that is

$$p(x) = \lim_{\Delta \to 0^+} \frac{\Pr(x \leq X < x + \Delta)}{\Delta} = \int_x^{x+\Delta} p(x)\,\mathrm{d}x. \tag{4.1}$$

The PDF $p(x)$ depends on the measurement unit used to quantify x and has the dimension of the inverse of x, such that $p(x)\,\Delta$—being a probability, i.e. a number between 0 and 1—is dimensionless. The empirical estimation of the PDF $p(x)$ is usually plotted with the horizontal axis scaled as a graded series for the variable under consideration and the vertical axis scaled for the values of $p(x)$.

- *Cumulative distribution function*. In many cases it is useful to consider the cumulative distribution function (CDF) of X, $P_{\leq}(x)$, defined by

$$P_{\leq}(x) = \Pr(X \leq x) = \int_{-\infty}^{x} p(y)\,\mathrm{d}y. \tag{4.2}$$

The CDF $P_{\leq}(x)$ gives the fraction of events with values less than (or equal) to x and increases monotonically with x from 0 to 1.

- *Complementary cumulative distribution function*. This is defined by

$$P_{>}(x) = \Pr(X > x) = 1 - \Pr(X \leq x) = \int_{x}^{\infty} p(y)\,\mathrm{d}y. \tag{4.3}$$

The complementary cumulative distribution function (CCDF) gives the fraction of events with values greater than x and decreases monotonically with x from 1 to 0.

4.2 Heavy-Tailed Distributions

Heavy-tailed distributions are probability distributions whose tails decay to 0 far slower than exponentially. In many applications it is the right tail of the distribution that is of interest, but a distribution may have a heavy left tail or both of its tails might be heavy.

The exponential distribution given by the PDF

$$p(x) = \lambda e^{-\lambda x}, \quad x \geq 0, \quad \lambda > 0, \tag{4.4}$$

is often considered as the boundary between classes of heavy-tailed and light-tailed distributions—although occasionally the term "heavy-tailed" is used for any distribu-

Table 4.1 Examples of heavy- and light-tailed distributions

Heavy-tailed	Lognormal, Weibull with exponent less than 1, power laws (with regularly varying tails)
Light-tailed	Exponential, Gaussian, Weibull with exponent greater than 1

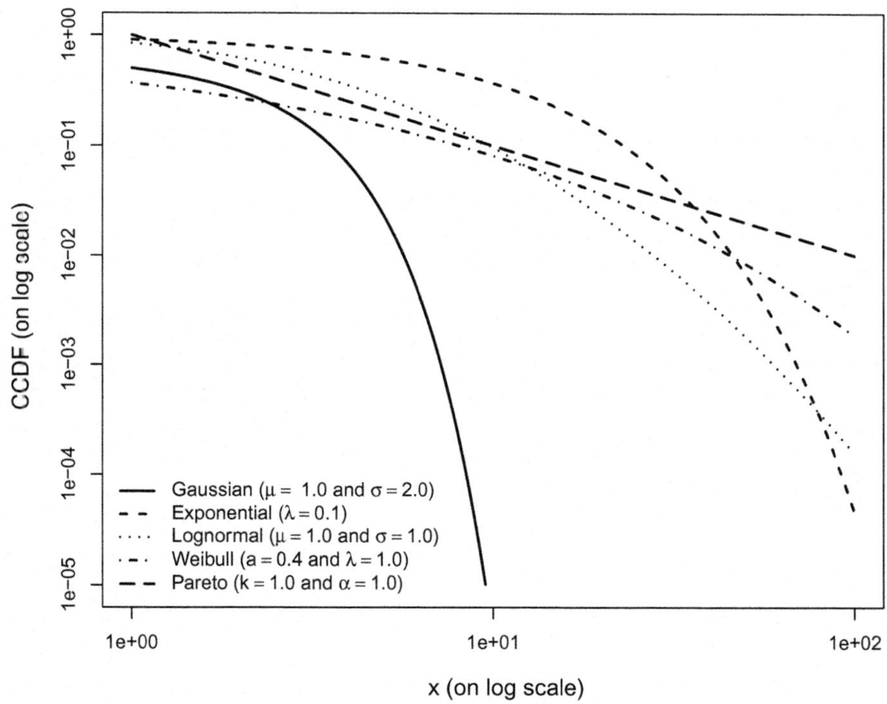

Fig. 4.1 Heavy- and light-tailed distributions: comparison of right tail behaviour

tion that has heavier tails than the Gaussian distribution. Typical examples of heavy- and light-tailed distributions are given in Table 4.1. Their (right) tail behaviour is compared in Fig. 4.1.

The class of heavy-tailed distributions comprises, among others, the subset of distributions with *regularly varying* tails (Bingham et al. 1987). Intuitively, a "regularly varying" distribution of a real variable is a distribution whose behaviour near infinity is similar to the behaviour of a power-law function. Regularly varying distributions (also commonly referred to as "fat-tailed" distributions) are always heavy-tailed. Some distributions, however, have a tail which goes to zero slower than an exponential function (meaning they are heavy-tailed) but faster than a power (meaning they are not fat-tailed). An example is the lognormal distribution. Many other heavy-tailed distributions—*in primis* the power-law distributions—are, instead, also fat-tailed.

For light-tailed distributions and distributions with no regularly varying heavy tails, all moments exist and are finite. In contrast, for regularly varying distributions the moments exist only up to (and excluding) their tail indices.

Some more details about specific examples of heavy-tailed distributions are given in the following list.

- The *lognormal distribution*. This is given by the PDF

$$p(x) = \frac{1}{x\sigma\sqrt{2\pi}} e^{-\frac{[\ln(x)-\mu]^2}{2\sigma^2}}, \quad x > 0, \tag{4.5}$$

  for parameters $\mu \in \mathbb{R}$ and $\sigma > 0$. All moments of the lognormal distribution are finite. The obvious advantage of the lognormal distribution is that, following a simple transformation, the enormous armature of inference for Gaussian distributions is readily available: indeed, a (positive) random variable X has a lognormal distribution with parameters μ and σ if and only if $\ln(X)$ has a Gaussian distribution with mean μ and variance σ^2. Hence, by taking the logarithm of the data points, the techniques developed for the Gaussian distribution can be used to estimate the parameters of the lognormal distribution. In particular, the location parameter μ is equal to the mean of the logarithm of the data points, and the shape parameter σ is equal to the standard deviation of the data set after transformation. The lognormal distribution has been widely used in many applications.[1]
- The *Weibull distribution*. It has the PDF

$$p(x) = a\lambda x^{a-1} e^{-\lambda x^a}, \quad x \geq 0, \tag{4.6}$$

  where $a, \lambda > 0$. The exponent a controls the thin versus heavy nature of the right tail; in particular:

  - for $a = 2$, the Weibull distribution has the same asymptotic right tail as the Gaussian distribution;
  - for $a = 1$, expression (4.6) recovers the pure exponential distribution;
  - for $a < 1$, the right tail of the Weibull is fatter than an exponential.

  Hence, the Weibull is a versatile distribution "interpolating" between thin-tailed distributions—such as the Gaussian or the exponential—when $a \geq 1$ and heavy-tailed distributions if (and only if) $a < 1$. Although there are many ways to estimate

[1] In the economic field, for example, Gibrat (1931) observed that the size distribution of French manufacturing establishments closely resembled the lognormal distribution. This led him to suggest a "law of proportionate effect" (see Sect. 4.3.5.1). Later, Aitchison and Brown (1954, 1957) argued that the lognormal hypothesis is particularly appropriate for the distribution of incomes, although much depends on the definition of income and the particular part of the distribution in which one happens to be interested—indeed, the above-cited authors consider the lognormal functional form most appropriate for modelling the distribution of earnings in fairly homogeneous sections of the workforce, but when examining the distribution of income from all sources they find in many instances that lognormality remains a reasonable assumption for the bulk of the incomes, whereas the upper tail appears to be governed by a different probabilistic law.

Table 4.2 Statistical distributions mentioned in this chapter. For each distribution we give the basic functional form of the probability density/mass function, $p(x)$, the cumulative distribution function, $P_{\leq}(x)$, and the raw moment, $\langle X^r \rangle$

Distribution		$p(x)$	$P_{\leq}(x)$	$\langle X^r \rangle$
Continuous	Gaussian[a]	$\frac{1}{\sigma\sqrt{2\pi}} e^{-\frac{(x-\mu)^2}{2\sigma^2}}$, $x \in \mathbb{R}, \quad \mu \in \mathbb{R}, \quad \sigma > 0$	$\frac{1}{2}\left[1 + \text{erf}\left(\frac{x-\mu}{\sigma\sqrt{2}}\right)\right]$	$\frac{1}{\sqrt{\pi}} \int_{-\infty}^{\infty} x^r e^{-u^2}\, \mathrm{d}u$, $r \geq 0$
	Exponential[b]	$\lambda e^{-\lambda x}, x \geq 0, \quad \lambda > 0$	$1 - e^{-\lambda x}$	$\frac{\Gamma(r+1)}{\lambda^r}, r \geq 0$
	Lognormal[a]	$\frac{1}{x\sigma\sqrt{2\pi}} e^{-\frac{[\ln(x)-\mu]^2}{2\sigma^2}}$, $x > 0, \quad \mu \in \mathbb{R}, \quad \sigma > 0$	$\frac{1}{2}\left\{1 + \text{erf}\left[\frac{\ln(x)-\mu}{\sigma\sqrt{2}}\right]\right\}$	$e^{r\mu + \frac{r^2\sigma^2}{2}}, r \geq 0$
	Weibull[b]	$a\lambda x^{a-1} e^{-\lambda x^a}$ $x \geq 0, \quad a > 0, \quad \lambda > 0$	$1 - e^{-\lambda x^a}$	$\lambda^{-\frac{r}{a}} \Gamma\left(1 + \frac{r}{a}\right), r \geq 0$
	Pareto	$\frac{\alpha k^\alpha}{x^{\alpha+1}}, x \geq k, \quad k, \alpha > 0$	$1 - \left(\frac{x}{k}\right)^{-\alpha}$	$\frac{\alpha k^r}{\alpha - r}, r < \alpha$
	Laplace[c]	$\frac{1}{2\lambda} e^{-\frac{\lvert x-\theta \rvert}{\lambda}}$, $x \in \mathbb{R}, \quad \theta \in \mathbb{R}, \quad \lambda > 0$	$x \leq \theta : \frac{1}{2} e^{-\frac{\lvert x-\theta \rvert}{\lambda}}$ $x \geq \theta : 1 - \frac{1}{2} e^{-\frac{\lvert x-\theta \rvert}{\lambda}}$	$r! \sum_{j=0}^{r} \frac{1+(-1)^{j+r}}{2j!} \theta^j \lambda^{r-j}$, $r \geq 0$
Discrete	Zipf[d]	$\frac{x^{-s}}{\zeta(s)}, x \in \mathbb{Z}_{>0}, \quad s > 1$	$\frac{H_{x,s}}{\zeta(s)}$	$\frac{\zeta(s-r)}{\zeta(s)}, r < s - 1$

[a] erf $(\cdot)$ denotes the *error function* (http://mathworld.wolfram.com/Erf.html)
[b] $\Gamma(\cdot)$ denotes the *gamma function* (http://mathworld.wolfram.com/GammaFunction.html)
[c] $r!$ denotes the *factorial* of the non-negative integer r, defined as $r! \equiv r \times (r-1) \times \cdots \times 2 \times 1$ (http://mathworld.wolfram.com/Factorial.html)
[d] $H_{x,s}$ is a *generalized harmonic number* (http://mathworld.wolfram.com/HarmonicNumber.html); $\zeta(\cdot)$ is the *Riemann zeta function* (http://mathworld.wolfram.com/RiemannZetaFunction.html)

the parameters a and λ based on a random sample $X = (x_1, \ldots, x_n)$, maximum likelihood estimation is generally the most popular method. However, the maximum likelihood estimators of the Weibull parameters are not available in closed form, which implies that no explicit solution to the likelihood equations exists and numerical methods have to be used. In contrast, notwithstanding its heavy-tailed nature, the Weibull distribution has all its moments finite.[2]

- The *power-law distributions*. These are the canonical example of heavy-tailed distributions. Power-law distributions occur in many areas of scientific interest, including economic analysis, and their identification in empirical data is often interpreted as evidence for (or suggestion of) complex underlying processes. Although power law-distributions are attractive for their simplicity—they are straight lines on log-log plots—a technical difficulty is that not all moments exist for these distributions, which means, among other things, that the central limit theorem can no

[2] The Weibull distribution has received maximum attention in the engineering literature. In physics, it is known as the "stretched exponential distribution". In the economic literature the Weibull is probably less prominent, but D'Addario (1974) noticed its potential for income data—although it has been used only sporadically as an income distribution (some applications can be found in Bartels and van Metelen 1975; Bartels 1977; Espinguet and Terraza 1983; McDonald 1984; Atoda et al. 1988; Bordley et al. 1996; Brachmann et al. 1996; Tachibanaki et al. 1997). The Weibull has also been used by Di Guilmi et al. (2004, 2005) to study the empirical distribution of business cycle phases, that is of expansions and contractions. The authors find that in both cases the best fitting distribution is Weibull, although the parameters identifying the Weibull fitting models differ between upturn and downturn episodes.

longer hold. Also, demonstrating that data do indeed follow a power-law distribution is not as straightforward as it might appear, as it involves more than simply fitting. Indeed, several alternative functional forms can appear to follow a power-law form over some extent, such as the above-mentioned lognormal and Weibull distributions. Thus, validating a power-law distribution as a possible adequate representation of a given data set requires more sophisticated statistics. For these reasons, in the following section we shall review the basic definitions and properties of power-law distributions as well as the commonly used statistical methods for discerning and quantifying them in empirical data. We shall also focus on some of the underlying generative models that lead to these distributions.

Table 4.2 summarizes the basic properties for the above-listed distributions and other parametric models that will be touched upon later on.

4.3 Power-Law Distributions

A first goal of research on economic complexity has been the determination of the ways in which complex systems represent an alternative to standard (neoclassical) economic theory. At the same time, economic complexity has from its inception been strongly motivated by the desire to explain empirical phenomena.

One of the main areas of work on the complexity/empirical interface consists of the identification of data patterns that conform with the features of complex systems (Durlauf 2005). Specifically, a major effort of this work has been devoted to detect where *power laws*, which represent a particular class of probability distributions, occur in various economic data (Brock 1999).

The power-law literature has identified a number of interesting statistical properties of different economic data and has made a valuable contribution in identifying a range of "facts" that should help constrain theoretical modelling, such as the presence of skewed and thick tailed densities in data that points toward the existence of pervasive heterogeneity over individual agents. The attempt to identify the presence of such statistical properties in economic data has to a substantial extent led by physicists, whose attention was primarily focused on analysis of financial markets because of the large quantities of data available at high frequencies.[3] However, power laws have also fascinated economists of successive generations, due to their occurrence in varied economic contexts such as income and wealth, the size of cities and firms, stock market returns, trading volume, international trade and executive pay.[4]

[3] Indeed, starting in the mid-1990s a new field of research has emerged within the physics community that has come to be known as "econophysics", where a major research activity is represented by efforts to find power laws in different socio-economic data sets. This literature is well surveyed by Săvoiu and Simăn (2013).

[4] See Gabaix (2009) for a survey of various power laws both within and outside economics.

Power laws have both practical importance and theoretical implications for economic research. For instance, a central argument maintained by Gabaix (2011) is that in an economy with fat-tailed distributions of agents' characteristics individual shocks do not die out in the aggregate, but create an amount of volatility that can be held responsible for a large part of macroeconomic fluctuations. This contrasts with existing research, which has focused on using economy-wide shocks to explain fluctuations of economic aggregates, arguing by the central limit theorem that shocks at the micro-level average out in the aggregate.

Roughly, the *central limit theorem* (*CLT*) states that the mean of n independent and identically distributed (i.i.d.) terms with a finite variance converges to a Gaussian distribution for an asymptotically large value of n regardless of the original distribution (e.g. Feller 1971). To be more precise, let $X_1, \ldots, X_n$ be a sequence of i.i.d. random variables with mean μ and variance σ^2. The CLT states that the distribution of the centred and normalized mean will have the standard Gaussian shape with zero mean and unit variance as n goes to infinity, that is

$$\frac{\bar{X}_n - \mu}{\sigma/\sqrt{n}} \xrightarrow{d} N(0, 1), \tag{4.7}$$

where $\bar{X}_n = (X_1 + \cdots + X_n)/n$ and $\xrightarrow{d}$ denotes convergence in distribution. Hence, in an economy where n agents have independent shocks, aggregate fluctuations should have a size proportional to $n^{-\frac{1}{2}}$. Given that modern economies can have millions of agents, this suggests that micro-level fluctuations will have a negligible aggregate effect if the fundamental hypotheses of the CLT are verified, i.e. if both independence and finite variance conditions of the n random variables X_i are satisfied as aggregate volatility decays according to $n^{-\frac{1}{2}}$.

When agents' characteristics are power-law distributed, however, the finite variance assumption cannot always be achieved and the main conditions under which the CLT holds are not satisfied. Therefore, other existing limit theorems must be considered when fat-tailedness makes the classical CLT break down. Lévy (1954) discovered that, in addition to the Gaussian law, there is a rich class of probability distributions allowing for fat tails and sharing the convergence condition. Accordingly, a less well-known version of the CLT, the *generalized central limit theorem* (*GCLT*), shows that if the finite variance assumption is dropped, the only possible resulting limit is a "Lévy α-stable law" (Nolan 2015). To be more rigorous, suppose $X_1, \ldots, X_n$ is a sequence of non-negative i.i.d. random variables having power-law tails with exponent $1 < \alpha \leq 2$ (implying finite mean but infinite variance). Then, as $n \to +\infty$,

$$\frac{\bar{X}_n - \mu}{a_n} \xrightarrow{d} L_\alpha(1, \beta, 0), \tag{4.8}$$

where the normalizing coefficient can be taken as $a_n \propto n^{-\left(1-\frac{1}{\alpha}\right)}$ (Uchaikin and Zolotarev 1999, p. 62). In the equation above, $L_\alpha(1, \beta, 0)$ is the four-parameter Lévy α-stable distribution with location parameter $\delta \in \mathbb{R}$ equal to zero and scale parameter $\gamma > 0$ equal to 1. $\beta \in [-1, 1]$ is the skewness parameter quantifying the asymmetry of the distribution, which is symmetric around zero when $\beta = 0$. The exponent $\alpha \in (0, 2]$, a.k.a. the index of stability, determines the rate at which the tails of the distribution taper off. The GCLT (4.8) applies under the same restrictions (except for the finiteness of the variance when $\alpha > 2$) of independence and of large n, but an important difference is observed between the Gaussian and stable non-Gaussian attractors: as $n \to +\infty$, the Gaussian law "attracts" all the probability density functions decaying as $|x|^{-\alpha}$ at large $|x|$ for $\alpha \geq 2$; similarly, as n gets large, all probability density functions whose tails decay according to a power law with exponent $\alpha < 2$ are attracted to the Lévy law. Therefore, there is an abrupt change in the tail behaviour of Lévy α-stable laws at the borderline case with exponent $\alpha = 2$: while for $\alpha < 2$ all the Lévy distributions are heavy-tailed, the case $\alpha = 2$ is special and represents the familiar, not heavy-tailed, Gaussian distribution $L_2(1, 0, 0) = N(0, 1)$, and the classical CLT (4.7) is recovered with the replacement $\alpha = 2$ in Eq. (4.8).

By the above reasoning, the fat-tailed (power-law) nature of individual-level shocks is important theoretically, as it determines whether the classical CLT applies. Indeed, Eq. (4.7) states that if the distribution of agents' characteristics has thin tails, then aggregate volatility decays according to $n^{-\frac{1}{2}}$. In contrast, Eq. (4.8) states that if the agents' characteristics distribution has fat tails ($\alpha < 2$), then aggregate volatility decays much more slowly than $n^{-\frac{1}{2}}$: it decays as $n^{-\left(1-\frac{1}{\alpha}\right)}$. Hence, purely microeconomic shocks do not die out in the aggregate, but have a rather concrete possibility to propagate throughout the economy so as to generate non-trivial macroeconomic fluctuations.

The rest of this section is structured as follows. Section 4.3.1 provides some basis for the analysis of power-law distributed data. Section 4.3.2 illustrates how to recognize power laws in empirical data, whereas Sect. 4.3.3 presents the main statistical techniques for identifying the lower bound to the power-law behaviour (Sect. 4.3.3.1) and fitting the power-law form to empirical distributions (Sect. 4.3.3.2). Then, Sect. 4.3.4 shows how to test the power-law hypothesis quantitatively and how to compare it with alternative distributions. Finally, Sect. 4.3.5 describes some of the mechanisms by which power-law behaviour can arise.

4.3.1 Some Basic Definitions and Properties

A non-negative random variable X is said to obey a *power law* if its realizations are drawn from a probability distribution

$$p(x) \propto x^{-(\alpha+1)}, \tag{4.9}$$

where $\alpha > 0$ is a constant parameter of the distribution known as the *scaling exponent*.[5] At the most basic level, there are two types of power-law distributions: *contin-*

[5]What is usually called a power-law distribution is simply the PDF associated with the CDF of the Pareto distribution, i.e.

uous, governing continuous real numbers, and *discrete*, where the quantity of interest can take only a discrete set of values—typically positive integers.

The continuous version, known as the *Pareto distribution*, is well studied in the literature and has the PDF

$$p(x) = \frac{\alpha k^{\alpha}}{x^{\alpha+1}}, \quad x \geq k, \tag{4.10}$$

where $k > 0$ is the scale parameter and $\alpha > 0$ is the shape parameter (e.g. Kleiber and Kotz 2003; Arnold 2015).[6] The discrete case has probability mass function (PMF)

$$p(x) = \Pr(X = x) = \frac{x^{-(s+1)}}{\zeta(s+1, k)}, \quad x \in \mathbb{Z}_{>0}, \quad k > 0, \quad s > 0, \tag{4.11}$$

where

$$\zeta(s+1, k) = \sum_{n=0}^{\infty} \frac{1}{(n+k)^{s+1}} \tag{4.12}$$

is the generalized zeta function.[7] For $k = 1$, $\zeta(s+1, k)$ reduces to the standard zeta function

$$\zeta(s+1) = \sum_{n=1}^{\infty} n^{-(s+1)} \tag{4.13}$$

and the distribution (4.11) becomes known as the *Zipf (or zeta) distribution* in honour of the American linguist Zipf (1949).

Figure 4.2 visualizes the Pareto (a) and Zipf (b) probability density/mass functions with scale parameter $k = 1$ and different values of the shape parameters α and s. Clearly, both the distributions are highly skewed to the right with a heavy tail. It is therefore reasonable to assume that a random variable following the Pareto/Zipf distribution contains extreme values. The effect of changing the shape parameters

---

(Footnote 5 continued)

$$p(x) \propto x^{-(\alpha+1)} = x^{-\zeta}.$$

Then, the exponent of the power-law distribution is $\zeta = \alpha + 1$, where α is the Pareto distribution shape parameter. To add to the confusion, some authors call $\alpha + 1$ the scaling exponent, that is the exponent of the density (4.9), while others find it easier to work with the exponent α of the CCDF $P_{>}(x) \propto x^{-\alpha}$. For the purposes of this chapter, we will not change here the nomenclature but will refer to the Pareto distribution shape parameter α as the power-law scaling exponent, with the hope that this caveat is sufficient to avoid confusion.

[6] The statistical distribution (4.10), usually referred to as the *strong Pareto law* (Mandelbrot 1960), has 100-year-plus history that dates back to the work of the Italian economist Pareto (1895). In his pioneering contributions at the end of the nineteenth century, Pareto (1896, 1897a, b) also suggested two variants of his distribution, occasionally called the three-parameter Pareto distributions. These further Pareto distributions, however, have not been used much in empirical economic (and other) studies.

[7] See http://mathworld.wolfram.com/HurwitzZetaFunction.html.

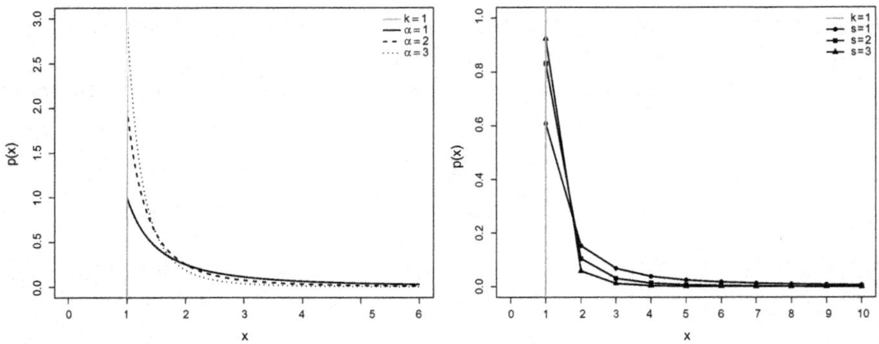

(a) Pareto (b) Zipf

Fig. 4.2 Power-law probability density/mass functions with scale parameter $k = 1$ and different values of the shape parameters α and s. In panel (**b**), the connecting lines do not indicate continuity

α and s is visible in the plots at the scale parameter k: the higher (lower) α and s, the higher (lower) the probability density/mass at k, and thus the thinner (fatter) the right tail.[8]

In many cases it is useful to consider the cumulative distribution function (CDF) of power-law distributed variables. In the continuous (Pareto) case, the CDF has the relatively simple structure

$$P_{\leq}(x) = 1 - \left(\frac{x}{k}\right)^{-\alpha}, \tag{4.14}$$

[8]At times, a power-law distribution is also called a *scale-free* distribution, because it is the only distribution that is the same whatever scale one looks at it on (e.g. Sornette 2012). To illustrate this fact, one can suppose to have some probability distribution $p(x)$ for a quantity x and to discover or somehow deduce that it satisfies the property that

$$p(kx) = kp(x)$$

for any k. That is, if one increases the scale or unit by which x is measured by a factor of k, the shape of the distribution $p(x)$ is unchanged, except for an overall multiplicative constant. Thus, for instance, an immediate consequence of the presence of the power-law tail in the probability distribution of incomes is that the probability that a random person from the richer part of the society is k times richer than another person with income x is independent of x, i.e.

$$\frac{p(kx)}{p(x)} = k^{-(\alpha+1)}.$$

Therefore, the power-law distribution is scale-free, reflecting a certain "self-similarity" of the structure of the richest class. The scale appears in the problem through the parameter k: for example, if $k = 10$ and $\alpha = 2$, then the power law predicts that the number of people ten times richer is roughly one thousand (10^{-3}) times smaller. The suppression factor is very sensitive to α. If the value of α moves toward unity, the suppression factor decreases, and for $k = 10$ it is only 10^{-2}. In other words, in economies with a smaller value of α the tail of the distribution is fatter. This leaves more space for rich individuals.

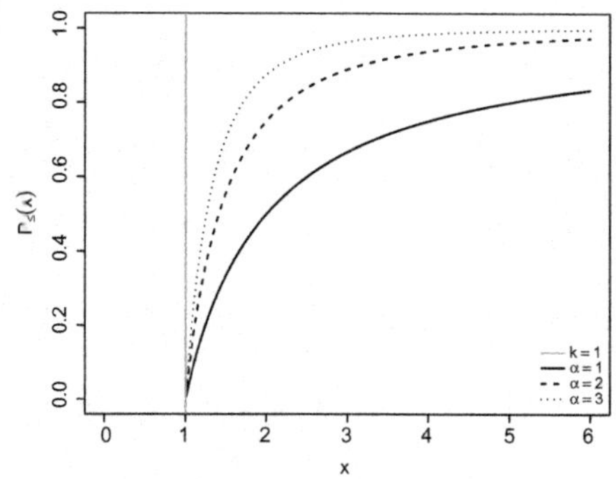

(a) Pareto

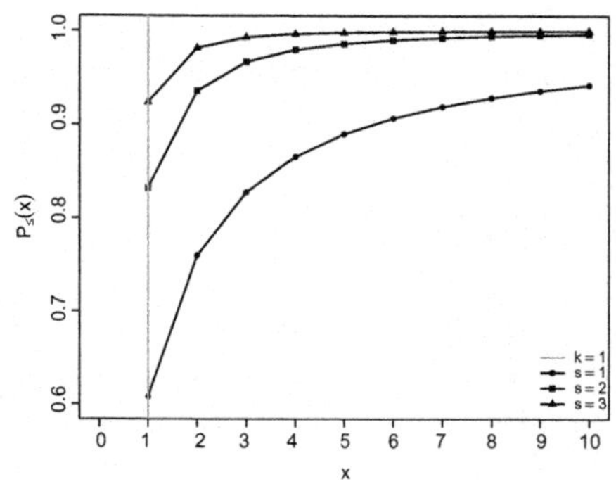

(b) Zipf

Fig. 4.3 Power-law cumulative distribution functions with scale parameter $k = 1$ and different values of the shape parameters α and s. In panel (**b**), the connecting lines do not indicate continuity

whilst for the discrete (Zipf) version it is given by

$$P_{\leq}(x) = \frac{H_{x,s+1}}{\zeta(s+1)}, \tag{4.15}$$

where $H_{x,s+1}$ is a generalized harmonic number.[9]

Figure 4.3 charts the Pareto/Zipf CDF for different values of α and s. As can be seen, the higher (lower) the value of α and s, the more (less) rapidly the CDF trends to 1.

The moments of power-law distributions are also of particular interest. For instance, in the Pareto case the rth moment equals

$$\langle X^r \rangle = \frac{\alpha k^r}{\alpha - k} \tag{4.16}$$

and exists only if $r < \alpha$. Therefore, when

- $0 < \alpha \leq 1$, the mean and higher-order moments diverge, i.e. $\langle X \rangle = \infty$;
- $1 < \alpha \leq 2$, the second and higher-order moments diverge, i.e. $\langle X^2 \rangle = \infty$;
- $2 < \alpha \leq r$, the rth and higher-order moments diverge, i.e. $\langle X^r \rangle = \infty$.

To understand the meaning of Paretian (power) laws with infinite population moments, one can use the *sequential moment estimation* method (Mandelbrot 1963; Willinger et al. 2004). This method plots the *running moment estimates*, that is the value of a moment estimate of the data is plotted as a function of the number of observations used in the estimation of the moment.

For example, Fig. 4.4 shows the sequential mean and standard deviation plots corresponding to same-sized ($N = 1{,}000$) distinct samples of a Paretian random vari-

[9]See http://mathworld.wolfram.com/HarmonicNumber.html.

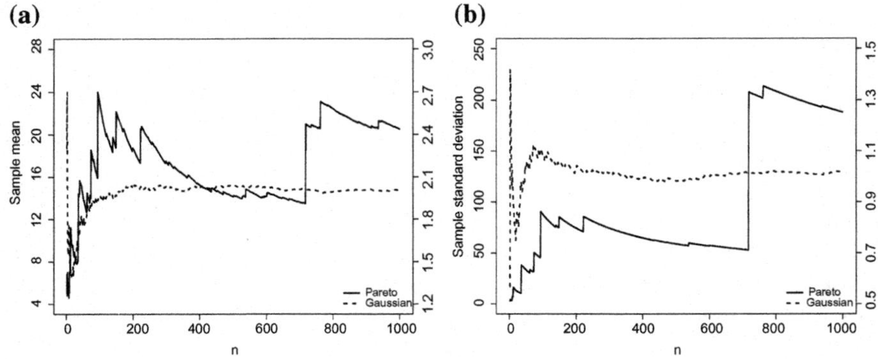

Fig. 4.4 Running moment estimates corresponding to same-sized ($N = 1{,}000$) distinct samples of a Paretian random variable with $k = 2$ and $\alpha = 1$ (left y-axis scale) and a Gaussian random variable with $\mu = 2$ and $\sigma = 1$ (right y-axis scale): **a** mean; **b** standard deviation. The figure gives an idea of how erratic and sample-dependent the moments of Paretian variables can be

able with $k = 2$ and $\alpha = 1$ and a Gaussian random variable with $\mu = 2$ and $\sigma = 1$, obtained by simply inverting series of random variables uniformly distributed in the interval $(0, 1)$.[10] As one can easily recognize, while in the Gaussian case the mean and standard deviation estimates exist, are finite, and converge robustly to their theoretical value as the number of observations increases, in the Paretian case the sample mean and standard deviation estimates do not converge as n increases, even if they always exist for any fixed n. This fact confirms that for a Paretian random variable with $\alpha = 1$ the first and second moments do not exist, i.e. the computer-simulated data set is a sample from an underlying distribution having mean and variance infinite.

Finally, power laws are conserved with respect to addition, multiplication, power transformation, minimization and maximization (e.g. Gabaix 2009; Sornette 2012). In particular, it can be proven that when two power-law distributed random variables are combined via the above algebraic transformations a new power law is generated from old ones whose exponent is preserved from the fatter-tailed power law, that is the one with the smallest exponent (Jessen and Mikosch 2006). For instance, if X is a power-law distributed random variable with $\alpha_X < \infty$ and Y is another power-law variable with an exponent $\infty > \alpha_Y \geq \alpha_X$, then $X + Y$, $X \cdot Y$ or $\max(X, Y)$ are still power laws with the same exponent α_X. This property also holds when Y is normal, lognormal or exponential, whose right tail is thinner than any power law.

[10]The "inversion method" relies on the principle that continuous CDFs range uniformly over the open interval $(0, 1)$. If u is a uniform random number on $(0, 1)$, then $x = P^{-1}(u)$ generates a random number x from any continuous distribution with the specified CDF P.

4.3.2 Recognizing Power-Law Distributions

Given a sample of data, the most common approach followed to probe for the power-law form of the empirical distribution is from visual inspection of a plot where the logarithm of data is plotted against the logarithm of their complementary cumulative probabilities, defined as

$$\hat{P}^n_> (x) = \frac{1}{N} \sum_{i=1}^{N} \mathbf{1}\{X_i > x\}, \tag{4.17}$$

where

$$\mathbf{1}\{X_i > x\} = \begin{cases} 1 & \text{if } X_i > x, \\ 0 & \text{otherwise.} \end{cases} \tag{4.18}$$

This is a natural estimator of the true CCDF (4.3) and it is essentially the CCDF of a distribution that puts mass $1/n$ on each data point.

If in doing a log-log plot of $\hat{P}^n_> (x)$ as a function of x one discovers a distribution that approximately falls on a straight line, then one can assert that the distribution follows a power law. For the specific case of a Paretian random variable, the plot will be exactly linear, as

$$\ln [P_> (x)] = \alpha \ln (k) - \alpha \ln (x) = C_\alpha - \alpha \ln (x), \tag{4.19}$$

where

$$P_> (x) = \left(\frac{x}{k}\right)^{-\alpha} \tag{4.20}$$

is the CCDF for the Pareto distribution.

Figure 4.5 shows the log-log scaled empirical CCDFs of two large data sets ($N = 10{,}000$) drawn from a Pareto distribution with $k = 1$ and $\alpha = 1.5$ and an exponential distribution with parameter $\lambda = 0.125$. As one can easily recognize, for the Paretian random variable the log-log plot exhibits a linear decrease by several orders of magnitude, whereas for the exponential case it shows a faster-than-linear decrease of the distribution, especially at the right-end tail.

Another graphical method for the identification of power-law probability distributions using random samples is the *Pareto quantile plot* (e.g. Beirlant et al. 1996b, 2004). Since a log-transformed Pareto random variable is exponentially distributed,[11] the Pareto quantile plot compare the log-transformed data to the corresponding quantiles of a standard exponential distribution (i.e. an exponential distribution with

[11] Formally, the Pareto distribution is related to the exponential distribution as follows: if X is Pareto-distributed with scale k and shape α, then $Y = \ln\left(\frac{X}{k}\right)$ is exponentially distributed with parameter $\lambda = 1/\alpha$.

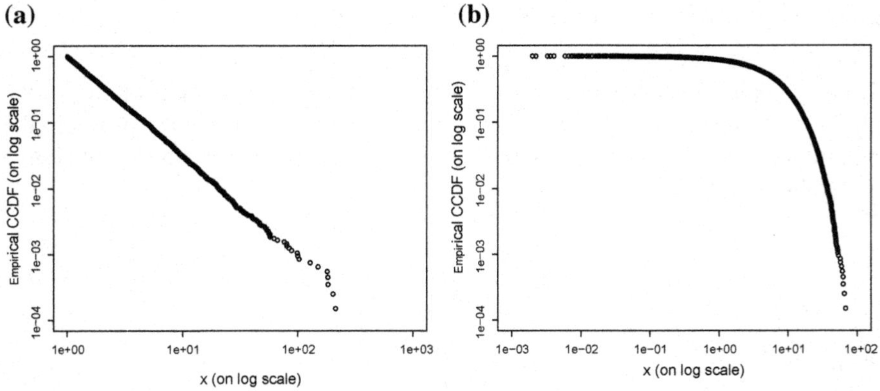

Fig. 4.5 Log-log scaled CCDFs of two large samples (N=10,000) drawn from different continuous distributions: **a** Pareto distribution with $k = 1$ and $\alpha = 1.5$; **b** exponential distribution with parameter $\lambda = 0.125$

parameter $\lambda = 1$) by plotting the former versus the latter. The quantiles of the standard exponential distribution are given by

$$-\ln\left(1 - \frac{i}{N+1}\right), \quad i = 1, \ldots, N, \tag{4.21}$$

thus yielding as coordinates for the Pareto quantile plot

$$\left\{-\ln\left(1 - \frac{i}{N+1}\right), \ln\left(x_i\right)\right\}, \quad i = 1, \ldots, N. \tag{4.22}$$

If the resulting plot suggests that the plotted points converge to a straight line, as in Fig. 4.6a, then a Pareto power-law distribution should be suspected.

The *mean excess plot* is an alternative way of graphically examining power-law probability distributions—a detailed description can be found in Beirlant et al. (1996a, 2004). This method consists of first sorting the data, such that $x_1 \leq \ldots \leq x_n$, and then computing for each observation x_i the empirical excess function

$$e_n\left(x_i\right) := \frac{1}{N-i} \sum_{j=i+1}^{N} \left(x_j - x_i\right), \quad i = 1, \ldots, N-1, \tag{4.23}$$

where N is the size of the random sample. The values of (4.23) are thus plotted against the corresponding x_i, and if the data follows a Pareto power-law distribution the plotted points will exhibit a positive linear trend, as shown in Fig. 4.6b.

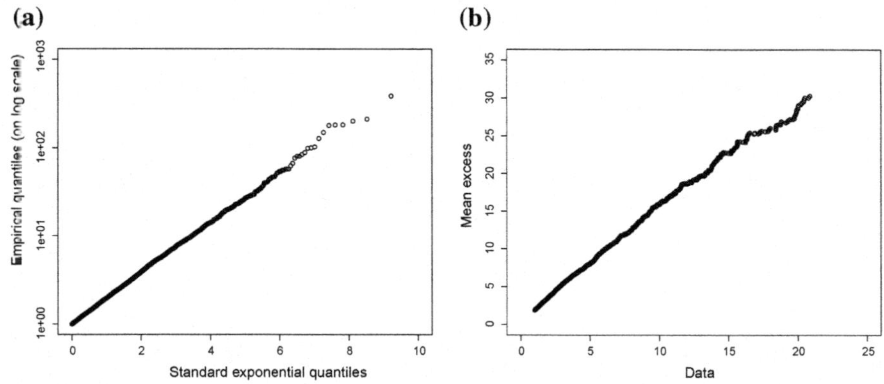

Fig. 4.6 Pareto quantile plot (**a**) and mean excess plot (**b**) for a large sample ($N = 10{,}000$) drawn from a Pareto distribution with $k = 1$ and $\alpha = 1.5$

4.3.3 Estimating Power-Law Distributional Parameters

4.3.3.1 Finding the Threshold

When power laws are used in practice, it is usually the case that only the upper *tail* of the empirical distribution follows a power law. Therefore, before estimating the scaling parameter α, all observations below some minimum point $x_{\min}$ need to be discarded, so that one is left with only those observations for which the power-law model is a valid one. Estimating the scale parameter k of the Pareto/Zipf distribution and finding the threshold $x_{\min}$ directly corresponds with each other, and since the estimate of α will be *conditioned* on the choice of $x_{\min}$—choosing too low a value for $x_{\min}$ reduces the statistical error on the scaling parameter α because more data are used, but it increases its bias because the power law normally holds only in the tail—it becomes clear that some care must be taken when choosing this value.

The most common ways of estimating $x_{\min}$ are either to select visually the point beyond which the empirical CCDF of the distribution becomes roughly straight on a log-log plot, or using a *Hill plot* as in Fig. 4.7a, which involves estimating the α parameter for all candidate values of $x_{\min}$ and choosing the smallest value of $x_{\min}$ beyond which the estimated parameter stabilizes to a constant.[12]

[12]See e.g. Drees et al. (2000) for more details about the Hill plot. The Hill estimator and other methods for estimating the scaling parameter α once the threshold $x_{\min}$ has been fixed will be discussed in Sect. 4.3.3.2. Figure 4.7a was obtained using random numbers from a *composite* lognormal-Pareto distribution, which takes a lognormal density up to an unknown threshold value θ and a two-parameter Pareto density with scaling parameter α thereafter. The idea of such a composite model comes from Cooray and Ananda (2005), to whom we refer the reader for technical details.

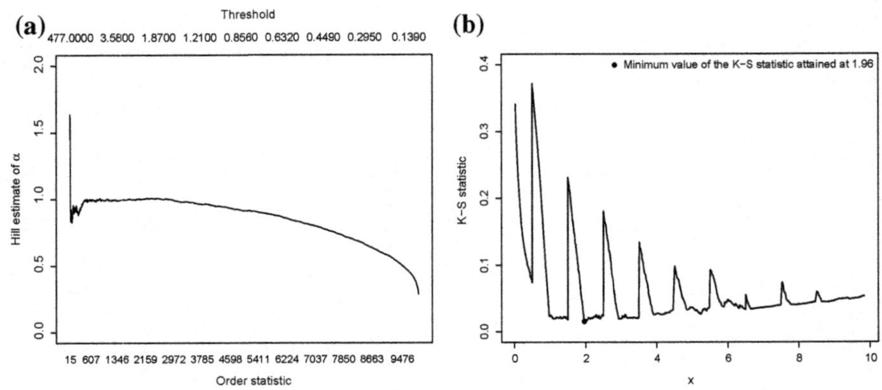

Fig. 4.7 Methods for finding the threshold. **a** Hill plot for 10,000 random observations from the composite lognormal-Pareto distribution with $\theta = 2$ and $\alpha = 1$. Notice that the left side of the graph clearly indicates the correct value of α in proximity of a threshold value equal to (or more than) θ. **b** K–S statistic versus ordered sample values for 5,000 random observations from the composite lognormal-Pareto distribution with $\theta = 2$ and $\alpha = 1$. Notice that the K–S statistic yielding the best fit to the tail data is very close to the true value of θ

Clearly, these graphical methods are highly subjective and error prone, and the same can be held true when judging by eye the degree of linearity on a Pareto quantile plot or mean excess plot and using as an estimate of the threshold $x_{\min}$ the leftmost point beyond which these plots form almost a straight line.

In the case of a strong discontinuity at the threshold, using traditional graphical diagnostics would lead to a discernible kink so that it would be easy to choose (with little uncertainty) a lower bound $x_{\min}$ for power-law behaviour in the data. In the more realistic case of a smooth transition at the threshold, however, the traditional diagnostics would be harder to interpret, and hence their results should not be trusted. Therefore, more objective and accurate approaches have been sought. Among these, the method put forward by Clauset et al. (2007, 2009) determines the optimal choice of $x_{\min}$ by minimizing the distance between the probability distributions of the data and the best-fit power-law model. The measure used for quantifying the distance between the two probability distributions is the Kolmogorov–Smirnov (K–S) statistic

$$D = \max_{x \geq x_{\min}} \left| \hat{P}^n_{\leq}(x) - P_{\leq}(x) \right|, \tag{4.24}$$

which is simply the maximum distance between the data and fitted model CDFs (for $x \geq x_{\min}$). The optimal estimate of the lower bound is then the value of $x_{\min}$ where D attains the minimum.[13] An example of application of this technique is given in

[13] As suggested by Clauset et al. (2009), the uncertainty in the estimate for $x_{\min}$ can be derived by making use of a non-parametric bootstrap method (Efron and Tibshirani 1993). That is, given a data set with sample size N, one can generate a synthetic data set by drawing uniformly at random from the original data a new sequence of points x_i, $i = 1, \ldots, N$. Using the method described above, one

Fig. 4.7b, which shows the K–S statistic as a function of the assumed value of $x_{\min}$ for 5,000 random observations drawn from a composite lognormal-Pareto distribution with $\theta = 2$ and $\alpha = 1$ (see footnote 12).[14] As the figure shows, the K–S statistic that yields the best fit to the tail data is very close to the true value of θ.[15]

4.3.3.2 Estimation of the Scaling Parameter

To estimate the scaling parameter α once the threshold $x_{\min}$ has been fixed is relatively straightforward.[16] Typically this parameter is extracted by observing that the Pareto power law implies the linear form (4.19).[17] Thus, if the doubly logarithmic plot of the empirical CCDF appear roughly straight above $x_{\min}$, then a straight line can be fitted to the data points beyond $x_{\min}$ using least squares (LS) linear regression, with the estimate of the scaling parameter α given by the absolute slope of the fitted straight line.[18] For example, the LS fit of a straight line to Fig. 4.8a gives $\alpha = 0.985$, which is clearly compatible with the known value of $\alpha = 1$ from which the data were generated.

(Footnote 13 continued)
then estimates $x_{\min}$ for this surrogate data set. By taking the standard deviation of all the estimates over a large number of repetitions of this process, the uncertainty in the original estimated parameter can thus be quantified.

[14]For the ease of presentation, the limits of the horizontal axis in panel (b) of the figure have been adjusted so as to visually magnify the first part of the graph.

[15]Several other statistically principled methods for the estimation of the threshold $x_{\min}$ have been proposed in the literature. For instance, Beirlant et al. (1996a, b,) developed a procedure that analytically determines the optimal choice of $x_{\min}$ by minimizing a non-parametric estimate of the asymptotic mean squared error (AMSE) for the maximum likelihood estimator of α proposed by Hill (1975; see also Sect. 4.3.3.2). Furthermore, Danielsson et al. (2001) proposed a bootstrap method to find the optimal $x_{\min}$ for the Hill estimator with respect to the AMSE, which has less analytical requirements than the approach proposed by Beirlant et al. (1996a, b). Finally, a robust criterion for choosing $x_{\min}$ and estimating the scaling parameter was developed by Dupuis and Victoria-Feser (2006). Nevertheless, these techniques are computationally time consuming and sometimes unstable, and are therefore not further discussed here.

[16]Parameter estimation for power-law type distributions is covered in depth in Johnson et al. (1994) and Arnold (2015). Here we shall only include the classical regression-type estimator and maximum likelihood estimation. For the method of moments, quantile and Bayes estimators, as well as methods based on order statistics, we refer the interested reader to the above-mentioned works. Some recent developments are also discussed by Alfons et al. (2013).

[17]Here we limit our attention to the methods for estimating the scaling parameter that are specific to *continuous* data. The discrete counterpart follows similar arguments, except for some additional technical conditions. A review of estimation methods that work for discrete data is contained in Clauset et al. (2009). We do not even consider the case of binned data sets, i.e. sequences of counts of observations over sets of non-overlapping ranges which occur when direct measurements are unavailable (because impractical or impossible) and this is simply the form of the data received, or when one recovers measurements from existing histograms. Readers interested in pursuing the topic further are encouraged to consult the work by Virkar and Clauset (2014), who adapt the statistical framework of Clauset et al. (2009) to the less common but important case of binned empirical data.

[18]Many software packages exist that can perform this kind of fitting, provide estimates and standard errors for the slope, as well calculate indicators for the quality of the fit.

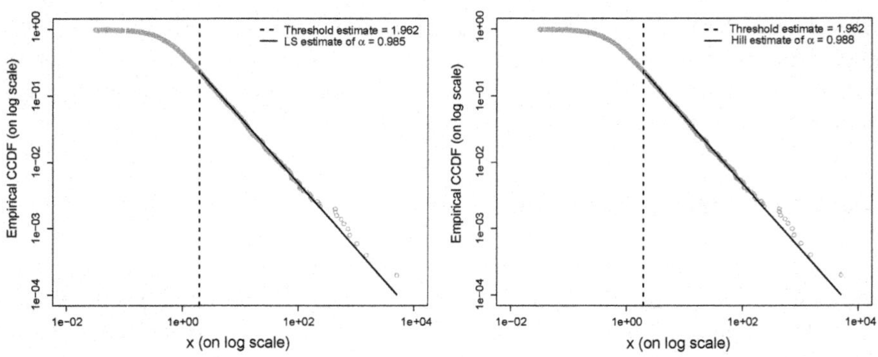

(a) LS regression (b) Hill estimator

Fig. 4.8 Estimation of the scaling parameter. Points represent the complementary cumulative distribution for 5,000 random observations distributed according to a composite lognormal-Pareto distribution with $\theta = 2$ and $\alpha = 1$. Solid lines represent the Pareto power-law fits to the data using the methods described in the text. Dashed lines denote the lower threshold estimated using a Kolmogorov–Smirnov approach (Clauset et al. 2007, 2009)

An alternative, simple and reliable method for extracting α is to employ the formula

$$\alpha_{\text{Hill}} = \frac{k}{\sum_{i=1}^{k} \ln(x_{N-k+i}) - k \ln(x_{N-k})}, \quad i = 1, \ldots, N, \quad k \leq N. \tag{4.25}$$

Here the quantities x_i are the sample elements put in descending order and k is the number of observations larger than $x_{\min}$. Equation (4.25) was introduced by Hill (1975) and is referred to as the *Hill estimator*, which is well-known to be asymptotically normal (Hall 1982) and consistent—meaning that $\alpha_{\text{Hill}} \to \alpha$ as $N \to \infty$ (Mason 1982). It is constructed as a maximum likelihood estimator *conditional* on some known threshold level $x_{\min}$, and coincides exactly with the maximum likelihood estimator for the shape parameter of the Pareto distribution when $x_{\min}$ corresponds to the smallest value of x, i.e. when $k = N$. An error estimate for α_{Hill} can be derived by exploiting the asymptotic distribution theory of the Hill estimator as $\frac{\alpha_{\text{Hill}}}{\sqrt{k}}$ (e.g. Lux 1996). Applying Eq. (4.25) to 5,000 lognormal-Pareto distributed random numbers as in Fig. 4.8b gives an estimate of $\alpha = 0.988$, which agrees well with the known value of 1.

4.3.4 *Testing a Set of Data for Power-Law Distribution*

Since it is possible to fit a power-law distribution to *any* data set, it is appropriate to test whether the observed data could *plausibly* be considered to follow a power law. Many empirical studies of power-law distributed data have attempted to test the power-law hypothesis *qualitatively*, based for instance on graphical visualizations of the data such as a log-log plot of their complementary cumulative distribution. But this could lead to claims of power-law behaviour that do not hold up under closer scrutiny, because even data that are drawn from a non-power-law distribution can produce samples that resemble power-law distributions on a log-log plot. This is the case, for instance, with data drawn from a lognormal distribution, where a log-log plot may appear linear for several orders of magnitude if the variance of the corresponding normal distribution is large (Mitzenmacher 2004). Therefore, to say with certainty whether a power law is a plausible hypothesis for the data, a more *quantitative* approach is desirable.

A standard way for testing empirical data against a hypothesized power-law distribution is to use a *goodness-of-fit* test based on the K–S statistic (4.24), which generates a p-value that quantifies the plausibility of the hypothesis.[19] Since the distribution of the K–S statistic is hard to obtain analytically, the p-value for the fit can be found by bootstrapping, i.e. by generating a large number of power-law distributed data sets with scaling parameter α and lower bound $x_{\min}$ equal to those of the distribution that best fits the observed data and then "re-inferring" the model parameters (Clauset et al. 2009).[20] When testing against the power-law distribution, the hypotheses are

$$\begin{aligned} H_0 &: \text{data are generated from a power-law distribution,} \\ H_1 &: \text{data are not generated from a power-law distribution.} \end{aligned} \tag{4.26}$$

Therefore, if the resulting p-value is larger than the chosen significance level, then the power law is a plausible hypothesis for the data; otherwise, if it is smaller, the model is rejected and another distribution may be more appropriate.

As a demonstration of this approach, we consider a data set with $N = 1{,}000$ observations drawn at random from a composite lognormal-Pareto distribution with $\theta = 2$ and $\alpha = 1$. For fitting a power-law model to the distribution's upper tail, we use the distance-based method for automatically identifying the point $x_{\min}$ above which the power-law behaviour holds and the Hill estimator for α (see Sect. 4.3.3). We calculate that $x_{\min} = 1.01$ and $\alpha_{\text{Hill}} = 1.00$. Given this hypothesized model, we compute the distance D between the estimated model and the original data set using the K–S goodness-of-fit statistic (4.24), which yields $D = 0.02$. Then, using a semi-parametric bootstrap, we generate 100 data sets with N values that follows a Pareto power-law distribution with parameter α_{Hill} at and above the estimated threshold

[19] Other measures for quantifying the "distance" between the distribution of the empirical data and the hypothesized model have been proposed and are in common use. Readers interested in pursuing the subject further may wish to consult the review by D'Agostino and Stephens (1986).

[20] For each generated data set the K–S statistic must to be computed relative to the best-fit power-law model for *that* data set, not relative to the original distribution from which the data set was drawn. In this way, it is ensured that the same calculation that has been performed for the real data set is performed also for each generated data set. This is a crucial requirement if an unbiased estimate of the p-value is sought (Capasso et al. 2009).

x_{min}, but follows the original distribution below x_{min}. After fitting the Pareto power-law model to each generated data set and calculated the associated K–S statistic, we are left with a p-value for the goodness-of-fit test equal to 0.78, meaning that the original data can be firmly considered to follow the Pareto power-law distribution in the upper tail at any of the usual significance levels (1 %, 5 %, and 10 %).[21]

A large p-value for the power-law model, however, provides no information about whether some other distributions might be an equally plausible (or even a better) explanation. Hence, demonstrating that such alternatives are worse models of the data can strengthen the statistical argument in favour of the power law. As a way to accomplish this task, the test proposed by Vuong (1989) examines if the differences between a fitted model and the others are statistically significant. The approach is based on testing the null hypothesis H_0 that the competing models are equally close to the true data generating process against the alternative hypothesis H_1 that one model is closer. The test statistic is

$$\mathcal{R} = \sum_{i=1}^{N} \ln \left[\frac{p_1(x_i; \theta_1)}{p_2(x_i; \theta_2)} \right], \tag{4.27}$$

$\theta_{j=1,2}$ being the maximum likelihood estimator of the unknown parameters for the model j, and is asymptotically distributed as a standard normal under the null hypothesis, that is

$$\text{under } H_0 : V = \frac{\mathcal{R}}{\sigma\sqrt{N}} \xrightarrow{d} N(0,1), \tag{4.28}$$

where

$$\sigma = \sqrt{\frac{1}{N}\sum_{i=1}^{N}\left\{\ln\left[\frac{p_1(x_i;\theta_1)}{p_2(x_i;\theta_2)}\right]\right\}^2 - \left\{\frac{1}{N}\sum_{i=1}^{N}\ln\left[\frac{p_1(x_i;\theta_1)}{p_2(x_i;\theta_2)}\right]\right\}^2}. \tag{4.29}$$

Hence, chosen a critical value z from the standard normal distribution corresponding to the desired level of significance, if $|V| \leq z$ the null that models are the same cannot be rejected, whereas if $V > z$ model 1 can be considered better than model 2, and the reverse is true if $V < -z$.

An example of comparing competing distributions is shown in Fig. 4.9, where the best-fit Pareto, lognormal and exponential models (all with $x_{min} = 1.30$) have been found for the randomly generated data of the previous example.[22] As can be seen, the

[21] The p-value is simply the fraction of the times the resulting K–S statistic is larger than the value for the original data.

[22] Parameter estimation for the Pareto distribution uses the Hill estimator conditional on $x_{min} = 1.01$ (see Sect. 4.3.3.2). For the lognormal and exponential distributions, an appropriate normalization constant C is used so that $\int_{x_{min}}^{\infty} Cp(x)\,\mathrm{d}x = 1$. The normalization constant does not count as a parameter, because it is fixed once the values of the other parameters are estimated, and x_{min} does not count as a parameter because we know its value from the distance-based approach proposed by Clauset et al. (2007, 2009). Normalization constants for both the lognormal and the exponential

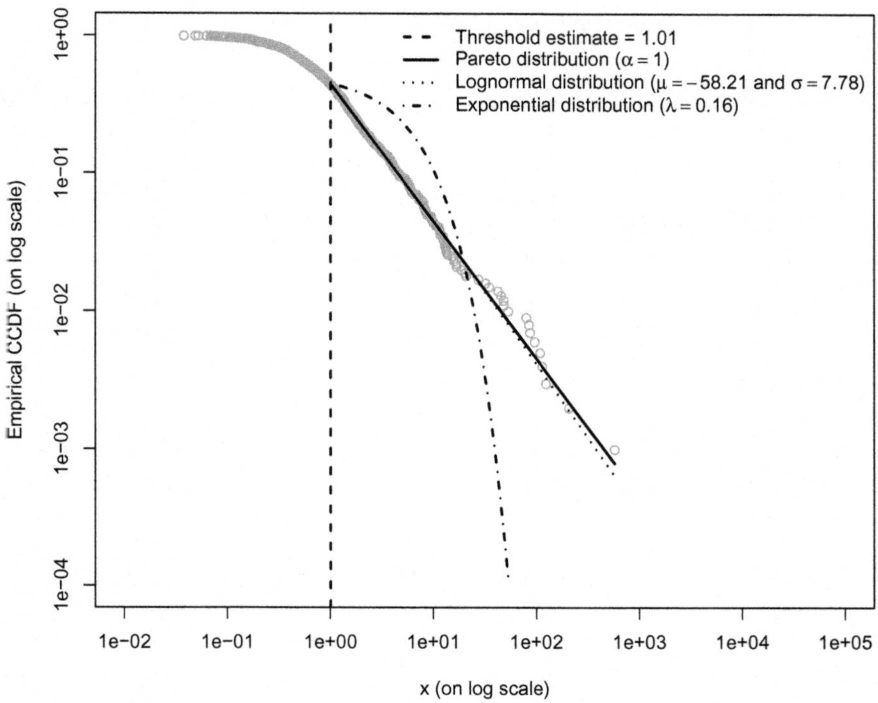

Fig. 4.9 Log-log scaled CCDF for 1,000 random observations distributed according to a composite lognormal-Pareto distribution with $\theta = 2$ and $\alpha = 1$. Solid, dotted and dotted-dashed lines represent, respectively, the Pareto, lognormal and exponential best fits. Dashed line denotes the lower threshold estimated using a Kolmogorov–Smirnov approach (Clauset et al. 2007, 2009)

Pareto and lognormal distributions perform equally well, whereas the exponential model is a poor fit for the tail data. Investigating this formally by means of the method proposed by Vuong (1989) gives a p-value of 0.90 and a test statistic that is close to zero (-0.13), which means we cannot reject the null hypothesis that the Pareto and lognormal models are observationally equivalent, whereas in the case of the exponential distribution the Vuong test gives a p-value and a test statistic of, respectively, 0.00 and 4.14, meaning we can reject the null hypothesis and conclude that the Pareto model is closer to the true distribution than the exponential one.

(Footnote 22 continued)
distributions can be found in Clauset et al. (2009). Once we are given with the value of $x_{\min}$, the method of "matching moments" which sets the distribution moments equal to the data moments and solves to obtain estimates for the distribution parameters is used to calculate our estimates. For the lognormal, the location parameter μ is equal to the mean of the logarithm of the data points, and the shape parameter σ is equal to the standard deviation of the data set after transformation (see Sect. 4.2). For the exponential, the estimate of λ is just the reciprocal of the sample mean.

4.3.5 Models of Generation of Power-Law Distributions

There is a large body of models capable of explaining the processes of generation of power-law distributions that span from physics (Bouchaud 2001; Mitzenmacher 2004; Newman 2005; Sornette 2006) to economics (Gabaix 2009). Here we shall explore the role of random multiplicative processes as key mechanisms that explain distributional power laws. Readers interested in pursuing the topic further may consult the above references for a review of other mechanisms by which power-law behaviour can arise.

4.3.5.1 Multiplicative Processes

Power-law distributions can be obtained as steady-state solutions of stochastic processes. The stochastic theory, one of the oldest (and still popular) theories of distribution, relies for the skewed shape of economic distributions mainly or solely on chance, luck and random occurrences. The main authorship of this theory is attributed to Gibrat (1931), who viewed the evolution of firms' size (sales, employees, valued added, assets) as a multiplicative random process in which the product of a large number of individual random variables tends to the *lognormal* distribution.

The connection between multiplicative processes and the lognormal distribution can be described as follows. Suppose that

$$x_t^i = \left(1 + r_{t-1}^i\right) x_{t-1}^i, \tag{4.30}$$

where x_t^i is the size of firm i at time t and $\left\{r_t^i\right\}_{t=0,1,\ldots,T-1}$ are the per-period rates of growth in firm's size. Denoting the firm's per-period growth factors by $\lambda_t^i = \left(1 + r_t^i\right)$, the above expression can be rewritten as

$$x_t^i = \lambda_{t-1}^i x_{t-1}^i, \tag{4.31}$$

where $\left\{\lambda_t^i\right\}_{t=0,1,\ldots,T-1}$ are independent, identically distributed, continuous and non-negative random variables. Taken literally with no other ingredient, expression (4.31) leads to an ensemble of values x_t^i over all possible realizations of the multiplicative factors $\left\{\lambda_t^i\right\}_{t=0,1,\ldots,T-1}$ which is distributed according to the lognormal distribution. Indeed, by iterating (4.31), the firm's size at time T is

$$x_T^i = x_0^i \lambda_0^i \lambda_1^i \lambda_2^i \cdots \lambda_{T-1}^i = x_0^i \prod_{j=0}^{T-1} \lambda_j^i, \tag{4.32}$$

where x_0^i represents the starting size of firm i. If the λ_t^i's are all governed by independent lognormal distributions $\Lambda_i(\lambda)$, then x_T^i is approximately lognormal as the product of lognormal distributions is again lognormal. However, lognormal distrib-

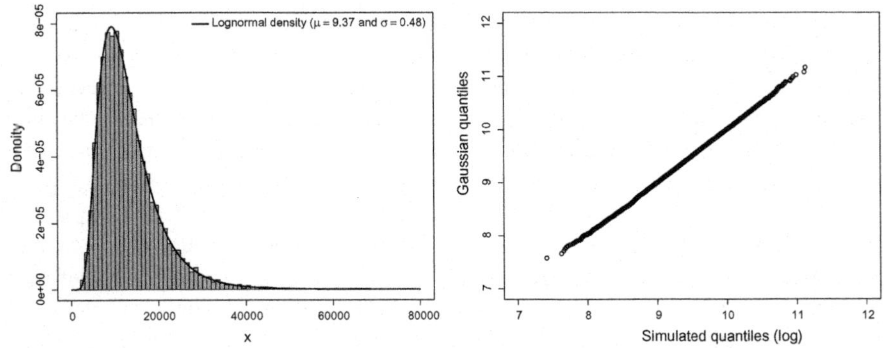

(a) Histogram (b) Lognormal quantile plot

Fig. 4.10 The final time step distribution obtained from the simulation of the multiplicative stochastic process (4.31). The solid line in panel (**a**) denotes the lognormal density with parameter values obtained by "matching moments" (see footnote 24)

utions may be obtained even if the λ_t^i's are not themselves lognormal by the additive form of the CLT. Indeed, from the logarithm of (4.32)

$$\ln\left(x_T^i\right) = \ln\left(x_0^i\right) + \sum_{j=0}^{T-1} \ln\left(\lambda_j^i\right) \tag{4.33}$$

one gets via the CLT that $\sum_{j=0}^{T-1} \ln\left(\lambda_j^i\right)$ converges to a Gaussian distribution for sufficiently large t if the $\ln\left(\lambda_j^i\right)$'s are independent and identically distributed variables with finite mean and variance; hence, for large times t, x_T^i is well approximated by a lognormal distribution.

In the industrial organization and economic geography literature this result is also known as the Gibrat "law of proportionate effect", stating that if growth rates of firms' size in a fixed population (i.e. abstracting from entry and exit dynamics) are independent of size and uncorrelated, the resulting distribution is lognormal. This is clearly seen in Fig. 4.10, which exhibits the simulated distribution for the multiplicative system (4.31) at time $T = 100$, where λ_t^i is a random draw from a Gaussian distribution with $\mu = 1.02$ and $\sigma = 0.05$.[23] The simulation has been run for $N = 10{,}000$ firms, whose size has been initialized to 100. As one can easily recognize, both the panels of Fig. 4.10 show every sign of being lognormal.[24]

[23]The value $\mu = 1.02$ ensures that the experimentally observed firms' size increases in the overall system at each time step of the simulation, whereas the standard deviation $\sigma = 0.05$ is large enough to enable occasionally values which are smaller than 1.

[24]Since a random variable X has the lognormal distribution with parameters $\mu \in \mathbb{R}$ and $\sigma \in (0, \infty)$ if $\ln(X)$ has the Gaussian distribution with mean μ and standard deviation σ, the lognormal density

Lognormal and power-law distributions are intrinsically connected. Indeed, small variations in the underlying model can change the result from one to the other.[25] As a consequence, many variations of the model (4.31) have been developed in the literature. The main result of this strand of research was to show that even small variations from the pure multiplicative stochastic process lead to a *power-law* distribution. As a matter of example, Champernowne (1953) offered an explanation for the Pareto power-law distribution of income similar in character to the "law of proportionate effect". His model, later on generalized and extended by Simon (1955), views income determination as a Markov process—income for the current period depends only on one's income for the last period and random influence—and relies upon the subdivision of incomes into discrete ranges as well as the specification of a constant matrix of transition probabilities—otherwise, no stationary distribution will emerge from the Markov process. Champernowne showed that if the income intervals defining each class are assumed to form a geometric progression, then the equilibrium distribution of income tends to that given by a discrete Pareto distribution.

The main difference between the multiplicative model (4.31) and the Champernowne model is that while in the former income can become arbitrarily close to zero through successive decreases, in the latter model there is a minimum income corresponding to the lowest class below which one cannot fall. Generally, for each economic system one can assume the existence of a positive cut-off $x_{t-1}^{*} > 0$ for the minimal income of each individual, i.e. there is some threshold income which one has to posses to fulfil minimal needs and function in the system. In welfare economies it is provided by the social security system through the economic effects of subsidies, securities, and services.

A very general extension to Champernowne model is contained in Levy and Solomon (1996a, b), who showed that a power-law distribution can be obtained by adding a reflection condition to the stochastic multiplicative model (4.31), i.e. by assuming that each x_{t-1}^{i} is bounded from below to a threshold

$$x_{t-1}^{*} = \frac{c}{N} \sum_{i=1}^{N} x_{t-1}^{i} = c \left\langle X_{t-1} \right\rangle \tag{4.34}$$

proportional to current average income $\langle X_{t-1} \rangle$. Operationally, each time the generic multiplicative process (4.31) returns a value x_t^i smaller than x_{t-1}^{*}, the actual value of x_t^i is restored to

(Footnote 24 continued)
in panel (a) of Fig. 4.10 uses parameter estimates obtained by first taking logarithms of the simulated data and then equating μ and σ to the mean and standard deviation of the log-transformed simulated data (see Sect. 4.2). The lognormal quantile plot in panel (b), instead, has been drawn by first taking logarithms of the simulated data and then using the Gaussian quantile plot with the same parameter estimates.

[25] A rich and long history about generative models leading to either power-law or lognormal distributions, spanning many fields, can be found in work from decades ago. See, for instance, Aitchison and Brown (1957) and Sahota (1978); see also Kleiber and Kotz (2003), Mitzenmacher (2004) and Newman (2005) for pointers to some of the recent and historically relevant scientific literature on the subject.

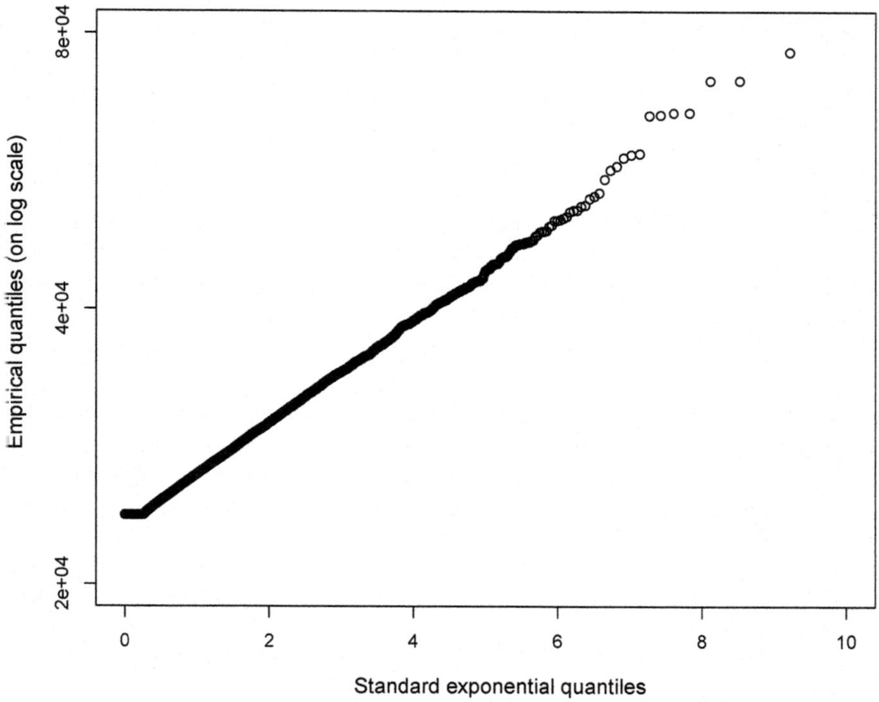

Fig. 4.11 Pareto quantile plot for the final time step distribution obtained from the simulation of the multiplicative stochastic process (4.36)

$$x_t^i = x_{t-1}^* = c\,\langle X_{t-1}\rangle\,, \tag{4.35}$$

where the fraction c is fixed in time.[26] This mechanism can be also viewed as a way of killing off an individual and introducing a new one at the same time, thus incorporating a perfectly balancing "birth and death" process. Then, the multiplicative model (4.31) formally changes to

$$x_t^i = \begin{cases} \lambda_{t-1}^i x_{t-1}^i & \text{if}\, x_t^i \geq c\,\langle X_{t-1}\rangle\,, \\ c\,\langle X_{t-1}\rangle & \text{if}\, x_t^i < c\,\langle X_{t-1}\rangle\,. \end{cases} \tag{4.36}$$

Numerical results probing the properties of the multiplicative stochastic model with reflecting lower bound are shown in Fig. 4.11 for the final time step $T = 100$ and values $c = 0.9$, $N = 10{,}000$ and $x_0^i = 100$. As in the previous simulation, the random factor λ_t^i is extracted from a Gaussian probability distribution with $\mu = 1.02$ and $\sigma = 0.05$. One can see that the lower cut-off in fact works, and the resulting

[26] Clearly, if c is time independent, x^* varies in time.

distribution is no longer lognormal but can be approximated by a Pareto power-law function.

Kesten (1973) considered the following mixture of multiplicative and additive processes

$$x_t^i = \lambda_{t-1}^i x_{t-1}^i + b_{t-1}^i, \tag{4.37}$$

with $\{\lambda_t^i\}_{t=0,1,\dots,T-1}$ and $\{b_t^i\}_{t=0,1,\dots,T-1}$ being positive independent random variables. Clearly, for $b_{t-1}^i = 0$ the simple linear stochastic Eq. (4.37) recovers the model (4.31); for $b_{t-1}^i \neq 0$, it generates an ensemble of values x_t^i for which the power-law tail behaviour

$$p(x_t) \propto x_t^{-(1+\alpha)} \tag{4.38}$$

can be observed. The term b_{t-1}^i can be thought of as an effective repulsion from the origin—i.e. a re-injection of the dynamics—and thus acts similarly to the barrier x_{t-1}^* in the previous model (4.36), making the multiplicative process with the reflective barrier and the Kesten model deeply related.[27] The reconstructed final time step ($T = 100$) density of the Kesten process (4.37) for λ_{t-1}^i and b_{t-1}^i uniformly sampled in the intervals [0.48, 1.48] and [0, 1], respectively, and values $N = 10{,}000$ and $x_0^i = 100$ is shown in Fig. 4.12, where a clear power-law behaviour in the tail can be observed from the double logarithmic plot of the cumulative distribution.

Finally, Blank and Solomon (2000) incorporate both entry and exit dynamics by assuming that agents disappear from the system if they fall below the threshold (4.34) and that at each period t

$$\Delta N = N_{t+1} - N_t = K\left(\sum_{i=1}^{N_{t+1}} x_{t+1}^i - \sum_{i=1}^{N_t} x_t^i\right) = K\left(x_{t+1}^{\text{tot}} - x_t^{\text{tot}}\right) \tag{4.39}$$

new individuals enter the system with the size x_{t-1}^*. This model—with a variable number of components whose size evolves according to the multiplicative stochastic rule—also leads to a power-law distribution, as one can easily recognize from Fig. 4.13, which shows the Pareto quantile plot comparing the distribution of the simulated data to the power-law distribution for $T = 100$.

4.4 The Laplace Distribution

In recent years part of the research in macroeconomics has analysed the statistical properties of aggregate output growth-rate distribution in a cross section of countries, i.e. ignoring time dimension. In particular, works belonging to this line of research have shown that GDP log growth rates have a *tent-shaped* distribution, which is characterized by a high singular mode and heavy tails similar to the Laplace distribution

[27] See Sornette (1998) on this subject; see also Sornette and Cont (1997) and Takayasu et al. (1997).

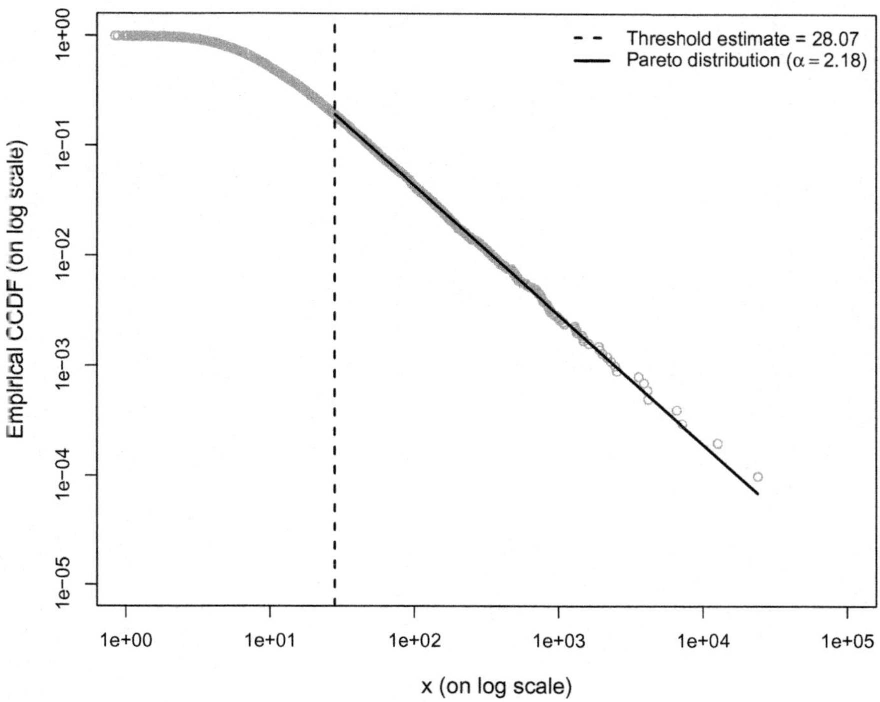

Fig. 4.12 The final time step distribution obtained from the simulation of the Kesten process (4.37). The solid line represents the Pareto power-law fit to the simulated data using the Hill estimator described in Sect. 4.3.3.2. The dashed line denotes the lower threshold estimated using a Kolmogorov–Smirnov approach (Clauset et al. 2007, 2009)

(e.g. Canning et al. 1998; Lee et al. 1998; Castaldi and Dosi 2004).[28] This kind of evidence was also found at lower levels of aggregation, namely in the case of the cross-sectional distribution of firms' growth rates, where the observed tent-shaped Laplace distribution appears robust to various measures of growth indicators—including value added, sales and employment—as well as over different levels of industry aggregation (see, among others, Stanley et al. 1996; Amaral et al. 1997; Lee et al. 1998; Bottazzi and Secchi 2003a, b; Castaldi and Dosi 2004; Fu et al. 2005; Sapio and Thoma 2006; Dosi and Nelson 2010).[29] Since the Laplace has higher spike and

[28] More recently, the research on the subject has expanded to investigate the distributional properties of aggregate output growth-rate *time series*, i.e. for individual countries over time (see Fagiolo et al. 2007a, b, 2008). The main finding from these studies is that in many industrialized countries the growth-rate time-series distribution can be well approximated by a Laplace density with tails much fatter than those of a Gaussian distribution. This implies that the pattern of economic growth over time tends to be quite lumpy: large growth events, either positive or negative, seem to be more frequent than what a Gaussian model would predict.

[29] There are, however, some documented variations in the observed tent-shaped distribution of firms' growth rates. In a study on Danish firms, for instance, Reichstein and Jensen (2005)

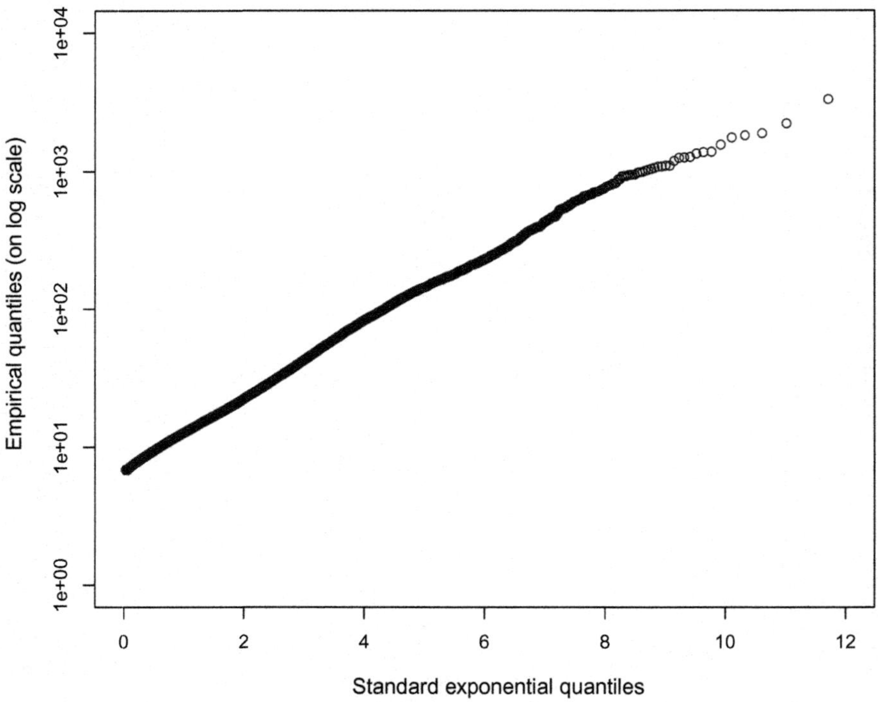

Fig. 4.13 Pareto quantile plot for the final time step distribution of the simulated Blank and Solomon (2000) model with $c = 0.4$, $K = 0.1$, $x_0^i = 100$ and $N_0 = 100$. The λ_t^i's have been drawn from a Gaussian distribution with $\mu = 1.02$ and $\sigma = 0.05$. The final system size is N = 121,185

thicker tails compared to the Gaussian distribution, these results indicate that—no matter the level of aggregation—the growth dynamics of complex organizations such as countries and firms is characterized by gains or losses from growth episodes that play a role statistically more significant than expected from a Gaussian distribution.[30]

(Footnote 29 continued)
provide evidence of substantial skewness along with signs of heavier tails than are accounted for by the Laplace distribution—especially for the right tail containing the fastest growing firms. Tails fatter than those of a Laplace were also found in studies such as Bottazzi et al. (2011), who remark that «[...] the Laplace distribution of growth rates cannot be considered as a universal property valid for all sectors. Looking at French manufacturing, we observe growth rates distributions with tails that are consistently fatter than those of the Laplace» (Bottazzi et al. 2011, p. 2). In their investigation, Bottazzi et al. (2011) use a more general group of probability densities, known as the Subbotin (1923) family of distributions, which allows for both skewness and "super-Laplace" tails in growth-rate distributions and encompasses both the Laplace and the Gaussian functions as special cases.

[30]Delli Gatti et al. (2005) present an agent-based model that replicates the Laplace distribution of both the firms' and aggregate output growth rates. They show that the power-law of firms' size implies that growth is Laplace distributed and also that small micro-shocks can aggregate into macro-shocks to generate recessions.

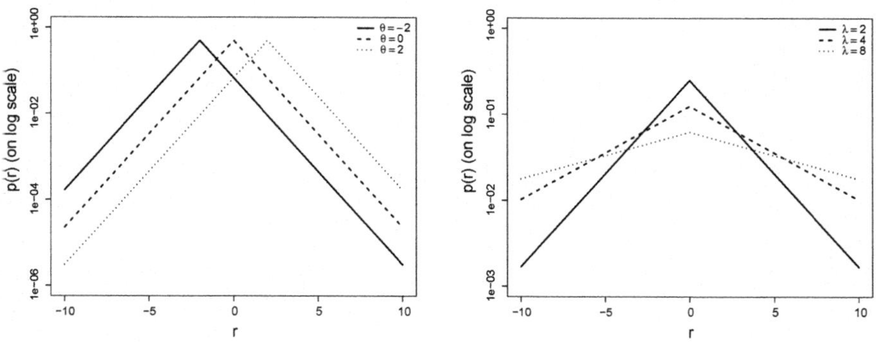

(a) $\lambda = 1$ (b) $\theta = 0$

Fig. 4.14 Laplace density function for different values of location (**a**) and scale (**b**). Note the appearance of a "tent shape" when the y-axis is expressed in logs

More precisely, if the annual growth rate is $r_t^i = \ln\left(\frac{x_t^i}{x_{t-1}^i}\right)$, where x_{t-1}^i is the GDP of a country or the size of a firm in year $t-1$, then for all years the probability density of r is consistent with a Laplace distribution given by the function

$$p(r) = \frac{1}{2\lambda} e^{-\frac{|r-\theta|}{\lambda}}, \quad -\infty < r < \infty, \tag{4.40}$$

where $\theta \in (-\infty, \infty)$ and $\lambda > 0$ are location and scale parameters, respectively. From Fig. 4.14a, it is apparent that changing the location simply shifts the probability density curve to the right or to the left. From Fig. 4.14b, we see that the scale parameter determines the width of the distribution.[31]

The distribution is symmetric about θ, i.e. for any real r we have

$$p(\theta - r) = p(\theta + r). \tag{4.41}$$

Consequently, as in the case of other symmetrical distributions, Laplace's location is the same as its mean, median, and mode. Figure 4.15 compares the Laplace against the Gaussian distribution. Recall that the Gaussian distribution has an expected value of μ and a variance equal to σ^2. Suppose we fix the mean of the Gaussian to equal the mean of the Laplace distribution, and then also match the variances of the two. In Fig. 4.15, both the distributions have an expected value of 4 and variance equal to 8.[32] As can be seen, the Laplace has higher spike and slightly thicker tails compared

[31]The Laplace distribution is the distribution of differences between two independent variates with identical exponential distributions (e.g. Kotz et al. 2001). It is also sometimes called the *double exponential distribution*, because its shape reminds one of two exponential distributions (with an additional location parameter) spliced together back-to-back.

[32]The variance of the Laplace distribution is $2\lambda^2$, hence the scale parameter has been taken equal to 2 for the Laplace density of Fig. 4.15.

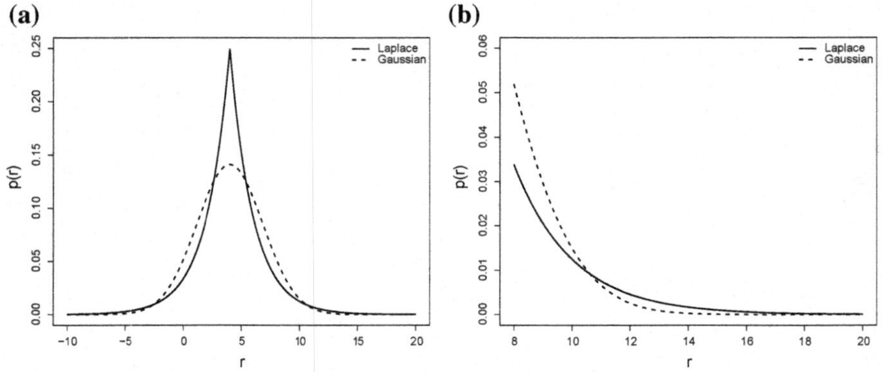

Fig. 4.15 Laplace and Gaussian densities

to the Gaussian. The latter property is particularly visible in panel (b) of the figure, which provides a magnification of the right tail on (8, 20).

Parameter estimation for the Laplace model presents few difficulties. Given a sample $R = (r_1, \ldots, r_N)$ coming from the Laplace distribution (4.40), the maximum likelihood estimator of θ is the sample median, whereas the maximum likelihood estimator of λ is

$$\lambda = \frac{1}{N} \sum_{i=1}^{N} |r_i - \theta| \, . \tag{4.42}$$

Figure 4.16 provides an example using 10,000 random observations generated from a Laplace-distributed population with parameters $\theta = 1$ and $\lambda = 2$. Clearly, the estimated values of the Laplace parameters are very close to the "true" values from which the data were generated. For comparison, a Gaussian distribution with the same mean and standard deviation as the simulated data is superimposed on the plot. However, while the Gaussian distribution is expressed in terms of the squared difference from the mean, the Laplace density is expressed in terms of the absolute difference from the median. Consequently, the Laplace distribution has a steeper peak and tails that asymptotically approach zero more slowly than the Gaussian.

To test whether a given data set is plausibly drawn from a Laplace distribution, one can use the K–S statistic (4.24). The hypothesis regarding the Laplace distributional form is rejected if the statistic D is greater than the critical value obtained from a table. For example, the calculated value of the K–S statistic that quantifies the distance between the estimated Laplace model and the simulated data of Fig. 4.16 is 0.72, whereas the critical value at the 5 % significance level is approximately 0.91.[33] Hence, as expected, the null hypothesis is not rejected for the Laplace-distributed

[33] For the tables of critical values, see Puig and Stephens (2000).

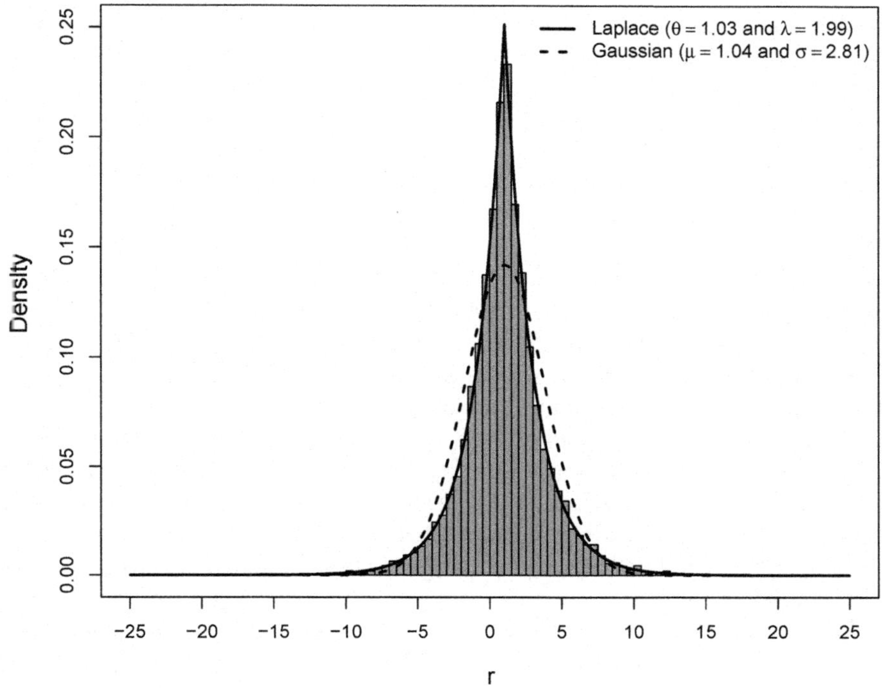

Fig. 4.16 Histogram with superimposed Laplace and Gaussian densities for 10,000 random observations from the Laplace distribution with $\theta = 1$ and $\lambda = 2$

data, while it is rejected for the Gaussian distribution—the corresponding value of D is 6.71, which is far beyond the 5 % critical value of around 0.9.[34]

Finally, distribution selection criteria can be used to distinguish between the Laplace and a number of alternative models. Among these criteria, the negative log-likelihood value $l = -\ln(L)$, minimized to determine the values for the free parameters, as well as the values of Akaike (1973) and Schwarz (1978) information criteria (AIC and BIC) typically provide a way to judge whether a distribution is a better explanation of the data than some other reasonable alternatives. Model selection criteria such as the AIC and BIC will select, when comparing models with the same number of parameters, the model with the largest l according to the formula

$$(2 \times l) + (d \times k), \tag{4.43}$$

where k represents the number of parameters in the fitted model and $d = 2$ for the usual AIC or $d = \ln(N)$, N being the number of observations, for the so-called BIC. When comparing models fitted by maximum likelihood to the same data, the smaller the AIC or BIC the better the fit. When comparing models using the log-likelihood

[34] For a practical guide to testing for normality by means of the K-S statistic, see Stephens (1974).

Table 4.3 Selection criteria for Laplace and Gaussian distributions using 10,000 random observations generated from a Laplace-distributed population with parameters $\theta = 1$ and $\lambda = 2$

	Laplace	Gaussian
l	$-23,797$	$-24,526$
AIC	47,597	49,056
BIC	47,612	49,070

criterion, the larger the l the better the fit. As a matter of example, Table 4.3 reports the values of l, AIC and BIC obtained for the same simulated data as in Fig. 4.16. As expected, it emerges that all the selection criteria agree on the Laplace distribution as the one to be preferred over the Gaussian.

We want to conclude this part by trying to answer a question the reader may have at this point. The literature seems often to suggest the Pareto distribution as a good approximation of firms' size and the Laplace distribution for growth rates. Is there a link between the two or are they separated phenomena? The second explanation may certainly be a possibility that we have followed in the presentation of this chapter, as there are separate stochastic processes generating the two distributions.

Regarding the first possibility, the existence of a link, a possible starting point is a couple of well-known statistical theorems that we have briefly mentioned before: (*i*) the logarithm of a Pareto random variable follows an exponential distribution (see footnote 11); (*ii*) the difference of two independent exponential random variables generates a Laplace distribution (see footnote 31). In other words, if we generate two independent Pareto distribution, say X_1 in period 1 and X_2 in period 2, then taking the logs $x_1 = \ln(X_1)$ and $x_2 = \ln(X_2)$ the difference

$$l = x_2 - x_1 \tag{4.44}$$

follows a Laplace (or double exponential) distribution. The problem with this theorem is the independence assumption. Can this theorem be generalized to the case involving *dependent* random variables? The analysis in Palestrini (2007) shows that the way of generating a double exponential random variable[35] by taking the difference of two exponential random variables can be generalized to dependent random variables having the $(t, t+1)$ joint distribution

$$\Pr(x_t > x_1, x_{t+1} > x_2) = e^{-\alpha_1 x_1 - \alpha_2 x_2 - \lambda \max(x_1, x_2)}, \tag{4.45}$$

where λ is a measure of dependence. In other terms, $\lambda = 0$ means independence, whereas with $\lambda > 0$ there is positive dependence as it is the case with firms' *log* size.

[35]This double exponentiality means that the tails have exponential shape but the distribution has a positive probability mass at zero because the generating joint probability distribution explained below has a singularity when $x_2 = x_1$. The probability mass at zero can be computed as in Bottazzi (2008).

The distribution (4.45) is known as the *Marshall-Olkin bivariate exponential distribution* after the analysis in Marshall and Olkin (1967), who proved that (*i*) this joint distribution has exponential marginals and, more important, (*ii*) it is the distribution satisfying the bivariate version of the "memoryless property" of exponential random variables, i.e.

$$\begin{aligned}\Pr\left(x_t > \bar{x}_1 + k, x_{t+1} > \hat{x}_1 + k | x_t > k, x_{t+1} > k\right) = \\ = \Pr\left(x_t > \bar{x}_1, x_{t+1} > \hat{x}_1\right).\end{aligned} \tag{4.46}$$

Summarizing the theorem in Palestrini (2007), the Pareto distribution together with the memoryless property are compatible with double exponential growth rates. As noted by the author, this theorem is very sensitive to the hypotheses. The scaling free property is not always a feature of the entire support of the firms' size distribution and the memoryless property may be a bad approximation of actual data. For this reason, we have chosen in this chapter to explain these two important stylized facts as separated.

4.5 Exercise

Exercise 1

Suppose to have a set of 5,000 observations, which have been randomly generated from a composite lognormal-Pareto distribution with $\theta = 2$ and $\alpha = 1$ (see footnote 12 and various examples throughout the text; also look at the source codes of the relevant examples available on the book's website). Obtain parameters via a maximum-likelihood estimation procedure for the distributions listed in Table 4.1. Plot the complementary CDF of the data and the fitted models on log-log axes. [Hint: in `R`, functions for fitting by maximum likelihood the non-power-law distributions of Table 4.1 are implemented in the package `fitdistrplus` (Delignette-Muller and Dutang 2015), the documentation of which the reader is referred to for more details. For the power-law model, use the methods of Sect. 4.3.3.]

Exercise 2

In `R`, load the example data set `Labour` from package `Ecdat`. The data set consists of 569 Belgian firms and includes information for 1996 on the total number of employees, their average wage, the amount of capital and a measure of output (Verbeek 2012, Chap. 4). Consider both the total number of employees and the amount of capital as proxies for size of firms and perform some exploratory graphical analysis of the data using the methods of Sect. 4.3.2. Does the data appear visually to follow a power law?

Exercise 3
Consider the same data of the previous exercise and assume the amount of capital—measured by total fixed assets (in million euros) at end of 1995—as a proxy of firm size. Estimate the lower bound $x_{\min}$ on power-law behaviour using the distance-based approach described in Sect. 4.3.3.1 and the scaling parameter α using the Hill estimator (4.25). Next, calculate the goodness of fit between the original data and the estimated power law using the method described in Sect. 4.3.4. Is the fit a good match to the tail data? Finally, fit the lognormal and exponential distributions to the data above the value of $x_{\min}$ for the power-law model and compare the latter with such alternative hypotheses using the method proposed by Vuong (1989). Can these alternatives be ruled out as a fit to your data or, if neither is ruled out, which one is the better fit? [Hint: see footnote 22 and look at the source code for Fig. 4.9 available on the book's website.]

Exercise 4
Repeat the same exercise as above, but assume the total number of employees as a proxy of firm size. Summarize/discuss the results you get. [Hint: the number of workers in a factory is a *discrete* numerical variable, hence the appropriate discrete counterparts of the methods presented in the relevant parts of the chapter should be used. These are readily implemented in the `R` software package `poweRlaw` (Gillespie 2015), the documentation of which the reader is referred to for more details. For further guidance, see also Clauset et al. (2009).]

Exercise 5
Using the `R` script available from the book's website, simulate the multiplicative stochastic process (4.31) for $N = 10{,}000$, $T = 100$, $\mu = 1.02$ and $\sigma = 0.05$. Provide a graphical comparison of the density curves estimated for time steps $t = 25$, $t = 50$, $t = 75$ and $T = 100$. Do they resemble a lognormal distribution? Which difference is more apparent when comparing the shape of the plotted densities? [Hint: find the parameter values of the lognormals by "matching moments" (see Sect. 4.2 and footnote 24).]

Exercise 6
In `R`, load the example data set `siemens` from package `evir`. These data are the daily log returns on Siemens share price from Tuesday 2nd January 1973 until Tuesday 23rd July 1996. Find which distribution the data fits more between a Laplace and a Gaussian. Provide the corresponding histogram with fitted density curves and compare the candidate distributions using selection criteria. [Hint: to improve performance of fitting functions, consider centring and scaling your data.]

Conclusion

So far only a small minority in the economic profession has embraced the Agent Based (AB) perspective in economic analysis. This may be due to the "wait and see" attitude of those who want to see the approach well established in the profession before embracing it. Hesitation, however, may also come from "cultural inertia": while in other disciplines the explanatory power of computer simulations has been long recognized, most economists remained dismissive of any scientific work that was not based on strict mathematical proof until one or two decades ago. We believe cultural interia should not block our quest for new tools to understand economic phenomena that exert such a powerful influence on our lives. Many interesting problems in macroeconomics and finance which are hard to analyze with traditional analytical tools can be insightfully disentangled using numerical analysis through computer simulations. By explaining the logic and main tools of the AB modelling approach, the main aim of this book is to show to undergraduate and Ph.D. students, and to interested scholars as well, the potential of the AB approach in providing an alternative line of attack to macroeconomic and financial studies, capable of tracing new unexplored routes that were previously unviable due to the limitations of traditional tools.

A. Caiani et al. (eds.), *Economics with Heterogeneous Interacting Agents*,
New Economic Windows, DOI 10.1007/978-3-319-44058-3

References

Aitchison, J., & Brown, J. A. C. (1954). On criteria for descriptions of income distribution. *Metroeconomica, 6*, 88–107.

Aitchison, J., & Brown, J. A. C. (1957). *The lognormal distribution with special reference to its use in economics*. New York: Cambridge University Press.

Akaike, H. (1973). Information theory and an extension of the likelihood ratio principle. In B. N. Petrov & F. Csaki (Eds.), *Proceedings of the second international symposium of information theory* (pp. 257–281). Budapest: Akademiai Kiado.

Akerlof, G. (1970). The market for lemons: qualitative uncertainty and the market mechanism. *Quarterly Journal of Economics, 84*.

Alfarano, S., Lux, T., & Wagner, F. (2005). Estimation of agent-based models: the case of an asymmetric herding model. *Computational Economics, 26*(1), 19–49.

Alfons, A., Templ, M., & Filzmoser, P. (2013). Robust estimation of economic indicators from survey samples based on pareto tail modeling. *Journal of the Royal Statistical Society: Series C (Applied Statistics), 62*, 271–286.

Allais, M. (1953). Le comportement de l'homme rationnel devant le risque: critique des postulats et axiomes de l'école américaine. *Econometrica: Journal of the Econometric Society*, 503–546.

Amaral, L. A. N., Buldyrev, S. V., Havlin, S., Salinger, M. A., Stanley, H. E., & Stanley, M. H. (1997). Scaling behavior in economics: the problem of quantifying company growth. *Physica A: Statistical and Theoretical Physics, 244*, 1–24.

Ando, A., & Modigliani, F. (1963). The life cycle hypothesis of saving: aggregate implications and tests. *The American Economic Review*, 55–84.

Anufriev, M., & Hommes, C. (2012). Evolutionary selection of individual expectations and aggregate outcomes in asset pricing experiments. *American Economic Journal: Microeconomics, 4*(4), 35–64.

Arnold, B. C. (2015). *Pareto Distributions* (2nd ed.). Boca Raton FL: CRC Press.

Arrow, K. J. (1951). An extension of the basic theorems of classical welfare economics. *In Second Berkeley Symposium on Mathematical Statistics and Probability, 1*, 507–532.

Arrow, K. J., & Debreu, G. (1954). Existence of an equilibrium for a competitive economy. *Econometrica: Journal of the Econometric Society*, 265–290.

Arthur, W. B. (2006). Out-of-equilibrium economics and agent-based modeling. *Handbook of computational economics, 2*, 1551–1564.

Arthur, W. B., Durlauf, S. N., & Lane, D. A. (1997). *The economy as an evolving complex system II* (Vol. 28). MA: Addison-Wesley Reading.

A. Caiani et al. (eds.), *Economics with Heterogeneous Interacting Agents*,
New Economic Windows, DOI 10.1007/978-3-319-44058-3

Assenza, T., Delli Gatti, D., & Grazzini, J. (2015). Emergent dynamics of a macroeconomic agent based model with capital and credit. *Journal of Economic Dynamics and Control*, *50*(C), 5–28.

Atoda, N., Suruga, N., & Tachibanaki, T. (1998). Statistical inference of functional forms for income distribution. *Economic Studies Quarterly*, *39*, 14–40.

Axtell, R. L. (2001). Zipf distribution of us firm sizes. *Science*, *293*(5536), 1818–1820.

Barabási, A.-L., & Albert, R. (1999). Emergence of scaling in random networks. *Science*, *286*(5439), 509–512.

Bardsley, N. (2010). *Experimental economics: Rethinking the rules*. Princeton: Princeton University Press.

Bargigli, L., Gallegati, M., Riccetti, L., Russo, A. (2014). Network analysis and calibration of the "leveraged network-based financial accelerator". *Journal of Economic Behavior & Organization*, *99*, 109–125. doi:10.1016/j.jebo.2013.12.018

Bargigli, L., & Tedeschi, G. (2014). Interaction in agent-based economics: a survey on the network approach. *Physica A: Statistical Mechanics and its Applications*, *399*, 1–15.

Bartels, C. P. A., van Metelen, H. (1975). *Alternative Probability Density Functions of Income: A Comparison of the Lognormal-, Gamma- and Weibull-distribution with Dutch Data*. Research Memorandum 29, Faculty of Economics, Vrije Universiteit, Amsterdam.

Bartels, C. P. A. (1977). *Economic aspects of regional welfare: income distribution and unemployment*. Leiden: Martinus Nijhoff.

Beirlant, J., Goegebeur, Y., & Teugels, J. L. (2004). *Statistics of extremes: theory and applications*. West Sussex UK: Wiley.

Beirlant, J., Vynckier, P., & Teugels, J. L. (1996a). Excess functions and estimation of the extreme-value index. *Bernoulli*, *2*, 293–318.

Beirlant, J., Vynckier, P., & Teugels, J. L. (1996b). Tail index estimation, Pareto quantile plots, and regression diagnostics. *Journal of the American Statistical Association*, *31*, 1659–1667.

Benabou, R., & Laroque, G. (1992). Using privileged information to manipulate markets: Insiders, gurus, and credibility. *The Quarterly Journal of Economics*, 921–958.

Bernanke, B., & Gertler, M. (1989). Agency costs, net worth and business fluctuations. *American Economic Review*, *89*, 14–31.

Bernanke, B., & Gertler, M. (1990). Financial fragility and economic performance. *Quarterly Journal of Economics*, *105*, 87–114.

Bernanke, B., & Gertler, M. (1995). Inside the black box: the credit channel of monetary transmission. *Journal of Economic Perspectives*, *9–4*, 27–48.

Bernanke, B., Gertler, M., & Gilchrist, S. (1999). The financial accelerator in a quantitative business cycle framework. In J. Taylor & M. Woodford (Eds.), *Handbook of macroeconomics* (Vol. 1). Amstrdam: North Holland.

Bingham, N. H., Goldie, C. M., & Teugels, J. L. (1987). *Regular variation*. Cambridge UK: Cambridge University Press.

Blank, A., & Solomon, S. (2000). Power laws in cities population, financial markets and internet sites (scaling in systems with a variable number of components). *Physica A: Statistical Mechanics and its Applications*, *287*, 279–288.

Blume, L. E., & Durlauf, S. N. (2005). *The economy as an evolving complex system, III: current perspectives and future directions*. Oxford: Oxford University Press.

Bordley, R. F., McDonald, J. B., & Mantrala, A. (1996). Something new, something old: Parametric models for the size distribution of income. *Journal of Income Distribution*, *6*, 91–103.

Boswijk, H. P., Hommes, C. H., & Manzan, S. (2007). Behavioral heterogeneity in stock prices. *Journal of Economic Dynamics and Control*, *31*(6), 1938–1970.

Bottazzi, G. (2008). On the relationship between firms' size and growth rate. *Economics Bulletin*, *3*, 1–7.

Bottazzi, G., Coad, A., Jacoby, N., & Secchi, A. (2011). Corporate growth and industrial dynamics: evidence from french manufacturing. *Applied Economics*, *43*, 103–116.

Bottazzi, G., Dosi, G., & Rebesco, I. (2005). Institutional architectures and behavioral ecologies in the dynamics of financial markets. *Journal of Mathematical Economics*, *41*(12), 197–228.

Bottazzi, G., & Secchi, A. (2003a). Common properties and sectoral specificities in the dynamics of U.S. manufacturing firms. *Review of Industrial Organization, 23*, 217–232.

Bottazzi, G., & Secchi, A. (2003b). Why are distributions of firm growth rates tent-shaped? *Economic Letters, 80*, 415–420.

Bouchaud, J.-P. (2001). Power laws in economics and finance: some ideas from physics. *Quantitative Finance, 1*, 105–112.

Bouchaud, J.-P., Mézard, M., & Potters, M. (2002). Statistical properties of stock order books: empirical results and models. *Quantitative Finance, 2*(4), 251–256.

Brachmann, K., Stich, A., & Trede, M. (1996). Evaluating parametric income distribution models. *Allgemeines Statistisches Archiv, 80*, 285–298.

Brock, W. A. (1999). Scaling in economics: A reader's guide. *Industrial and Corporate Change, 8*, 409–446.

Brock, W. A., & Hommes, C. (1997). *A Rational Route to Randomness. Econometrica, 65*(5), 1059–1096.

Brock, W. A., & Hommes, C. H. (1998). Heterogeneous beliefs and routes to chaos in a simple asset pricing model. *Journal of Economic Dynamics and Control, 22*(89), 1235–1274.

Browning, M., Hansen, L. P., & Heckman, J. J. (1999). Micro data and general equilibrium models. *Handbook of macroeconomics, 1*, 543–633.

Caiani, A., Godin, A., Caverzasi, E., Gallegati, M., Kinsella, S., Stiglitz, J. E. (2015). Agent Based-Stock Flow Consistent Macroeconomics: Towards a Benchmark Model. Working paper, SSRN.

Caldentey, R., Stacchetti, E. (2007). Insider trading with stochastic valuation. *SSRN 986405*.

Campbell, J. Y., & Kyle, A. S. (1993). Smart money, noise trading and stock price behaviour. *The Review of Economic Studies, 60*(1), 1–34.

Canning, D., Amaral, L. A. N., Lee, Y., Meyer, M., & Stanley, H. E. (1998). Scaling the volatility of gdp growth rates. *Economic Letters, 60*, 335–341.

Capasso, M., Alessi, L., Barigozzi, M., & Fagiolo, G. (2009). On approximating the distributions of goodness-of-fit test statistics based on the empirical distribution function: The case of unknown parameters. *Advances in Complex System, 12*, 157–167.

Castaldi, C. Dosi, G. (2004). *Income Levels and Income Growth: Some New Cross-Country Evidence and Some Interpretative Puzzles*. Working Paper 18, Laboratory of Economics and Management, Sant'Anna School of Advanced Studies, Pisa. http://www.lem.sssup.it/WPLem/files/2004-18.pdf.

Catullo, E., Gallegati, M., & Palestrini, A. (2015). Towards a credit network based early warning indicator for crises. *Journal of Economic Dynamics and Control, 50*, 78–97.

Chakraborty, A., & Yilmaz, B. (2008). Microstructure bluffing with nested information. *The American Economic Review, 98*(2), 280–284.

Champernowne, D. G. (1953). A model of income distribution. *The Economic Journal, 63*, 318–351.

Chiarella, C., & Iori, G. (2002). A simulation analysis of the microstructure of double auction markets. *Quantitative Finance, 2*(5), 346–353.

Chiarella, C., Iori, G., & Perelló, J. (2009). The impact of heterogeneous trading rules on the limit order book and order flows. *Journal of Economic Dynamics and Control, 33*(3), 525–537.

Christiano, L. J., Trabandt, M., Walentin, K. (2010). Dsge models for monetary policy analysis. In Friedman, B. M. and Woodford, M., (Eds.), *Handbook of Monetary Economics*, (vol 3, pp. 285–367). Elsevier.

Cincotti, S., Raberto, M., Teglio, A. (2010). Credit money and macroeconomic instability in the agent-based model and simulator Eurace. Economics Discussion Papers 2010-2014, Kiel Institute for the World Economy (IfW).

Clauset, A., Shalizi, C. R., & Newman, M. E. J. (2009). Power-law distributions in empirical data. *SIAM Review, 51*, 661–703.

Clauset, A., Young, M., & Gleditsch, K. S. (2007). On the frequency of severe terrorist events. *Journal of Conflict Resolution, 51*, 58–88.

Cont, R. (1998). *Statistical finance: empirical study and theoretical modeling of price variations in financial markets*. Ph.D. thesis, Universite de Paris XI.

Cont, R. (2001). Empirical properties of asset returns: stylized facts and statistical issues. *Quantitative Finance*, *1*(2), 223–236.

Cont, R., Potters, M., Bouchaud, J.-P. (1997). *Scale Invariance and Beyond: Les Houches Workshop, Mar 10–14, 1997*, Chapter Scaling in Stock Market Data: Stable Laws and Beyond, pp. 75–85. Springer.

Cooray, K., & Ananda, M. M. A. (2005). Modeling actuarial data with a composite lognormal-pareto model. *Scandinavian Actuarial Journal*, *2005*, 321–334.

Csardi, G., & Nepusz, T. (2006). The igraph software package for complex network research. *Complex Systems*, 1695.

Dacorogna, M. M., Müller, U. A., Nagler, R. J., Olsen, R. B., & Pictet, O. V. (1993). A geographical model for the daily and weekly seasonal volatility in the foreign exchange market. *Journal of International Money and Finance*, *12*(4), 413–438.

D'Addario, R. (1974). Intorno ad una funzione di distribuzione. *Giornale degli Economisti e Annali di Economia*, *33*, 205–214.

D'Agostino, R. B., & Stephens, M. A. (1986). *Goodness-of-fit techniques*. New York: Marcel Dekker.

Danielsson, J., de Haan, L., Peng, L., & de Vries, C. (2001). Using a bootstrap method to choose sample fraction in tail index estimation. *Journal of Multivariate Analysis*, *76*, 226–248.

Dawid, H. (2005). Agent-based models of innovation and technological change. In Tesfatsion, L. & Judd, K.L (Eds.), *Handbook of Computational Economics 2*, pp. 1236–1267. North-Holland.

De Long, J. B., Shleifer, A., Summers, L. H., & Waldmann, R. J. (1990). Noise trader risk in financial markets. *Journal of Political Economy*, 703–738.

Debreu, G. (1951). The coefficient of resource utilization. *Econometrica: Journal of the Econometric Society*, 273–292.

Debreu, G. (1954). Representation of a preference ordering by a numerical function. *Decision Processes*, *3*, 159–165.

Debreu, G. (1960). Topological methods in cardinal utility theory. *Mathematical Methods in the Social Sciences*, *1959*, 16–26.

Debreu, G. (1974). Excess demand functions. *Journal of Mathematical Economics*, *1*(1), 15–21.

Delignette-Muller, M. L., & Dutang, C. (2015). `fitdistrplus`: an `R` package for fitting distributions. *Journal of Statistical Software*, *64*, 1–34.

Delli Gatti, D., Desiderio, S., Gaffeo, E., Cirillo, P., & Gallegati, M. (2011). *Macroeconomics from the bottom-up*. Berlin: Springer Science & Business Media.

Delli Gatti, D., Di Guilmi, C., Gaffeo, E., Giulioni, G., Gallegati, M., & Palestrini, A. (2005a). A new approach to business fluctuations: heterogenous interacting agents, scaling laws and financial fragility. *Journal of Economic Behavior & Organization*, *56*, 489–512.

Delli Gatti, D., Di Guilmi, C., Gaffeo, E., Giulioni, G., Gallegati, M., & Palestrini, A. (2005b). A new approach to business fluctuations: heterogeneous interacting agents, scaling laws and financial fragility. *Journal of Economic behavior & organization*, *56*(4), 489–512.

Delli Gatti, D., Di Guilmi, C., Gaffeo, E., Giulioni, G., Gallegati, M., & Palestrini, A. (2005c). A new approach to business fluctuations: heterogeneous interacting agents, scaling laws and financial fragility. *Journal of Economic Behavior & Organization*, *56*(4), 489–512.

Delli Gatti, D., Gallegati, M., Giulioni, G., & Palestrini, A. (2003). Financial fragility, patterns of firms? entry and exit and aggregate dynamics. *Journal of Economic Behavior & Organization*, *51*(1), 79–97.

Delli Gatti, D., Gallegati, M., Greenwald, B., Russo, A., & Stiglitz, J. (2010a). The financial accelerator in an evolving credit network. *Journal of Economic Dynamics and Control*, *34–9*, 1627–1650.

Delli Gatti, D., Gallegati, M., Greenwald, B., Russo, A., & Stiglitz, J. E. (2010b). The financial accelerator in an evolving credit network. *Journal of Economic Dynamics and Control*, *34*.

Di Guilmi, C., Gaffeo, E., & Gallegati, M. (2004). Empirical results on the size distribution of business cycle phases. *Physica A: Statistical Mechanics and its Applications*, *333*, 325–334.

Di Guilmi, C., Gaffeo, E., Gallegati, M., & Palestrini, A. (2005). International evidence on business cycle magnitude dependence: an analysis of 16 industrialized countries, 1881–2000. *International Journal of Applied Econometrics and Quantitative Studies*, *2*, 5–16.

Diamond, P. A. (1965). The evaluation of infinite utility streams. *Econometrica: Journal of the Econometric Society*, *1*, 170–177.

Ding, Z., & Granger, C. W. (1996). Modeling volatility persistence of speculative returns: a new approach. *Journal of Econometrics*, *73*(1), 185–215.

Ding, Z., Granger, C. W., & Engle, R. F. (1993). A long memory property of stock market returns and a new model. *Journal of Empirical Finance*, *1*(1), 83–106.

Dosi, G., Fagiolo, G., & Roventini, A. (2010). Schumpeter meeting Keynes: a policy-friendly model of endogenous growth and business cycles. *Journal of Economic Dynamics and Control*, *34*(9), 1748–1767.

Dosi, G., Napoletano, M., Roventini, A., Stiglitz, J. E., Treibich, T. (2015). Expectation formation, fiscal policies and macroeconomic performance when agents are heterogeneous and the world is changing. Working papers, Large Scale Crisis 1929-2008, Ancona Conference, 2015.

Dosi, G., & Nelson, R. R. (2010). Technical change and industrial dynamics as evolutionary processes. In B. H. Hall & N. Rosenberg (Eds.), *Handbook of the economics of innovation* (Vol. 1, pp. 51–127). Amsterdam: North-Holland.

Drees, H., de Haan, L., & Resnick, S. (2000). How to make a hill plot. *The Annals of Statistics*, *28*, 254–274.

Duffy, J. (2006). Agent-based models and human subject experiments. *Handbook of Computational Economics*, *2*, 949–1011.

Dupuis, D. J., & Victoria-Feser, M.-P. (2006). A robust prediction error criterion for pareto modelling of upper tails. *The Canadian Journal of Statistics*, *34*, 639–658.

Durlauf, S. N. (2005). Complexity and empirical economics. *The Economic Journal*, *115*, 225–243.

Efron, B., & Tibshirani, R. J. (1993). *An introduction to the bootstrap*. New York: Chapman and Hall.

Erdős, P., & Rényi, A. (1960). On the evolution of random graphs. *In Publication ofhte Mathematical Institute of the Hungarian Academy of the Sciences*, *5*, 17–61.

Espinguet, P., & Terraza, M. (1983). Essai d'extrapolation des distributions de salaires français. *Economie Appliquée*, *36*, 535–561.

Fagiolo, G., Napoletano, M., & Roventini, A. (2007a). Sulle distribuzioni dei tassi di crescita dell'output aggregato: un'analisi per sati uniti e italia. *Rivista Internazionale di Scienze Sociali*, *115*, 215–241.

Fagiolo, G., Napoletano, M., & Roventini, A. (2007b). The european physical journal b. How do output growth rate distributions look like? *Some Time-Series Evidence on OECD Countries*, *57*, 205–211.

Fagiolo, G., Napoletano, M., & Roventini, A. (2008). Are output growth-rate distributions fat-tailed? some evidence from oecd countries. *Journal of Applied Econometrics*, *23*, 639–669.

Feller, W. (1971). *An introduction to probability theory and its applications* (2nd ed.). New York: Wiley.

Figlewski, S. (1979). Subjective information and market efficiency in a betting market. *The Journal of Political Economy*, 75–88.

Flannery, M., & Rangan, K. (2006). Partial adjustment toward target capital structures. *Journal of Financial Economics*, *79–3*, 469–506.

Frank, M., & Goyal, V. (2008). Tradeoff and pecking order theories of debt. In B. Espen Eckbo (Ed.), *The handbook of empirical corporate finance*. Amstrdam: North Holland.

Frank, M., & Goyal, V. (2014). The profits-leverage puzzle revisited. *Review of Finance*, 1–39.

Friedman, M. (1957). The permanent income hypothesis. In A. Theory (Ed.), *of the Consumption Function* (pp. 20–37). Princeton: Princeton University Press.

Fu, D., Pammolli, F., Buldyrev, S. V., Riccaboni, M., Yamasaki, K., Matia, K., et al. (2005). The growth of business firms: theoretical framework and empirical evidence. *Proceedings of the National Academy of Sciences of the United States of America*, *102*, 18801–18806.

Gabaix, X. (2009). Power laws in economics and finance. *Annual Review of Economics, 1*, 255–294.

Gabaix, X. (2011). The granular origins of aggregate fluctuations. *Econometrica, 79*, 733–772.

Gabaix, X., Gopikrishnan, P., Plerou, V., & Stanley, H. E. (2003). A theory of power-law distributions in financial market fluctuations. *Nature, 423*(6937), 267–270.

Gabaix, X., Gopikrishnan, P., Plerou, V., Stanley, H. E., et al. (2006). Institutional investors and stock market volatility. *The Quarterly Journal of Economics, 121*(2), 461–504.

Galbraith, J. W., & Zernov, S. (2009). Extreme dependence in the nasdaq and s&p 500 composite indexes. *Applied Financial Economics, 19*(13), 1019–1028.

Gibrat, R. (1931). *Les inégalités économiques. Applications: aux inégalités des richesses, à la concentration des entreprises, aux population des villes, aux statistiques des familles, etc., d'une loi nouvelle: la loi de l'effet proportionnel*. Librairie du Recueil Sirey, Paris.

Gigerenzer, G., Todd, P. M., & Group, A. R. (2000). *Simple heuristics that make us smart*. Oxford: Oxford University Press. Number 9780195143812 in OUP Catalogue.

Gilbert, N., Pyka, A., & Ahrweiler, P. (2002). Innovation networks - a simulation approach. *Journal of Artificial Societies and Social Simulation, 4*(3),

Gillespie, C. S. (2015). Fitting heavy tailed distributions: the `poweRlaw` package. *Journal of Statistical Software, 64*, 1–16.

Gode, D. K., & Sunder, S. (1997). What makes markets allocationally efficient? *The Quarterly Journal of Economics, 112*(2), 603–630.

Gorman, W. M. (1953). Community preference fields. *Econometrica: journal of the Econometric Society*, 63–80.

Gorman, W. M. (1961). On a class of preference fields. *Metroeconomica, 13*(2), 53–56.

Graham, J., & Harvey, C. (2001). The theory and practice of corporate finance. *Journal of Financial Economics, 60*, 187–243.

Granger, C. W., Ding, Z. (1994). Stylized facts on the temporal and distributional properties of daily data from speculative markets. *UCSD Department of Economics Discussion Paper*, pages 94–19.

Greenwald, B. C., & Stiglitz, J. E. (1993). Financial market imperfections and business cycles. *Quarterly Journal of Economics, 108*(1), 77–114.

Grilli, R., Tedeschi, G., Gallegati, M. (2014). Network approach for detecting macroeconomic instability. In *2014 Tenth International Conference on Signal-Image Technology and Internet-Based Systems (SITIS)*, pp. 440–446. IEEE.

Guvenen, F. (2011). *Macroeconomics with heterogeneity: a practical guide*. Technical report: National Bureau of Economic Research.

Hall, P. (1982). On some simple estimates of an exponent of regular variation. *Journal of the Royal Statistical Society: Series B (Methodological), 44*, 37–42.

Haruvy, E., Lahav, Y., & Noussair, C. N. (2007). Traders' expectations in asset markets: experimental evidence. *The American Economic Review, 97*(5), 1901–1920.

Heathcote, J., Storesletten, K., & Violante, G. L. (2009). Quantitative macroeconomics with heterogeneous households. *Annual Review of Economics, 1*(1), 319–354.

Hill, B. M. (1975). A simple approach to inference about the tail of a distribution. *The Annals of Statistics, 3*, 1163–1174.

Hommes, C. (2013). *Behavioral rationality and heterogeneous expectations in complex economic systems*. Cambridge: Cambridge University Press.

Ijiri, Y., Simon, H. A. (1977). *Skew distributions and the sizes of business firms*, vol. 24. North Holland.

Iori, G. (2002). A microsimulation of traders activity in the stock market: the role of heterogeneity, agents? interactions and trade frictions. *Journal of Economic Behavior & Organization, 49*(2), 269–285.

Jackson, M. (2008). *Social and Economic Networks*. Princeton: Princeton University Press.

Jessen, A. H., & Mikosch, T. (2006). Regularly varying functions. *Publications de l'Institut Mathématique, 80*, 171–192.

Johnson, N. L., Kotz, S., & Balakrishnan, N. (1994). *Continuous univariate distributions* (2nd ed., Vol. 1). New York: Wiley.

Kahneman, D., & Tversky, A. (1972). Subjective probability: a judgment of representativeness. *Cognitive Psychology*, *3*(3), 430–454.

Kahneman, D., & Tversky, A. (1979). Prospect theory: an analysis of decision under risk. *Econometrica: Journal of the Econometric Society*, 263–291.

Kernighan, B. W. (1988). *The C programming language* (2nd ed.). New Jersey: Prentice Hall. Prentice Hall Professional Technical Reference.

Kesten, H. (1973). Random difference equations and renewal theory for products of random matrices. *Acta Mathematica*, *131*, 207–248.

Keynes, J. M. (1936). *The general theory of interest, employment and money*. London: Macmillan.

Kirman, A. (1991). Epidemics of opinion and speculative bubbles in financial markets. In M. Taylor (Ed.), *Money and financial markets*. Oxford: Blackwell.

Kirman, A. (1993). Ants, rationality, and recruitment. *The Quarterly Journal of Economics*, *108*(1), 137–156.

Kirman, A., Moulet, S., Schulz, R. (2008). Price Discrimination and Customer Behaviour: Empirical Evidence from Marseille. working paper or preprint.

Kiyotaki, N., & M. J.,. (1997). Credit cycles. *Journal of Political Economy*, *105–2*, 211–248.

Kleiber, C., & Kotz, S. (2003). *Statistical size distributions in economics and actuarial sciences*. New York: Wiley.

Kotz, S., Kozubowski, T. J., & Podgórski, K. (2001). *The laplace distribution and generalizations: a revisit with applications to communications, economics, engineering, and finance*. Basel: Birkhäuser.

Krueger, D., Mitman, K., and Perri, F. (2015). Macroeconomics and heterogeneity, including inequality. Technical report, forthcoming in Handbook of Macroeconomics.

LeBaron, B., Arthur, W., & Palmer, R. (1999). Time series properties of an artificial stock market. *Journal of Economic Dynamics and Control*, *23*(9–10), 1487–1516.

LeBaron, B., & Yamamoto, R. (2008). The impact of imitation on long memory in an order driven market. *Eastern Economic Journal*, *34*(4), 504–517.

Lee, Y., Amaral, L. A. N., Canning, D., Meyer, M., & Stanley, H. E. (1998). Universal features in the growth dynamics of complex organizations. *Physical Review Letters*, *81*, 3275–3278.

Lei, V., Noussair, C. N., & Plott, C. R. (2001). Nonspeculative bubbles in experimental asset markets: Lack of common knowledge of rationality vs. actual irrationality. *Econometrica*, *69*(4), 831–859.

Leijonhufvud, A. (1981). *Information and coordination: essays in macroeconomic theory*. Oxford: Oxford University Press.

Lenzu, S., & Tedeschi, G. (2012). Systemic risk on different interbank network topologies. *Physica A: Statistical Mechanics and its Applications*, *391*(18), 4331–4341.

Levy, M., & Solomon, S. (1996a). Power laws are logarithmic Boltzmann laws. *International Journal of Modern Physics C*, *7*, 595–601.

Levy, M., & Solomon, S. (1996b). Spontaneous scaling emergence in generic stochastic systems. *International Journal of Modern Physics C*, *7*, 745–751.

Lévy, P. (1954). *Théorie de l'addition des variables aléatoires*. Paris: Gauthier-Villars.

LiCalzi, M., & Pellizzari, P. (2003). Fundamentalists clashing over the book: a study of order-driven stock markets. *Quantitative Finance*, *3*(6), 470–480.

Lillo, F., & Farmer, J. D. (2004). The long memory of the efficient market. *Studies in Nonlinear Dynamics & Econometrics*, *8*(3), 1.

Liu, Y., Cizeau, P., Meyer, M., Peng, C.-K., & Stanley, H. E. (1997). Correlations in economic time series. *Physica A: Statistical Mechanics and its Applications*, *245*(3), 437–440.

Lucas, R. E. (1972). Expectations and the neutrality of money. *Journal of Economic Theory*, *4*(2), 103–124.

Lucas, R. E. (1976). Econometric policy evaluation: A critique. In *Carnegie-Rochester Conference Series on Public Policy*, (vol. 1, pp. 19–46). Elsevier.

Lux, T. (1996). The stable paretian hypothesis and the frequency of large returns: an examination of major german stocks. *Applied Financial Economics*, *6*, 463–475.

Lux, T. (1998). The socio-economic dynamics of speculative markets: interacting agents, chaos, and the fat tails of return distributions. *Journal of Economic Behavior & Organization, 33*(2), 143–165.

Lux, T., & Marchesi, M. (2000). Volatility clustering in financial markets: a microsimulation of interacting agents. *International Journal of Theoretical and Applied Finance, 3*(04), 675–702.

Malkiel, B. G., & Fama, E. F. (1970). Efficient capital markets: a review of theory and empirical work. *The Journal of Finance, 25*(2), 383–417.

Mandelbrot, B. (1960). The pareto-lévy law and the distribution of income. *International Economic Review, 1*, 79–106.

Mandelbrot, B. (1963). New methods in statistical economics. *The Journal of Political Economy, 71*, 421–440.

Mantel, R. R. (1974). On the characterization of aggregate excess demand. *Journal of Economic Theory, 7*(3), 348–353.

Marinsek, D., Pahor, M., Mramor, D., & Lustrik, R. (2015). Do european firms behave as if they converge toward a target capital structure? *Journal of International Financial Management & Accounting*.

Marshall, A. W., & Olkin, I. (1967). A multivariate exponential distribution. *Journal of the American Statistical Association, 62*, 30–44.

Mason, D. (1982). Laws of large numbers for sums of extreme values. *Annals of Probability, 10*, 754–764.

McDonald, J. B. (1984). Some generalized functions for the size distribution of income. *Econometrica, 52*, 647–665.

Merton, R.C., Samuelson, P. A. (1992). Continuous-time finance.

Milgrom, P. R. (2004). *Putting auction theory to work*. Cambridge: Cambridge University Press.

Mitzenmacher, M. (2004). A brief history of generative models for power law and lognormal distributions. *Internet Mathematics, 1*, 226–251.

Muth, J . F. (1961). Rational expectations and the theory of price movements. *Econometrica: Journal of the Econometric Society*, 315–335.

Newman, M. E. (2003). The structure and function of complex networks. *SIAM Review, 45*(2), 167–256.

Newman, M. E. J. (2005). Power laws, pareto distributions and zipf's law. *Contemporary Physics, 46*, 323–351.

Nolan, J. P. (2015). *Stable Distributions – Models for Heavy Tailed Data*. Birkhäuser, Boston MA. In progress, Chapter 1 online at http://academic2.american.edu/~jpnolan/stable/chap1.pdf.

Pagan, A. (1996). The econometrics of financial markets. *Journal of Empirical Finance, 3*(1), 15–102.

Palan, S. (2013). A review of bubbles and crashes in experimental asset markets. *Journal of Economic Surveys, 27*(3), 570–588.

Palestrini, A. (2007). Analysis of industrial dynamics: a note on the relationship between firms' size and growth rate. *Economics Letters, 94*, 367–371.

Pareto, V. (1895). La legge della domanda. *Giornale degli Economisti, 10*, 59–68.

Pareto, V. (1896). La courbe de la répartition de la richesse. Reprinted in G. Busino, editor, *Œeuvres complètes de Vilfredo Pareto, Tome 3: Écrits sur la courbe de la répartition de la richesse*, pp. 1–15, Librairie Droz, Geneva, 1965.

Pareto, V. (1897a). Aggiunta allo studio della curva delle entrate. *Giornale degli Economisti, 14*, 15–26.

Pareto, V. (1897b). Cours d'économie politique, vol. 2, lausanne: F. *Rouqe and Paris: F. Pichon*.

Pogrebna, G. (2006). Auctions versus bilateral bargaining: Evidence from a natural experiment. *SSRN 954891*.

Potters, M., & Bouchaud, J.-P. (2003). More statistical properties of order books and price impact. *Physica A: Statistical Mechanics and its Applications, 324*(1), 133–140.

Press, W. H., Teukolsky, S. A., Vetterling, W. T., & Flannery, B. P. (1992). *Numerical recipes in C: The art of scientific computing* (2nd ed.). New York, NY, USA: Cambridge University Press.

Puig, P., & Stephens, M. A. (2000). Tests of fit for the laplace distribution, with applications. *Technometrics*, *42*, 417–424.

Pushkin, D. O., & Aref, H. (2004). Bank mergers as scale-free coagulation. *Physica A: Statistical Mechanics and its Applications*, *336*(3), 571–584.

Raberto, M., Cincotti, S., Focardi, S. M., & Marchesi, M. (2001). Agent-based simulation of a financial market. *Physica A: Statistical Mechanics and its Applications*, *299*(1), 319–327.

Recchioni, M. C., Tedeschi, G., & Gallegati, M. (2015). A calibration procedure for analyzing stock price dynamics in an agent-based framework. *Journal of Economic Dynamics and Control*, *60*, 1–25.

Reichstein, T., & Jensen, M. B. (2005). Firm size and firm growth rate distributions–the case of denmark. *Industrial and Corporate Change*, *14*, 1145–1166.

Riccetti, L., Russo, A., & Gallegati, M. (2013). Leveraged network-based financial accelerator. *Journal of Economic Dynamics and Control*, *37*(8), 1626–1640.

Riccetti, L., Russo, A., and Gallegati, M. (2014). An Agent Based Decentralized Matching Macroeconomic Model. *Journal of Economic Interaction and Control.*, On-line version.

Roth, A. E., & Erev, I. (1995). Learning in extensive-form games: experimental data and simple dynamic models in the intermediate term. *Games and Economic Behavior*, *8*(1), 164–212.

Sahota, G. S. (1978). Theories of personal income distribution: a survey. *Journal of Economic Literature*, *16*, 1–55.

Sallans, B., Pfister, A., Karatzoglou, A., & Dorffner, G. (2003). Simulation and validation of an integrated markets model. *Journal of Artificial Societies and Social Simulation*, *6*(4),

Sapio, S. and Thoma, G. (2006). *The Growth of Industrial Sectors: Theoretical Insights and Empirical Evidence from U.S. Manufacturing*. Working Paper 9, Laboratory of Economics and Management, Sant'Anna School of Advanced Studies, Pisa. http://www.lem.sssup.it/WPLem/files/2006-09.pdf.

Schwarz, G. E. (1978). Estimating the dimension of a model. *Annals of Statistics*, *6*, 461–464.

Shiller, R. J., Fischer, S., & Friedman, B. M. (1984). Stock prices and social dynamics. *Brookings Papers on Economic Activity*, *1984*(2), 457–510.

Simon, H. A. (1955). On a class of skew distribution functions. *Biometrika*, *42*, 425–440.

Simon, H. A. (1957). *Models of man: social and rational; mathematical essays on rational human behavior in society setting*. New York: Wiley.

Smith, V. L. (1965). Experimental auction markets and the walrasian hypothesis. *The Journal of Political Economy*, 387–393.

Sonnenschein, H. (1972). Market excess demand functions. *Econometrica: Journal of the Econometric Society*, pp. 549–563.

Sornette, D. (1998). Multiplicative processes and power laws. *Physical Review E*, *57*, 4811–4813.

Sornette, D. (2006). *Critical Phenomena in natural sciences. chaos, fractals, selforganization and disorder: concepts and tools* (2nd ed.). Berlin and New York: Springer.

Sornette, D. (2012). Probability distributions in complex systems. In A. R. Meyers (Ed.), *Computational complexity: theory, techniques, and applications* (pp. 2286–2300). New York: Springer.

Sornette, D., & Cont, R. (1997). Convergent multiplicative processes repelled from zero: power laws and truncated power laws. *Journal de Physique I France*, *7*, 431–444.

Stanley, M. H., Amaral, L. A. N., Buldyrev, S. V., Havlin, S., Leschhorn, H., Maass, P., et al. (1996). Scaling behavior in the growth of companies. *Nature*, *379*, 804–806.

Stephens, M. A. (1974). EDF statistics for goodness of fit and some comparisons. *Journal of the American Statistical Association*, *69*, 730–737.

Stiglitz, J., & Greenwald, B. (2003). *Towards a new paradigm in monetary economics*. Cambridge: Cambridge University Press.

Stiglitz, J. E. (2004). Comments, in milgrom, p. putting auction theory to work.

Stiglitz, J. E., & Weiss, A. (1981). Credit rationing in markets with imperfect information. *The American Economic Review*, *71*(3), 393–410.

Stöckl, T., Huber, J., & Kirchler, M. (2010). Bubble measures in experimental asset markets. *Experimental Economics*, *13*(3), 284–298.

Subbotin, M. T. (1923). On the law of frequency of errors. *Matematicheskii Sbornik, 31*, 296–301.

Săvoiu, G., & Simăn, I. I. (2013). History and role of econophysics in scientific research. In G. Săvoiu (Ed.), *Econophysics: background and applications in economics, finance, and sociophysics* (pp. 3–16). Oxford UK and Waltham MA: Academic Press.

Tachibanaki, T., Suruga, T., & Atoda, N. (1997). Estimations of income distribution parameters for individual observations by maximum likelihood method. *Journal of the Japan Statistical Society, 27*, 191–203.

Takayasu, H., Sato, A.-H., & Takayasu, M. (1997). Stable infinite variance fluctuations in randomly amplified Langevin systems. *Physical Review Letters, 79*, 966–969.

Taylor, S. J. (2007). Modelling financial time series.

Team, R. C. (2015). *R: A Language and Environment for Statistical Computing*. https://www.R-project.org/.

Tedeschi, G., Gallegati, M., Mignot, S., & Vignes, A. (2012). Lost in transactions: the case of the boulogne s/mer fish market. *Physica A: Statistical Mechanics and its Applications, 391*(4), 1400–1407.

Tedeschi, G., Iori, G., & Gallegati, M. (2009). The role of communication and imitation in limit order markets. *The European Physical Journal B, 71*(4), 489–497.

Tedeschi, G., Iori, G., & Gallegati, M. (2012a). Herding effects in order driven markets: the rise and fall of gurus. *Journal of Economic Behavior and Organization, 81*(1), 82–96.

Tedeschi, G., Iori, G., & Gallegati, M. (2012b). Herding effects in order driven markets: the rise and fall of gurus. *Journal of Economic Behavior & Organization, 81*(1), 82–96.

Tedeschi, G., Vitali, S., & Gallegati, M. (2014). The dynamic of innovation networks: a switching model on technological change. *Journal of Evolutionary Economics, 24*(4), 817–834.

Tesfatsion, L. (2006). Agent-based computational economics: a constructive approach to economic theory. *Handbook of computational economics, 2*, 831–880.

Tesfatsion, L. (2013). Web site on validation of ace.

Tesfatsion, L. et al. (2014). Elements of dynamic economic modeling: Presentation and analysis. Technical report, Working Paper 14001, Department of Economics, Iowa State University.

Tesfatsion, L., Judd, K. L. (2006). *Handbook of computational economics: agent-based computational economics*, vol. 2. Elsevier.

Theil, H. (1954). *Linear aggregation of economic relations*. Amsterdam: North-Holland Publishing co.

Tversky, A., & Kahneman, D. (1973). Availability: a heuristic for judging frequency and probability. *Cognitive Psychology, 5*(2), 207–232.

Tversky, A., & Kahneman, D. (1989). *Rational choice and the framing of decisions*. Berlin: Springer.

Uchaikin, V. V., & Zolotarev, V. M. (1999). *Chance and stability: stable distributions and their applications*. Utrecht: VSP International Science Publishers.

Vaglica, G., Lillo, F., Moro, E., & Mantegna, R. N. (2008). Scaling laws of strategic behavior and size heterogeneity in agent dynamics. *Physical Review E, 77*(3), 036110.

Verbeek, M. (2012). *A guide to modern econometrics* (4th ed.). Chichester UK: Wiley.

Virkar, Y., & Clauset, A. (2014). Power-law distributions in binned empirical data. *Annals of Applied Statistics, 8*, 89–119.

Vuong, Q. H. (1989). Likelihood ratio tests for model selection and non-nested hypotheses. *Econometrica, 57*, 307–333.

Walras, L. (1874). *Éléments d'économie politique pure*, vol. 7. L. Corbaz.

Willinger, W., Alderson, D., Doyle, J. C., Li, L. (2004). More normal than normal: scaling distributions and complex systems. In Ingalls, R. G., Rossetti, M. D., Smith, J. S., Peters, B. A. (Eds.), *Proceedings of the 2004 Winter Simulation Conference*, pp. 130–141, Piscataway. IEEE Press.

Zipf, G. K. (1949). *Human Behavior and the Principle of Least Effort*. Cambridge MA: Addison-Wesley.

Zovko, I., Farmer, J. D., et al. (2002). The power of patience: a behavioural regularity in limit-order placement. *Quantitative Finance, 2*(5), 387–392.

Index

A. Caiani et al. (eds.), *Economics with Heterogeneous Interacting Agents*,
New Economic Windows, DOI 10.1007/978-3-319-44058-3

Printed by Printforce, the Netherlands